ROMANY AND TOM

ROMANY
AND TOM

BEN WATT

B L O O M S B U R Y
LONDON • NEW DELHI • NEW YORK • SYDNEY

'Home is So Sad' from *The Complete Poems of Philip Larkin* by Philip Larkin, edited
by Archie Burnett. Copyright © 2012 by The Estate of Philip Larkin. Reprinted by
kind permission of Farrar, Straus and Giroux, LLC, and Faber & Faber, Ltd.
'The Song of the Wandering Aengus' by W. B. Yeats is reprinted by kind permission
of United Agents on behalf of The Executors of the Estate of Grainne Yeats.
'Slough' from *Collected Poems* by John Betjeman © The Estate of John Betjeman
1955, 1958, 1962, 1964, 1968, 1970, 1979, 1981, 1982, 2001. Reproduced by kind
permission of John Murray (Publishers).

Bloomsbury Circus is an imprint of Bloomsbury Publishing plc
50 Bedford Square
London
WC1B 3DP

www.bloomsbury.com

Bloomsbury Publishing, London, New Delhi, New York and Sydney
A CIP catalogue record for this book is available from the British Library

Hardback ISBN 978 1 4088 4527 1
Trade paperback ISBN 978 1 4088 5319 1

10 9 8 7 6 5 4 3 2 1

Typeset by Hewer Text UK Ltd, Edinburgh
Printed and bound in Great Britain by CPI Group (UK) Ltd, Croydon CR0 4YY

For Jennie

Preface

We only ever see the second half of our parents' lives – the downhill part. The golden years we have to piece together. It's hard to think of our parents as young – or maybe I mean young adults – when everything stretched out in front of them and was possible. The versions of them that we see and judge every day have been shaped by experiences they've had, but which we have never known: the times they were hurt; the days they won; the times they compromised. For so much of it, we were simply *not there*.

So who are we to judge? Maybe we don't know them at all. And yet they must be – or were – only ordinary people like ourselves. Or the ones, as their kids, we may become. We all walk on common ground.

These days, in the age of infinite digital storage, an ordinary life is being documented every second of every day. Lofts and blanket drawers are stuffed full of video and audio cassettes, MiniDiscs, digital audio tapes, hard drives, smart cards and DVDs of all our unviewed photographs and eight-hour wedding receptions. Future generations will get sick of hearing about us.

But the ones who came just before us have left fewer foot-prints: a handful of private letters in a hat box; a voice captured on a slowly oxidising crumbling reel to reel; three minutes of a single holiday on a tiny spool of Super 8. They are the disappearing generation. We need to read the things they will eventually throw away, to listen out for the offhand remark and the moments of lucidity. We might even learn something. About them. And ourselves.

I tell this story from first-hand and second-hand experience: the moments I lived through; the handed-down stories; the photographs and the letters; the rummaging in the attic; a few public archives. It's a true story, or as true as any of our own stories are.

It is about my parents. And me.

There he was. I watched him from the doorway. He was in the last of the beds on the left. It was a small ward, just a handful of people, and the air was tangy and sweet with the smell of ointment and iodine. He was sitting up, but collapsed into his pillows. Was he smaller than I remembered? Or was the bed just bigger? In his hands he held the mask of his nebuliser, although the tube had fallen out, and he was trying to fix it. His fingers looked pale, even from the door. Those matchwood fingers. Still perfectly shaped. *Don't wrinkle your brow. Is it so hard? A square peg for a round hole?* He looked momentarily boyish. A nurse sped past me. People spoke and coughed. An alarm sounded elsewhere.

I walked across the room and stood at the foot of his bed. He hadn't seen me yet. I could hear his breathing now; it was a flimsy wheeze of air; a faint wind whistling through a crack in an upstairs door. His blue pyjama jacket was misbuttoned and stretched open. Beautiful curls of white chest hair showed against the sallow droop of old skin, all soft and furrowed and smooth. An image came to me of marram grass and sand dunes the colour of a lion's mane; and I pictured empty motor-oil bottles on the tideline, a stretch of beach, salt rime, gulls squabbling by a barnacled breakwater strewn with kelp, blasted shards of bleached timber and the winter sea at Climping in West Sussex where we'd spent some of my childhood weekends in a borrowed cottage.

His hair was ungroomed; that wasn't like him. It had lost the pristine shape I'd known from all the years I'd watched him comb it, glossed with Vitalis hair tonic from the glass shelf in the bathroom, teased with the steel tines into the low quiff to meet the swept-back sideburns, once folded in with a flat palm, but now roughly cropped with a prison barber's touch into little blunted badger-hair shaving brushes on either side of his head.

'Hello, old son,' I said.

He looked up, surprised. 'Ben!' His hands dropped to the bedclothes. His small green eyes stopped straining and caught the light, watery and glistening. His face was childlike and thrilled. 'What . . . how did you know I was *here*?'

I felt a spark down in my stomach. I was thrilled he was thrilled. His white sheet was badly stained. Was it blood? 'Roly told me,' I said. 'I wanted to come earlier in the week but I couldn't, but I am here now. I came on the train.' I made it sound as if I'd come as quickly as I could, which was a lie; I had in fact been putting it off; several days had passed since he had been admitted. It didn't seem serious at the beginning, and I'd hoped if I left it a few days it would all blow over, and I wouldn't have to confront anything. 'Here, let me help you,' I said. I sidled round the bed and took the parts of the mask from his hands and slipped the tube back into the collar, fitted the mask to his face and tightened the strap a little. 'How are you then?'

He tugged the mask down. 'Oh Ben, Ben . . .'

I could sense him groping for words, as if he first had to corner and take hold of each one. 'You're OK, though?' I said.

'You know what . . .'

I let him pause.

He swallowed and stared ahead and breathed with his lips open, before turning slightly and grabbing three mouthfuls of air to the side, as a swimmer might, head twisting above the waterline. Each pull was followed by a muffled wheeze. Then the words came: not bitter; no bleeding heart; just matter-of-fact. 'I'm at the end of my tether.'

In his voice I heard just a hint of the Glasgow accent he had shrugged off all those years ago when he left home – a fiery and ambitious teenage jazz musician called up by the wartime RAF – and it reminded me of his mother, Jean, my grandma, and how she visited three times a year from Scotland when I was a boy. She flew down on BEA. Her clothes smelled alien. Camphor and talcum powder. I pictured her twin sets, her thick nylon stockings the colour of strong tea, the sugar-dusted travel sweets in her handbag, how she always spread her marmalade to the very outer edges of her toast; she never used butter; that was far too extravagant. I used to be anxious when she embraced me – the perfumes, the rough weave of her skirt, the powdery down on her face, the sloping shapelessness of her shoulders – but she had a soft button nose and uncomplaining eyes that seemed full of fortitude and kindness. To me anyway.

I was looking at him. He resembled her so much now, and it struck me how the eloquence of his words had stopped me in my tracks – especially now – especially knowing how the naming of things eluded him, how sentences often had no endings, how faces and things passed through his head like streaks of light and shadow, momentarily recognisable, then gone; especially with him here, in this arbitrary part of England, not really anywhere near somewhere you could

3

call his home, nearing the reckoning, an oxygen mask around his neck.

I reached out and found myself laughing and ran my hand across his fine tangled white hair. His scalp was scaly but vulnerable to the touch. There was a moment's silence, and then he said, 'And I've had enough of *fatso* over there.'

The word made him splutter, and I listened to his chest list and heave like a laden ship. But he didn't seem to care about being overheard; in fact everything he had said had been delivered in the same unstudied tone.

My eyes flicked up to the bed opposite, where a woman – I guessed late twenties – was lounging absent-mindedly on the sheets. She seemed to be half in and half out of her bed. Her hair was hanging limply in coils around her face in a grown-out perm. She wore a tightly stretched apricot-coloured bed-jacket with the sleeves pulled up to her elbows, and tracky bottoms and compression stockings, and was eating a chocolate digestive from a half-finished torn packet lying on the bedclothes, while a man was sitting in the chair by the bedside, picking something from his ear and rubbing it on the knee of his jeans.

I looked back at my dad and glared at him. So hard on the wrong kind of strangers. No change there. I glanced around the room. No one appeared to have taken offence. Relieved, I leaned over and kissed him on the forehead. 'Well, it's nice to see you, old man,' I said. 'Roly and Mum should be here soon too.' I sat next to the bed and patted his leg through the blanket. It felt like a stick. He smiled at me, then I saw his shoulders relax and he rolled his head towards the window. After a few moments his eyes had closed and I could hear small jets of air being exhaled from his nose.

I got up quietly and walked out into the lobby and tried to catch the eye of one of the nurses on the ward station; they seemed to be deliberately avoiding eye contact. A junior doctor in chinos was running his eye over a patient's notes. The desk was a chaotic jumble of files, plastic cups, elastic bands, newspapers, specimen jars, biros.

'Excuse me,' I said.

One of the nurses looked up.

I smiled and tried to seem genial yet experienced. 'Any chance of some info on my dad? I'm his son. He's "Tommy Watt". End bed.'

'His nurse'll be along in a minute.' She turned away and finished off a story she was sharing with a colleague.

I loitered for a few moments, reading the washable white board on the wall: *Week commencing: Monday 15 May 2006.* Below it were the names of the patients in the different beds and basic instructions written in coloured marker pens. A female nurse appeared in a hurry in a disposable white plastic apron. She was clutching an aspiration kit and a clipboard. The woman on the desk nodded towards her as if to say, 'That's her.' I stepped into her path.

'I'm Tommy's son,' I said, gesturing to his bed. 'How is he doing?'

She stopped and looked at me and sighed heavily and a bit grumpily. 'Oh, he's not bad. A bad night. Still a fever.' Her accent was strong. Filipino? 'But his *chest* . . .' She rolled her eyes.

'Tell me.'

'COAD. Very difficult.'

'COAD?'

'Chronic obstructive airways disease.'

'Chronic ob . . . ' I started to repeat the words.

She jumped in. 'You know what *emphysema* is?'

I nodded.

'OK. So, *that*. *And* bad bronchitis. Together. Not good. Not good at all.' She began to move away. 'And he's been shouting. Shouting at *everyone*. You tell him to be nice, will you?'

I nodded.

She smiled back thinly, and bustled off.

I walked back to his bedside. His eyes were open again. For a moment I thought he might have forgotten I'd arrived and express fresh surprise, but he saw me and smiled. I ambled to the window and looked out at the small car park below and watched people coming and going. Two dusty minicabs were dropping off: a red Vauxhall Vectra; an old Orion with no hubcaps. I saw the supportive arm on an elbow, the cautious steps, the overnight bag. Two women were under the glass awning: the older one in leggings and wedge flip-flops; the younger in a dressing gown and podgy animal slippers.

I heard soft footsteps and the rustle of clothes behind me and turned round. It was Roly, my half-brother. He had my mum on his arm. His cheeks were flushed, his blue eyes congenial, a collared shirt under a dark zip-neck fleece, loose softened jeans, casual cushion-soled shoes. One hand was slipped into his pocket and he wore his vicar's smile – the one that looks part welcoming, part serene and insular, and if it could speak would say, 'It's a funny old life.' I thought how he'd always had it, even before he was ordained and got his parish, when he was just the family peacemaker. Lately we've begun an unexpected alliance – having moved in different orbits for most of our lives, nearly nine years between us, him the older. When things changed for the worse with my mum and dad we took on the role of their guardians, assuming Power of Attorney, talking on the phone, moving their money around, cancelling out-of-date electrical appliance insurance, tracking down ancient standing orders, working out state allowances, getting things ready for the last bit. We've got on well. He lives in the neighbouring village to the care home in the countryside north of Bristol where they moved in 2004. A familiar face at a tricky time. Dependable. It has meant a lot.

'All right?' he said affably, unlinking arms.

'Yes. Easy journey.'

My mum, eighty-two, approached the bed in her familiar shuffling flat-footed walk. She was wearing a loose-peaked velvet baker boy cap and a limp shower-proof walking jacket. As she saw me she moved her mouth into the shape of a smile, her lips together and stretched wide, making her cheeks and the corners of her eyes crease deeply behind her gold-rimmed glasses. I went towards her and reached out to kiss her. She kept the smile frozen on her face and turned her cheek to greet me. I kissed the warm skin, and pressed her shoulders for a moment. She held the pose as though waiting for a photograph to be snapped.

'Hello, Mum. How are you?

'As good as can be expected, darling.' Her voice was defensive. Slightly lugubrious.

We settled around the bed.

She took my dad's hand and rubbed her thumb along the back of it in the same way she had done to me fourteen years earlier when I was in hospital in the Intensive Care Unit, and on her face was the same self-absorbed look I had seen all those years ago: half connected and involved; half ready to go home.

My dad rolled his head to look at her and smiled. There was no detectable rancour. It appeared affectionate. She pulled a slow-motion rueful smile in return, dipping her head to one side then closing both eyes slowly and opening them again at him, as you might at a poorly child. But then a little murmur escaped from her closed mouth accompanied by a barely audible quick out-breath through the nose. I've heard it before; it says: 'Well, look at me, who'd have thought I'd be here in *this* situation?' And with it, the tiny moment of tenderness was compromised, and joined by an uneasiness, until it looked more like an evolved tolerance, and on her face was written a faint watermark of disappointment at how it had all turned out.

What were they like when we were not here? Was there a secret language and code we never saw, the ones that all couples have? Perhaps they had nicknames for each other we'd yet to even hear. Did they deliberately hide affection from us, imagining that it was somehow inappropriate in front of the children – even now – even in front of children who were forty-three- and fifty-two-year old men with children of their own? Or was it just as I saw it then – difficult and altered?

'Oh, look at your sheet. Did no one change it?' she said, looking at the dark stain.

'It's coffee,' he said.

Relief. Not blood then.

She stood and tugged at the sheet and thought about straightening it, but then looked uncomfortable and gave up.

'Would anyone like to see some pictures of the kids?' I said brightly.

'Oh yes,' said my dad enthusiastically, responding to the change in atmosphere.

I reached into my bag and pulled out my laptop. 'I have them on screen.' I put the laptop at the foot of the bed for a moment. 'Let me hitch you up so you can see, Dad.' I slipped my arms under his shoulders. The distance between his pyjamas and his body was further than I was expecting. His frame felt brittle. I remembered a day I had to pick up a dead blackbird from the lawn and how light it had seemed. He grimaced as I straightened him up. 'There we go,' I said.

I picked up the laptop, flipped it open and sat it on his lap.

'Is it a television?' my mum said.

'No, a computer, Mum, with photographs stored in it,' I said.

'*Really*. What *will* they think of next?'

There was something odd in the tone of her voice. Was she joking? It was as though she had said it because that's what she thought an eighty-two-year-old woman should say, or had said it like that for my dad's benefit, and actually knew exactly what it was. Or perhaps it was just as it sounded: all a mystery. I thought how even now I still found her hard to read.

I opened the folder with the photos in it and brought them up on to the screen. I chose a picture of Tracey to begin with.

'Ahhhh . . .' my dad said. '*Tracey*.'

His voice lingered on her name for a moment. It is strange to think how fond of her he became. I can remember when I first took her home and thrust her into the domestic cauldron of my late teens. It would have been 1982. My dad, then fifty-six, cooked that night. Lamb and potatoes were ceremonially roasted to near-dehydration point in the oven. Vegetables – three kinds – were heavily boiled then coated in a thick cheese sauce in separate dishes. He had been in the kitchen, as was his routine, since 5.30, 'preparing supper'. This meant some basic food preparation – in other words, peeling a few carrots – but was mainly an excuse for a string of large gin and tonics on his own to the accompaniment of jazz on the small red JVC radio-cassette player on the oak bureau. Zoot Sims, Toots Thielemans or Stan Getz were long-standing favourites. Wisps of intro-spective tenor saxophone and harmonica would drift under the kitchen door accompanied by the odd clanging saucepan lid. He could be a good cook but overcooked everything when he drank. By 7.30 he was usually well-oiled and ready for a confrontation. Just back from university for an end-of-term holiday we sat down for our first meal all together and he rounded on her at the narrow yellow-laminate kitchen table, and slurred a vintage opening salvo: 'So, Tracey, how long have you been a *socialist*?'

I looked up at my mum on the other side of the bed. Her grey teeth were misaligned. They looked different. 'Oh, Mum, did something happen to your tooth, the front one?' I said with concern in my voice, but she took it as a boxer takes an aggressive jab.

Her eyes flashed. 'What do you *expect*? I am *old*, darling. Nothing *works*,' she said, with affected affront. She looked at me coldly and pulling a face like an old crone, waggled the tooth at me with her index finger, as if she'd been braced for an attack of some kind and was getting in a quick retaliatory upper-cut.

I threw her a look of exasperation. She simply mimicked the look back at me.

I turned and caught Roly's eye.

'It was ever thus,' his vicar's face said equably.

I closed my eyes. I didn't want a scene. I took a slow breath, and absorbed the impact of the counter-punch silently, like a fighter swallowing down early punishment.

Turning to the laptop, I popped open a picture of Jean, my daughter. She is eight in the photograph, standing at the top of the battlements of Lulworth Castle, an iron weather-vane behind her and and a grey-green valley barrelling away to the sea beyond. She is wearing a pale blue shell jacket and is smiling without complication straight at the camera with a perfect unblemished face.

'Who is that?' my dad said.

If I have a regret it is that we had our children too late for my parents to enjoy them. They were in their early seventies – not old for some folk these days – but their frailty and inflexibility were already taking hold when the girls were born. I have pictures of them in the sunlit sitting room on the north London road where we lived at the time in which they are each holding one of the newborn twins swaddled up in hand-knitted cardigans and baby-grows. It is 1998. My dad looks well in the photograph – smart in the mustard corduroy shirt I'd bought him for his birthday; his hair and skin are good. He is smiling down at baby Jean, but on his face uncertainty is written among the warm creases of affection; it's as if he is saying, 'I am trying, but I won't be able to deal with this.' Was it just too late to put aside his own preoccupations? Had he simply forgotten how to cope? Or was he never going to be any good at it?

'It's Jean,' I said, 'in Dorset.'

'One of the *twins*, darling,' said my mum over-loudly.

'Really,' he said almost dreamily. 'How marvellous.'

It was obvious he wasn't sure who it was, or if he was, he had very few memories of her on which to draw. Bad health had made him more introspective. Grandchildren had slipped down the list of priorities. Apart from the occasional prompt from a framed photograph of a face in a pram on the sitting-room sideboard, they just hadn't been on his mind much these past few years.

I clicked the mouse and up came a picture of Jean's twin sister, Alfie. She is reaching both arms out towards the camera, her fingers outstretched, the pink tartan of her coat bunched on her shoulders, her face clear and mischievous.

'And that's Alfie, Dad.'

'Ahhh.' He paused. 'So clever . . . So clever . . . this machine.'

I looked at him. He was no longer looking at the screen. He

was running his finger along the edge of the laptop's keyboard, diverted and seduced by the technology. I remembered him breaking an awkward early silence on a hospital visit to see me when I was ill with the news that his new Laguna-blue Mazda 323 had power-steering and anti-lock brakes.

Breezily I clicked through more: holiday snaps; landscapes; the kids in dressing-up costumes and new school uniforms; days out. Facts and faces blurred into one, but when we got to a close-up of my son Blake, five at the time, my dad spoke up.

'There! Ahhh. The boy!'

He had a soft spot for Blake. In him, of all the children, it was as if he saw a glimmer of me. The young son. Unformed. A distant innocence. Is that too sentimental? In the photograph, Blake is standing reflectively on the deck of the small Brownsea Island Ferry, his hands on the white steel rail, squinting out across Poole Harbour on a salt-fresh spring day. He is wearing an orange Winnie-the-Pooh baseball cap that jumps out against the clear blue Dorset sky and the yellow wooden slats of the wheelhouse: a serious thoughtful face in cartoon colours. I thought of the day I visited the care home near Bristol when I went upstairs to find the two of them – my dad and Blake – lying on their backs side by side on the covers of my dad's single bed, each with their little feet crossed identically at the ankle. Blake must have been nearly four. They were gazing up at the ceiling, picking out animal shapes in the swirls of Artex plaster, seventy-five years between them. They were, as Blake said on the train home that day, 'being two mans together'.

I could sense my mum getting restless. She activated her speaking watch – her eyesight had been worsening – and the robotic voice announced that twenty minutes had passed. Roly had warned me this would be approaching her limit. I gently shut the lid on the laptop.

My dad's eyes were closing again.

My mum let out a long sigh. 'Is the car far, dear?' she said to Roly.

'No, not really. How are you doing?' he said.

'I think perhaps . . .' She trailed off. My dad's eyes were open again. 'I think maybe we should, don't you?' she said.

'As you wish,' said Roly, unperturbed. 'Shall I meet you downstairs?'

'Yes, you fetch the car.'

Roly raised his eyebrows at me, and rolled his eyes quickly. I raised my hand as if to say, 'It's fine.'

Then suddenly, my dad spoke. 'I think it is time . . .' he announced, with an unexpected authority that made all three of us stop what we were doing. Was this going to be a momentous announcement? A change to his will? An admission of guilt? We turned to him, but it was followed by a pause as the rest of the thought began to escape him. All the words must have been there together in the right order in his head a moment before, but now the ones at the end of the sentence he had planned were fainter, as if washed over by an incoming tide. We hung there for a few seconds, wondering if he might finish, watching him draw down air, and then just as suddenly as he had started I saw the remainder of the thought return like a boomerang and he said loudly, 'I think it is time that we stopped *fatso* over there from eating any more.'

I froze. Two people by the neighbouring bed looked round quizzically, a hint of irritation in their faces. The woman in the bed opposite – who had restarted on her chocolate digestives – carried on eating methodically, still idly leafing through a magazine. My mum was fastening the popper on her handbag.

Roly was smirking. I turned back to my dad to show my objection but he was already distracted, picking at something fascinating on the back of his hand. I felt the small ripple of adrenalin break and disperse.

Roly turned to go, stifling a smile.

'I'll bring Mum down in five minutes. Meet you at the door,' I said, still thankful no one had complained.

'Fine,' he said. And then in a louder voice, 'Bye, Tom. See you tomorrow.'

My dad looked up and smiled and nodded generously.

With Roly gone, I filled my mum in on some family news to pass the time. She was still wearing her coat and her bag was still on her lap. When it was time to go she looked at my dad complicatedly, her face a little thunderstorm, but spoke no words. Their eyes met.

'Yes, you go, Romany,' he said quite clearly and assertively. There was no animosity, no expectation that she should stay.

She kissed him tenderly on the temple, and for a brief moment, as her eyes closed and her lips touched his skin, her affection for whoever was in her mind – him, or a version of him – seemed unconditional. I looked at them. They were like two old inosculated trees: different stock but rooted in the same ground, until the branches and trunks had curled and conjoined, then grafted together. I wondered what kind of axe it would take to split them.

We turned to go.

'Back in a few minutes, Dad,' I said.

As we padded towards the lift, my mum said, 'Do you think there's a little shop down by the entrance?'

'Possibly. I didn't notice one though.'

'Do you think there's an *off-licence*?'

'Not in a hospital, Mum, no.'

We walked on in silence. Every brief trip out in someone's car dangled the slender possibility of a half-bottle.

Downstairs we stood by the doors waiting for Roly to pull up. People came and went.

'So strange,' she pondered. 'Having him in here . . .'

There was a pause. I felt a clot of sympathy rise in my throat, but she carried on before I could reply,

'. . . among these *awful* people.'

I stared straight ahead. The theatrically snobbish ennui chimed loud and familiar – languid, affected, dismissive, unlikeable – born of a deeper dissatisfaction I'd heard in her for years, a perceived sense of injustice swollen with time. She resented the moment not because she really found the circumstances repellent but because of how they hampered her, as if today had been just one more unfair cross for her to bear. I wondered – not for the first time – where it all came from, what she thought she was still owed, what had caused her such disappointment, and what brought it to the front of her mind, even now, with her own husband in a hospital bed upstairs, with them both in need of each other as never before. Did she still see her tragedy as the greater? Was this still *her* scene? I looked out towards the car park and wished she'd made peace with it all years ago. Or toughened up, or something.

Roly arrived.

I helped her into the car.

'Bye, then, Mum.'

She turned on a smile, gave a royal wave through the window, and they were gone.

Back upstairs my dad was still awake. I stroked his dry white hair again for a while. I was conscious of only being able to do such a thing unselfconsciously since I'd had kids of my own. The selfless affectionate act seemed to be part of being a parent, part of stepping to one side and putting someone else in the place of importance, of no longer always having to be at the heart of your own life all the time. With me, it also came from being used to hospitals now; I'd spent a long time in one of them in 1992. I recognised the equipment. I wasn't alarmed by the drips and drains and the sugary smell of illness. I had no urge to walk away the moment I stepped on to the ward. I knew the value of the warmth of human contact.

'You are a kind boy,' he said as I was leaving.

Later, I caught the train home, and, as it hurtled through the landscape, past the flashing trees, the blankets of wheat, the sheep walking slowly on the hillsides, I wondered if it would be the last thing that I'd ever hear him say to me.

2

ive years earlier, the first week of July 2001 had been hot and thundery. Headache weather. My mum and dad were living in Oxford, where they'd been since selling the family home in Barnes in south-west London at the end of the eighties. My dad was seventy-five. He'd smoked a packet of twenty cigarettes a day without filters for fifty years until he was nearly seventy, and was now spending most of his time sitting in a green leather armchair overlooking a nondescript urban stretch of the river with an oxygen tank within easy reach. His bed had been moved into a room on the same floor and he hadn't used the stairs in weeks. When he coughed, it was a condensed and heavy sound. His doctor had him on asthma inhalers; it sounded worse than that to me. 'Your father's low,' my mum would say. 'Not a word all day.' Some mornings he wouldn't even get up, or returned to his bed after only a couple of hours – twenty-seven shuffling footsteps from his armchair – like a sick dog to its basket. My mum was seventy-six. Robust yet weary. 'We can't go on like this,' she said bleakly on the phone to me one evening. 'Well, he can, but I can't.'

I knew we were at a fork in the road. Oxford had been a surprise choice to most of the family – the reasons only became clear to me later – and while my mum and dad had enjoyed more than twelve years of self-sufficiency, we were now all realising it was in the middle of nowhere compared with where the rest of us were living: Roly was north of Bristol; Jennie, my half-sister, was near Glastonbury; Toby, my half-brother, was near Esher in Surrey; Simon, my eldest half-brother, was in Edinburgh; and I was in London. None of us were in a position to respond quickly to an emergency, or pop out for some useful shopping, or casually drop round for moral support. It was also not lost on me that Tom was *my* father, not theirs. Although he'd been in their lives since they were children, he was only their stepfather – walking in out of nowhere before they were ten. It seemed clear which path was in front of me. And so on a warm and still morning a month later my mum caught the train up to London to view some possible flats for her and my dad near us.

Call me hopeful, but as I climbed – aged thirty-eight – into the car to collect her and drove along our street, beneath the flickering sunlight and shadows of the tall overhanging lime trees, I imagined I was making the drive to see them for the first time in a new flat near me, and the moment seemed full of possibility and change for the better – of fixing things and getting differences sorted out – as though all the years of hardened paint that overlaid us could be scraped away to reveal the original wood that made us up, mellowed with age and full of a forgotten warmth.

I should have known better. There was a familiar heaviness to her step as I glimpsed her coming towards me along the commuter-filled platform at Paddington. She was walking the self-aware solemn stately march I had seen her adopt so often in public, her shape reflected in the windows of the little blue-and-white Thames Turbo Express train from

Oxford. Her 'best' coat had been chosen for the occasion. It was a present from the actress-broadcaster Katie Boyle, given to her when they were working together editing an 'agony aunt' column at the *TV Times* in the early eighties – one of the final jobs handed to my mum after almost thirty years working as a freelance columnist and feature writer. A voluminous cream duvet of a coat from neck to knee, with rough-cut leather tie straps, and toggles for buttons, edged in fluffy mountaineering fur, it seemed completely at odds with the fine weather. Perhaps it was colder in Oxford, I thought. Or perhaps it was going to get worn whatever the weather; it was her *best* coat and it was a trip to *London* after all. Not a tall woman, perhaps five foot three, she wore on her head a crimson felt beret and her small wide archless feet padded along the platform in dark blue comfortable slip-on pumps secured with broad elastic straps. She was the last to the ticket barrier by quite a distance; bustling commuters were long gone. I smiled when I thought I was within her focal range. When she finally saw me, she cocked her head slightly to the side and threw one of her lightly pained, self-commiserating smiles back at me.

'Ready?' I said enthusiastically as she approached.

'Not really.'

In the car, she was quiet, one elbow on the window ledge, her fingers touching her brow. Every now and then she breathed in quickly and loudly and let out a long sigh, more like a huff. She did it unconsciously, I am sure, as another problem was turned over in her mind but not quite resolved, but it was a habit she had had for years, and to the outsider it could sound sudden and dramatic and intrusive; the instinct was to feel obliged to ask, 'What's *wrong?*' or, 'Everything *all right?*'

I ignored it.

'Are you happy to be coming to London?' I said.

'I am not sure "happy" is the word, dear.'

'Surely a bit of you is excited, no?'

'I think we are too old to be excited.'

We drove up on to Bishops Bridge.

'What about the theatre? It'll be on your doorstep again. You could look up some old friends. Elspet, perhaps.'

'One step at a time, dear.'

We cut along Clifton Road and then up and over the stepped terrace of Maida Vale, and soon we were pulling through iron art deco gateposts into the driveway of a huge, stately thirties mansion block on the Finchley Road. A muscular front-line of London plane trees held the thrumming traffic at bay. The estate agent was pacing up and down outside on his mobile.

We viewed two flats. One was almost on the top floor, looking south, with a panoramic outlook over Lord's Cricket Ground, but my mum said the windows were too high and they'd see nothing but empty sky from their armchairs. The second was on the first floor facing north, overlooking a side street; it was dark, empty and unfurnished and smelled faintly of cheese and decaying fruit. As she padded round the empty rooms I could see her struggling to imagine anything other than a long slow incarceration.

Outside we waited on the pavement at the lights on the Wellington Road. The sun was high and bright, bouncing off the bonnets and windscreens. My mum loosened her coat and rooted around in her handbag for her special sunglasses. One of her eyes was in worse shape than the other. 'Macular degeneration,' her doctor had said. 'Not uncommon, but not much we can do.' I'd looked it up. *Vision worsens in the centre of the eye; typical in old age; recognising faces becomes a problem; peripheral vision is better.* I could picture her tipping her head to one side like a bird on a lawn to read cooking instructions or an address on an envelope. Her house had taken on extra floor lamps and illuminated magnifiers in recent years, and silences were often broken by the sound of her digital talking watch ordered from the Royal National Institute for the Blind catalogue; one press of the button and a clipped and distorted Americanised female voice announced the time through a tiny speaker: *It's. Three. Fifty. Eight. Pee. Em.* I remembered being awake at night in their Oxford house, up in the spare room under the eaves, the pivot-roof window open, no sound but for the clicks of unfamiliar surroundings and the occasional car hissing past on the rain-slicked Thames Street below, and just as sleep had been overwhelming me again, I'd been startled awake by a voice in the dark from the room next door: *It's. Four. Twenny. Seven. Ay. Em.* She'd always been a light sleeper. I used to imagine her finger hovering over the button under the bedclothes. She kept biscuits in a tin next to the bed to keep her going through the night.

I looked at her on the pavement. Her doctor had told her that protecting what was left of her eyesight was the best she could do. Which explained the special sunglasses. In fact, 'sunglasses' does not really describe them; they were big, blacked-out, wraparound eye protectors, with side and brow shields, the shape worn by lab technicians or wood choppers, so big that they fitted *over* her normal bi-focals. They seemed perfect for my mum – medically recommended but also with a touch of the attention-seeker. It was wrong not to sympathise, but standing next to her at the pelican crossing I was unable to shake the thought that she looked a bit like an elderly European rock star.

Diagonally opposite was another large purpose-built modern block of flats. Bullnose biscuity-brown engineered bricks rose functionally above the loose-limbed trees of the Wellington Road. I think I'd once thought they were offices. Wide steps led up to the glass front doors past well-stocked planters. My mum nodded aristocratically at the porter in the entrance lobby, but I could sense her already flagging as we got into the lift up to the second-floor flat for our next viewing. The lift doors opened again and we padded across a navy fitted carpet, past a solitary weeping fig, and through a communal fire door.

'Cold corridor,' she said.

I felt the radiator. It was off. I hoped the flat would be warmer.

It was. In fact it seemed cosy. Honey-blond hardwood flooring threw a glow on to the white walls. We were drawn to the big aluminium double-glazed windows in the sitting room overlooking the gentle bustle of the tube station.

'Lovely big sky,' she said, clearing her throat.

'Isn't it,' I enthused.

'We need a view. The days can be very long, dear. Especially when the snooker is on.'

The compact fitted kitchen was right next to the sitting room, separated by sliding doors.

'Oh, praise be! Now *that's* easier,' she said mordantly. She opened the fridge, closed it, and then ran her fingers slowly along the worktop. She'd been ferrying food up and down the stairs in their Oxford house for too long. Meals used to be taken in the downstairs kitchen at the teak dining table, but recently my dad had been having everything in front of the TV on the first floor. I'd even been flirting with the idea of buying him a bean-bag lap-tray.

The estate agent showed her a large cupboard with a small window ('or third bedroom' as he put it, in that language of elastic dimensions that only estate agents use) where she tried to picture herself neatly set out with her electric typewriter and Romany pictures and scrapbooks. Down the hall was a double bedroom with a bathroom for her, and a separate bedroom and small bathroom for my dad.

'Will Dad like it?' I asked as we were leaving.

'Who knows?'

When I dropped her off back at Paddington, and watched her blow one of her mannered hangdog kisses through the windscreen, and then turn and get her bearings before trudging away from the taxi rank towards the familiar Edwardian three-faced clock and the trains, I found it hard to imagine how they were still coping, what with her eyesight and fluctuating moods, and the drinking (once mainly him, now often both of them) and the infirmities and the long afternoons of darts and snooker. I imagined a kind of auto-pilot: days navigated by instinct and accustomed routines; furniture in familiar places; the quirks of the kitchen appliances memorised. And while I thought I understood my mum's longing to escape, and have new support near by, I drove back over Bishops Bridge and worried about the change and what bewilderment it might bring.

Later that night I spoke to her on the phone.

'First impressions?'

'Very practical, if you need to hear something positive, dear,' she said. 'The last one, I mean. Seemed promising. Your father is in agreement with whatever I choose. I don't know if that makes it easier or not.'

'How did you describe it to him?'

'I could barely remember it by the time I got home. The train was packed. Quite unpleasant. Oh, I don't know. Bright, airy. A view of the sky. Everything handy. You'll have to fill me in on the detail. You know I'm half blind, dear. It's about the practicality. We're not looking for *St-Tropez*.'

I asked her to sleep on it.

Two days later, with the weather still fine, I went back to the flat with a handheld camcorder and filmed a walkthrough for them both to watch, hoping it might help them make up their minds, and ease the burden I felt that I might be rushing them into it. The thought of my mum returning and choosing anything else seemed remote. I tried to show everything as it was, impartially, but I couldn't help skimming across the condensation pockets trapped in one or two of the ageing double-glazed windows and instead made a point of hovering over things that I knew would matter to my dad, like the view, the electric razor power point, the master light switches, and the Sky TV coaxial socket.

I dubbed it on to a video cassette and posted it to them.

The next day my mum phoned.

'You father's calling it a masterstroke, darling,' she said. 'Very clever of you. Such a modern way of doing things. We've watched it *three* times. He wants you to know he thinks the place looks very *metropolitan* – that was the word he used – but *friendly* and *practical*. And we both agree there's no point hanging around waiting for something perfect. We are beyond that. Put in an offer, dear, and let's get it over with.'

3

'd hoped for a crisp December morning – blue skies, low sun – but it was mild and overcast, when, three and a half months later, I met a Pickfords removals van outside the block of flats with the biscuity-brown bullnose bricks. Everything was flattened in a neutral plain grey light.

The offer had gone in and had been accepted, and the deal completed over a leisurely twelve weeks. The Oxford house had been packed up; Roly had taken my mum and dad to a nearby hotel for a night ('As much as anything else,' he'd said, 'to get them out of the way and make sure they don't change their mind'); and I was planning to unpack everything and make the place recognisable and homely, while Roly collected them late morning, took his time and arrived late afternoon with it all done. 'A pub lunch should slow them down,' he'd said drily.

It was gone ten before the removals men had finally edged the lorry up against the pavement, swung the battered doors open, and begun glumly trundling boxes up the path to the front doors. For the next few hours I kept things moving, supervising furniture positions and unpacking possessions, and when the three workers had shuffled off midway through the day, I carried on on my own.

I wanted it to look perfect. I hung clean towels and quilted loo rolls in the bathrooms and filled the fitted wardrobes with their soft musty comfortable clothes, flattening all the boxes as I went, piling them like gym mats in the corridor outside. In the little kitchen I stocked the green glass-fronted cupboards with my mum's handed-down mismatched Romany china: gold-rimmed orphaned teacups, lidless serving dishes, odd cream jugs and faded soup plates. As I spread it out on the counter it looked like the contents of a car-boot sale, not a vintage collection of rare antiques, which was how she'd always proudly painted it. 'Gypsy heirlooms, darling. Makers' marks. Very desirable.'

It was a motley assortment; I suppose its diversity hadn't been helped by the night the kitchen cupboard fell off the wall. I must have been eleven years old. It was a Saturday night. We'd been happily watching TV in the other room; my dad was just back from the pub, and he was passing round the biscuits and we were all whistling the theme tune to *Parkinson* when we heard it; the crash was ear-splitting. Leaping from our chairs, we rushed into the darkened kitchen across the landing to find the crockery cupboard had dropped two feet on to the worktop below. My mum's cherished collection had been crammed on to the top shelf. 'You've been promising to fix those Rawlplugs for weeks,' she had reprimanded, suppressing a slight hysteria, while salvaging one of my great-grandma Tilly's saucers. 'I wouldn't have needed to if it weren't for all that knackered old china,' my dad had answered saltily.

I opened another box. Saucepans and oven dishes came out smelling pungent and waxy. Some were still ringed with tidemarks of soup, and flecked with specks of food. Cutlery was smeared. A few of the tumblers and mugs had lip-marks, and the frosted rings brought on by dishwashers used without rinsing agent and salt. It caught me off guard. I thought of my dad in his armchair with his oxygen, unable to get downstairs, and my mum with her degenerative eyesight doing the evening dishes, and suddenly they seemed old and frail. Was I convincing myself otherwise? I found the manual for the dishwasher and put everything I could fit inside on an intensive cycle, before sliding open the window and looking out at the traffic on the Wellington Road, wondering if any of this was a good idea.

The light was thickening. I turned back and glanced at my watch; they'd be well on their way. I pressed on, making up the beds and putting ornaments and framed photographs of the family on the window ledges and shelves. The Sky installer arrived as planned and within twenty minutes he was done, and the TV was plugged in and fully tuned, and I was moving round the flat to the comforting sound of racing from Lingfield Park. I thought of my mum and dad's Saturday-afternoon betting slips: each-way doubles and Yankees fixed to the green baize pin-board in our old kitchen; and the day I was told off at school for doing my geography test with a short stubby pencil taken from the bookie's.

In my dad's single bedroom, I neatly arranged his jazz tapes and CDs on the sideboard. I opened a suitcase expecting to find more clothes, only to find a dozen smart leather-bound manuscript folders, each with a black ribbon to tie it closed, and each embossed with the words *Tommy Watt Orchestra*. Underneath them was a stack of jumbled sheet music, some handwritten, some in a copyist's smart ink script. An arrangement of Neal Hefti's 'Girl Talk' slithered out on to the floor; above the intro was written 'Flutes?' in my dad's firm handwriting. I shuffled them all up together. The ream of blank manuscript paper on the bottom felt lovely in my hand. A wedge of cream-coloured, heavy-grade soft bond paper. The edges almost fibrous. It must have been expensive. The best you could buy, probably. It seemed so like him. Or the him I pictured when I was young: pin-sharp; immoderate; sometimes formidable. I stacked them in the bottom of his wardrobe; it seemed the appropriate place; it was where he used to keep them – below the duty-free cigarettes and his laundered shirts.

I considered hanging up some pictures and paintings, but I knew that was one of my mum's great pleasures – she was forever painstakingly reframing and rearranging things on the walls, particularly when they moved to Oxford – so instead I stacked them against the cupboard in her new tiny study. There were cut-out photo montages of the family she'd made herself, watercolours of Romany wagons and birdlife, cartoons and sketches by artists she knew from Fleet Street, black-and-white photographs of actors she'd interviewed and fancied over the years (Anthony Hopkins, Richard Burton, Gregory Peck), and a poster for one of my dad's jazz orchestra concerts – his name on it mischievously half burnt out by the tip of a teenage stepson's cigarette.

I unpacked her framed theatre-costume designs collected since her season as an actress at the Shakespeare Memorial Theatre in Stratford-upon-Avon in 1950. There was Mariano Andreu's painted sketch for a dress for Diana Wynyard in John Gielgud's 1949 production of *Much Ado About Nothing*, the material dropping gracefully off the shoulders at the back like the wings of a great white dove, a pencil annotation (*Beatrice 1er Acte*) still clear on the canvas. Behind it was a later watercolour from 1955 of a male costume, in burgundy and indigo, with *Titus . . . Sir Laurence Olivier* written across the top, and

Olivier's own signature dashed off across the bottom. A third, from 1950, entitled *Lady in Waiting to Queen Catherine in Henry VIII*, had two small swatches of the costume's material still pinned like butterflies to the canvas under the glass. On the back, held on by yellowing sticky-tape, was a photocopy of a photograph of my mum wearing the very same costume on stage in the production at Stratford. She must have been twenty-six. She looked raven-haired, dark-eyed, her face as pale as the moon, hawkishly beautiful, sitting on her haunches, stitching at the hem of the queen.

I sat at the desk and opened the scuffed cardboard Harrods gift box in which she kept her keepsakes and theatre souvenirs. The programmes inside were inexpensive – just folded sheets of pale yellow printed A4. One was headed *Shakespeare Memorial Theatre, Stratford-upon-Avon. 1950 Festival.* Underneath: *Julius Caesar; Measure For Measure; King Henry VIII.* I sifted among the sheaves of paper and found a typewritten page on the bordered foolscap she used to use with her old electric golf-ball typewriter:

I was one of only six women in a sixty-six strong company. The audiences were extraordinary. They queued all night, they queued all day. Fans lay is wait by the stage door, and they were just as delighted to get my autograph as Miss Ashcroft's.

The dressing room: first-night telegrams, picture post-cards and photographs bordered the mirrors; mascots, flowers, books and half-done crossword puzzles lay on the table, with pots of cold cream, cotton wool, powder and sticks of greasepaint. Square-toed Tudor shoes, green suede boots and patched ballet slippers jostled each other on the shoe-rack, and yellow woollen stockings, garters and white coifs hung on the towel rails. On the shelf above sat the wigs and hats of every shape and colour – demure gabled headdresses, golden fillets, blue felt waste-paper baskets, and white cambric cartwheels, and over the lamp-brackets were slung strange ropes of woollen pearls and exotic brass necklets made of bicycle-chain.

When the whole repertory of plays was running our costumes were exchanged daily according to the play that was being performed. The dressing room was thus constantly changing in mood and period. On Monday the racks were filled with dirty chrome and brown peasant costumes inspired by Bosch and Bruegel, which the producer would not allow to be cleaned because they looked more authentic when dirty. On Tuesday the rags and tatters of the Roman mob. By mid-week the barbaric splendour of Goneril's crimson velvet hung in solitary state. By Thursday the subdued browns and greys of Catherine of Aragon's sad Tudor ladies, and at the weekend the gorgeous-hued sapphire, primrose and cherry velvets of the Italian Renaissance.

I was struck by the eye for detail. I remembered looking up the season on the online British Theatre Archive Project and reading the ecstatic first-hand reviews of the audiences at the time. It was still ten years until Peter Hall would form the permanent year-round Royal Shakespeare Company, and the season in 1950 was seen by many back then as a milestone in British theatre history. I glanced down the cast list on one of the programmes. There were big names in the tiny roles – Robert Shaw and Robert Hardy as First and Second Gentleman – and the main parts were impressively star-studded – Alan Badel, Sir John Gielgud, and Harry Andrews.

The director was Anthony Quayle. The production was by Peter Brook.

I thought of how little it had meant to me when I was growing up and the struggle parents often have to impress their children with their past glories: all those box files and photos and scrapbooks kept for years in the hope at least one member of the family might be captivated. My mum once told me excitedly that *Harry Andrews* had offered her a lift to Stratford from Leamington station on her first day. I didn't know who Harry Andrews was. Much of what she said was a jumble of arcane words. 'I *danced* with Sir John in *Much Ado*, you know' was a favourite. It wasn't until I was seventeen that I took an interest in the theatre and decided to read drama at university, but even then I thought I knew best, and much of my mum's stuff was just old uninteresting history to me – even dancing with Gielgud. And then recently she had said to me, without any hint of sentimentality, 'They were the best years of my life. I was *accepted*.' And the word 'accepted' stayed with me.

I pictured her acting career slowed in its promising infancy by the Second World War, then stopped quickly in its tracks by family life. She'd had one child (Simon) with Ken – her first husband – in 1951, just after her debut season at Stratford, and was knitting booties for another one two years later and contemplating a gentle return to the stage, only to be told she ought to buy more wool as she was pregnant with triplets; it must have been such a shock. The hospital took an X-ray to confirm it. The spines showed up on the negative, as she used to say, like 'three little fish bones on a plate'. When she informed Ken of the news that evening at home, she told me the first words that came out of his mouth were 'How bizarre . . .' and then he turned away into the bay window and looked out on to the street in silence. Within a few months – in January 1954

– Toby, David Roualeyn ('Roly') and Jennie were born and turned her life upside down. It was on the front page of the *London Evening Standard: Triplets for Author's Wife*, ran the headline, with her picture above. Among all the excitement, she must have watched her dream of being an actress just melt away.

I put the papers back in the box and got up and walked into the hall. They'd be here soon. I looked around. It all seemed plausible: the front door with a little cupboard next to it for rubbish that could be collected by the porter from the outside without knocking; a place for coats and shoes and a big full-length wall-mirror for my mum in which to check herself before perhaps a matinée at the National Theatre; the easy-clean hardwood floors for soup spills; the compact fitted kitchen conveniently located next to the sitting room; the teak dining table that we almost left behind right there in its own perfect space in the sitting room; the books with the nicest spines I'd selected for the bookcase – some old Penguins, a biography of Jean Shrimpton, a hardback Brecht, an incomplete set of crumbling red-leather-bound Temple Shakespeares. But as I congratulated myself I noticed there were other things – chairs, a fruit bowl, those Portmeirion storage jars – that seemed to belong to other rooms I knew so well, the memories of which clung to me like smoke, and it was as if I'd stolen each item and repositioned it here in an unfamiliar place irresponsibly.

I leaned on the window ledge in the sitting room and watched a full number 13 double-decker bus, its lights glowing like a storm lantern in the gathering dusk, the windows misted, pull clear of the crossroads and disappear north towards Swiss Cottage, and I waited for them to arrive.

Shortly before five, the bell rang.

It was dark outside. As Roly brought them up in the lift, I ran round adjusting cushions, turning on table lamps, dimming the down-lights a little, muting the television and putting on some background jazz. It felt like a first date.

'I thought we were back at the hotel in Oxford until Roly told us where we were,' my mum said with a tight laugh, as we all greeted each other in the doorway.

They followed each other into the flat, my dad cautiously steadying himself on the door frame and watching where he put his feet, my mum overdoing the silent face of childish excitement at me, while pretending to tiptoe.

I showed them round.

'Do you like it?' I said, unable not to ask, as we finally settled in the sitting room after a brief tour, coats shed.

They looked tired and disorientated.

'Tom?' my mum said, as though she sensed I was expecting the final word on the matter, and it was his opinion that I was seeking.

My dad cleared his throat and looked round the room. He was out of breath. His face was chalky. He went to speak, then glanced at my mum, before dropping his head slightly and waving his hand in a limp surrender.

'Not now, darling,' my mum said, coming to his aid. 'It's been a long day. Ask us again in a day or two. I think we might as well be in Timbuktu.'

'Now what?' I said to Roly on the way down in the lift.

'Give it time,' he said.

I remembered us having a puppy once when I was young; that feeling when it was shut in the kitchen overnight for the first time, and I could sense it behind the door; and how I didn't know what it would make of the night; or what would have happened when we opened the door again in the morning.

I had that feeling as I drove home.

4

Three weeks after they moved in I invited my mum and dad up for Christmas lunch at our house; it was only five minutes away by car. Apart from a couple of scares with the unfamiliar waste-disposal unit and the immersion heater, things had gone uneventfully, if a little cautiously; or at least they hadn't told me otherwise. I collected them around eleven, wheeling my dad down in his shiny new wheelchair that I'd bought especially for their new life in London. The tyre-treads were still clean and supple, the footplates gleaming. As the flat door closed their breath was caught in the draught. A flurry of brackish sweetness. Burnt sugar.

We stood waiting for the lift. In the blunt sodium light of the lobby my dad looked terrible. His cheeks were criss-crossed under the skin with tiny broken crimson threads. His nose was blotchy and purple, and the skin on his forehead was red and desiccated as if he'd just brutishly rubbed his face with a bone-dry flannel. Perhaps he had. I looked at his clothes. Nothing smart. It wasn't like him. He'd pulled on a drab green fleece. I saw a smudge of mustard. My mum looked tired. Her dark grey hair was swept back off her forehead accentuating her sharp high cheekbones, her skin pale, but soft and sallow, her face fixed but watchful like a crow. She wore small turquoise studs in her ears, and was wrapped in a big brown woollen cardigan-coat that fell in folds like thick protective wings.

She roused herself. 'So clever, the wheelchair, Tom,' she said, enunciating each syllable so that he could hear her. I pictured her delivering it from a stage to the back of the upper circle. It was as though she wasn't related to him, a local church volunteer doing a good deed on Christmas Day for one of the old people.

'Yes. Clever,' he said.

'Fits easily in the lift, doesn't it?'

'Doesn't it.' He seemed to be used to this style of conversation. Efficient answers. Keep things moving. Did I sense a hint of embarrassment?

'So useful the way the wheels come off for the car,' she went on loudly.

'What's that?'

'The wheels – the way they come off. Very useful.'

'Very useful. Marvellous.'

We pushed open the glass doors and headed for the road.

'Ooh, it's quite brisk out, isn't it?'

'Brisk it is, Romany,' he said, his voice masterfully both dry *and* cheerful.

They were quiet on the journey. An estate car laden with presents pulled up alongside us at the traffic lights. My indicator silently winked, amber reflections in the silver gift-wrap on the parcel shelf.

At the house they parked themselves on the sofa amidst the Christmas tears and tantrums and torn wrapping-paper – our twin girls, Jean and Alfie, were nearly four years old. Blake, their little brother, was only nine months. My dad blinked and smiled and cupped his hand behind his ear every time someone spoke to him. My mum took Blake cautiously on her knee for a few minutes as though it were all new to her, before handing him back, a look of quiet relief on her face. I wondered if they both had terrible hangovers.

At lunch someone generously filled my dad's fat wine glass with a full-bodied red. St-Estèphe. *14%*. There was little I could do from the other end of the table. 'Stop worrying,' I said to myself. 'It's Christmas.' People were laughing. Someone blew on a kazoo. My mum jumped. I saw my dad swallow a mouthful then reach out through the hubbub and, with maximum concentration, pour another slug to top it up. Here comes trouble, I thought. Half an hour later, he went to stand up. His legs buckled and I saw him make a grab for the edge of the table. I was picking up a small rubber band and reading an abandoned Christmas motto when it happened. *Why do the Christmas elves wear seat belts? For Elf and Safety.* And as I finished it I saw his knees as they crumpled like a detonated wall. I caught him just in time and got him back into his chair. How long can this go on? I thought. And what's it like when I'm not there?

They lasted another half an hour in which time my mum managed a black coffee and my dad ate a handful of Quality Streets before I ushered them back to the car and drove them home.

Twenty minutes later as my mum said goodbye and went to close the door of their new flat I wanted to push it open again and remonstrate, or shout at them, or take a deep breath and sit down and talk calmly like someone from Social Services, but I did none of those things and just let her close it and stood silently in the cold corridor.

As a fifteen-year-old, alone in our old flat where I grew up, I would wait for them to come home from the pub on a school night, hearing the tyres approach on the road around ten, the car turning into the drive and stopping in the car-port, a stumble on the step, the key in the Yale lock, the heavy footsteps up the stairs to the flat, the overcompensation in their greeting, the fat-tongued words, their slight air of hostility as though they feared I would be censorious.

My mum wasn't a natural drinker. In fact, in the years with Ken, pubs were not in her social orbit at all; parties, dinners with theatrical friends, intellectuals and writers were more her thing, but to my dad socialising meant the pub and it always had done. Once they were married, my dad's choices dictated how they spent most of their leisure time, and pubs were top of the list.

Facing the village green and the graceful sweep of Barnes Pond with its curving white fence and green draping willows and swans, the Sun Inn was their favourite haunt as a drinking couple in the late sixties. I can remember being taken down on summer evenings – my earliest pub memory. I wasn't allowed inside, of course. Instead I was escorted through the gravel car park and the gate in the wall to the small empty silent wooden pavilion of the crown bowls club that backed on to the pub. I was given a Coke with a straw and a bag of roast-chicken-flavoured crisps, and cajoled into playing darts with perhaps another boy who might have been left loitering in there too, or – if the place was empty, which it usually was – I'd talk my dad into a quick game before he exited to drink in the bar with my mum and their current loose circle of drinking friends. I liked the darts: the wire mesh that separated the numbers; the little doors that folded back on which you could write the score in chalk; 'B' for Ben, 'D' for Dad. And I liked the smell of the old trestle tables, the earwigs, the mildew and the woodworm, the folded-up deckchairs stacked in the corner and the canvas bowls bags. It felt lived-in and oddly homely. After I got bored – if I was on my own – I ignored the *Keep Off* signs and tiptoed out under the pale urban stars on to the sumptuous, supple, yielding grass of the brick-walled bowls lawn, as flat as a snooker table. It was like walking on gentle springs, the turf so pliable and plump with dewy, sap-filled life. I walked right out into the middle, my heart thumping, and lay down on my back and stared up at the sky, listening to the distant muffled laughter from the pub. And on a clear night, I breathed in the cool, spotless air, and watch the winking red and white lights of the planes flying over south-west London into Heathrow, the TV aerials on the tops of neighbouring houses, the glow from the windows, other families passing through rooms, and I was aware that I didn't really like this part of my parents' life.

Not long after that Christmas, in January 2002, I fixed my mum and dad up with appointments with a new local doctor. It felt as if I was taking two vintage cars for a long-overdue MOT. Safety and roadworthiness were top of the list. I was worried about them in the new flat. 'It's still all a bit of a dream, dear,' my mum had said. 'Some days we have to remind ourselves where we are.'

My dad tried to keep it light and witty with the doctor, but she was more concerned with his shallow breathing and inability to use his inhaler properly, telling him flatly he must go back to using his spacer, which I know he thought made him look foolish. He grimaced quickly at me. She examined his 'frozen shoulder' and advocated physiotherapy and a steroid jab from a specialist. He nodded approvingly at me at the word 'specialist'. Pulling out his blood results, she said they showed enlarged red cells which were affecting his vitamin uptake. She also remarked that his blood pressure was a little high, and that the most likely cause of both was 'too much alcohol'. He pulled a serious face. She asked him to cut back. He nodded grimly. She finished by telling him to take regular aspirin, add some B12 and folic acid to his diet, and use the sleeping tablets – that he was swallowing like sweets – only when completely necessary, before remarking that his kidney and liver functions were 'on balance, satisfactory'. At this, he turned to me and beamed triumphantly.

As for my mum, the doctor linked her stories of recent gastric upsets to the powerful Vioxx painkillers she was taking for her rheumatism. The doctor suggested different medication, lined up a possible endoscopy, promised to monitor her eyesight, proposed additional calcium supplements, then finished by recommending a reduction in alcohol for her as well. It was all briskly unspectacular, and perhaps not the dressing-down I'd been expecting.

My mum and dad were ecstatic with the results. In the run-up to the check-ups, they'd feared what my mum had referred to more than once as an enforced 'booze embargo'. In fact, when I popped round to chat it all through with them the next day they seemed positively elated. Their faces seemed to be saying a little too smugly, 'No scolding allowed; doctor's note,' and they were each celebrating with a large brandy and a fresh slab of Cadbury Dairy Milk Caramel.

I took my dad to have his shoulder looked at. The specialist diagnosed a badly torn rotator cuff in the joint, but as he inserted the needle for the anti-inflammatory injection, he was more than surprised when blood spurted back up the syringe.

'Well, I wasn't expecting *that*. You must have had a nasty fall, Mr Watt,' he said, stepping back, blood on his cuff.

'Must I?' said my dad, blinking at him like a cartoon mole.

'When did it happen?'

'When did what happen?'

'The fall. Or could you have torn it in some other way? Would have needed some force for blood to still be in the joint like that.'

My dad looked at me and sucked his bottom lip in and gently shook his head.

'He has no memory of how he did it,' I said. I had an image of him tumbling down the stairs in Oxford or slipping in the shower and not telling anyone. Or just not telling me.

An operation to fix the tear was discussed. My dad said he couldn't face it. Instead we settled on management and pain-killers.

Back home I looked at all their appointments in the diary, and each one stood out like incontrovertible evidence of a new era of attempted control and reassurance. I was wearing the captain's armband now. Everything seemed part of the new plan: dynamic London; the fresh start; the compact flat; health checks; the wheelchair for my dad; a tube station for my mum. In spite of all the setbacks over the years – the repeated patterns of behaviour, the knowledge that very few old dogs learn new tricks – I was full of hope that all of it would help them turn a splendid corner, reanimated and inspired. I thought I could will it to happen.

On Sundays, during those first few weeks, I drove to Marks & Spencer in Camden and filled up an extra bag of food shopping for them – mainly ready-meals, some fruit and chocolate treats. I kept the fridge well stocked. Most weekends I had one of the kids with me. We'd park and take the lift up to the flat with the shopping, exchanging a couple of words with the porters. I discovered that the block was largely international lettings. The man in the flat opposite was Japanese, although my parents had barely seen him. Arab families passed us in the lobby. There was little eye contact from anyone and it started to bother me there was not much sense of community. It was the opposite of what I'd hoped, and I felt stupid for not thinking how the city might isolate them.

I warmed to the porters though. Jim, who was English, quieter and older, in – I guessed – his late fifties, had wiry white hair and apple cheeks, and a wobbling eye affected by nystagmus. Often poring over his newspaper, he seemed slightly unguarded and easily startled – perhaps not ideal attributes for a security porter. Luis – his shorter, swarthy partner – was younger and Portuguese, maybe mid thirties, and with his tie loosened I'm sure reckoned himself as a dead spit for a young Al Pacino on his Saturday night off. We talked mainly about football and the weather. They seemed to be keeping an eye out for my mum and dad. 'They are like a lord and a lady,' said Luis. It helped that my mum was inclined to tip them from time to time.

Up in the flat my mum always left something out for the kids to play with – a stuffed toy ('Why does Granny have a hippopotamus?'), a wind-up yapping crocodile ('Does she play with it too?'), a tin piggy bank, some Tupperware. My dad would be in his armchair in his pyjamas like a clapped-out Hugh Hefner with a 'pre-lunch brandy', which I imagined followed the 'post-breakfast brandy', and possibly even a small 'pre-breakfast brandy'. I ringed odd exhibitions and new plays in the newspaper and asked my mum to 'have a think about it', imagining she could manage a trip up to town. I copied out the telephone numbers of her oldest London friends and left them in big print on a piece of paper by the phone. 'Don't tell me off if I don't call them,' she said. 'It's a bit of a battle some days.'

In the kitchen I'd again try to show her how to work the dishwasher and the washer-dryer, but I could see her struggling with it all; they were different to the models they'd had in Oxford, which in themselves had probably taken several years to master. I looked at her and wondered if our memory, like an old notebook, must just fill up one day, leaving no room for new entries or instructions, no matter how clearly they are relayed. And I wondered if arbitrary pages, loosened by age, must then just start to fall out and go missing, and if – in the effort to keep going – we start making new assumptions to compensate, hazarding a guess, hoping no one will notice. Perhaps my mum was already cutting her losses, narrowing her options, mercifully using her remaining presence of mind to minimise risk, to avoid things that might be dangerous. Hot oil. That knife. But what about *without* presence of mind – when presence of mind is no longer there? When I thought of that, I worried I was asking too much of her, with all my painstaking guidance and tutelage in a new unfamiliar kitchen, so instead I hid the poultry shears and the modern vegetable peeler and wrote short cuts on pieces of paper and taped them to the control panels and the detergent-dispenser drawer of the dishwasher and the washer-dryer; but several weeks later I noticed neither machine had been used.

'I just use a bucket and rinse out a few smalls,' she said.

'What about the dishwasher, Mum?'

'Which one is that?'

I watched her shuffling around the small kitchen, misplacing a spoon, scribbling a note to herself and underlining it, peering shortsightedly at a letter from a utility company, or a circular that had landed alarmingly on the mat. I saw how control over all of it would slowly start to elude her.

And an image came to me of myself as a boy of eight lying awake in my room on a Saturday morning, safe under my candy-striped sheet and blankets, listening to the scuffling footfall of the pigeons on the flat roof above and the rustle of the leaves in the copper beech tree at the back, watching the corona of sunlight dance round the outline of the thin rough fabric curtains of my bedroom, listening to the sound of the water tank refilling, and knowing she'd be downstairs in the kitchen getting the day ready, purposeful and absorbed. And I saw myself getting up and going downstairs, across the bumpy linoleum landing, down the thinning red-patterned runner, past the painted woodchip wallpaper over which I ran my fingers, under the high skylight at the turn in the stairs where the water leaked every winter into saucepans and spread-out newspapers below, past the closed door to my mum and dad's bedroom at the foot of the stairs, with its humorous cardboard *No Molestar* sign snitched from a Mexican hotel hanging on the doorknob, and into the kitchen where she'd be quietly bustling. I could see myself taking my new copies of my Saturday football mags – *Shoot* and *Scorcher* – into the sitting room and lying on the floor to leaf through the pages, and my mum bringing me in some toast and jam ('Nice and quiet, please, darling, the house is asleep') and me looking up out through the window into an overcast sky and wondering why my dad got up so late and never wanted to talk to anyone for ages.

5

Back then my dad kept his piano in their bedroom but I didn't often hear him play it. Or sometimes he would start playing it and then I'd hear him stop. In the afternoons he'd go in there to work and I might hear the key turn in the lock on the inside, and then the creak of the double bed as he lay down, and he seemed to stay in there a long time in silence. In the holidays or at weekends I might be down in the garden playing on my own and I would look up at his bedroom window and notice that the curtains weren't drawn, which led me to believe he couldn't have been asleep, and I used to wonder what he must be doing in there. I came to the conclusion that he must be doing a lot of thinking.

And then one day I came home from school on a clear late-autumn afternoon and there was a different atmosphere in the flat. I could hear notes from the piano as I came up the stairs to the flat door. I went into the kitchen. My mum was bright and her face looked like someone had turned a light on inside it. She was arranging a cup and saucer on a tea-tray. 'Tea for the thirsty worker!' she chimed. 'You can pop your head round the door, but don't stay long. So much to do!'

I gently pushed open the bedroom door. Behind it a black gate-leg table had been set up at right angles to the small brown upright piano. A fresh ream of manuscript had been cracked open. Black-and-red-striped dark 2B pencils lay ready in a row next to an eraser. There was a steel sharpener, a tuning fork and a long wooden ruler that was four times the length of the pocket one I took to school. More manuscript was propped up along the music rack on the piano and several double sheets were spread open across the top. My dad had the fingers of his right hand spread wide and he was holding down several notes at once. He lifted his hand, then keeping the same shape, played the notes again and I saw his right foot hold down the right-hand pedal underneath. He lifted his hand from the keys, grabbed a pencil, and as the sound kept ringing in the room he lightly whistled a few notes and wrote them on the stave.

'Five saxophones, four trumpets, four trombones. Was there ever a better sound?' he said, still looking at what he was writing, but clearly for my benefit. Then he span round on his stool and grinned at me – a big grin, the pencil between his teeth – and I sensed my mum come in behind me with the tray of tea and she was grinning too.

That evening, after I'd done my homework, he took me to the Ship Inn at Mortlake to celebrate, though what we were celebrating I wasn't quite sure. The pub sat right on the river's edge in the shadow of the vast, brick, eight-storey Victorian maltings of the Watney's brewery. The maltings scared me. It loomed like a blank hulk above the towpath, featureless and threatening. I wondered how much grain must be piled high inside, soaking in the monstrous vats of water. When the tide was out, the foreshore was an oozing mud-pit of stones and washed-up plastic debris, and if a mist had dropped low on to the water's surface, as it often did in the cold dusk of an approaching winter night, I half expected to see a lighterman – or another river character I'd picked up from Dickens read aloud at school – sculling gently towards me, the rudder lines of his darkened boat slack in the turbid shallows. And yet, in spite of this, I got a thrill from being there, and loved the moment of expectation as we made the final turn in the car down Ship Lane, not knowing if the tide would be out, or in, and lapping at the very end of the road where we had to park, like a filthy tongue.

Looking back now, I know what it all meant. It was 1970. Work had been drying up for my dad since the mid-sixties; the work for modern composer-arrangers was in TV and pop, not in the thing he lived for – live ensemble jazz – and yet, just when it looked like it would never return, he had been offered the chance to revive the sound with his own new nine-piece band in nightly residency at the Dorchester in London. Everything seemed glamorous and important again.

In the fifties there were perhaps a hundred jazz big bands touring up and down the country, each sporting up to sixteen members – eight brass, five saxophones and a rhythm section; it was a unique and rich composite sound. But by the late fifties ballroom owners had realised that booking four or five young amateurs with electric guitars and amplification was a lot cheaper, and what's more it brought the new sound with it – the sound of rock 'n' roll. The big band age was dying. After a meteoric rise in the late fifties, the last notable event of any size that my dad had been involved with was a European Broadcasting Union concert at the Playhouse on Northumberland Avenue in London in 1966, where he'd directed an All-Star European big band including Albert Mangelsdorff on trombone and the Spanish tenor player Pedro Iturralde. The poster for it hung in the hallway at home when I was young. The names seemed exotic, weighty and serious, but my dad had wrinkled his nose when I'd asked him about it. It was as though it signified something disappointing.

In their heyday the big bands created a finishing school for young emerging players and acted as a bedrock for working jazz musicians. Before getting his break as a composer and arranger, my dad had cut his teeth playing piano with a whole list of them after moving to London following the Second World War, starting with Ronnie Munro's band in 1948 running through to Harry Roy's at the Café de Paris in 1953. Apart from the high quality of musicianship, the bands also brought a huge camaraderie, and for a generation of young men still used to the rigours of wartime deployment, the ballsy convivial communal effort of jazz orchestras must have felt like second nature. Archer Street in Soho was a magnet for any jazz musician looking for work. Crowds of them gathered during the day exchanging stories, picking up bookings. If the police were diverted by one of the frequent break-ins at one of the jeweller's in nearby Burlington Arcade, it would be accompanied by the sound of two hundred musicians whooping and whistling. 'I never wanted to go to bed,' my dad once said. 'You'd play until the small hours, go back to someone's flat, play cards until dawn, and then you wanted to be back at it by late morning. It was a drug.'

We stood just above the foreshore at the Ship Inn, the sun melting behind the silhouettes of the trees on Dukes Meadows on the far side of the river. My dad seemed in a good mood. I was allowed a second Coke. He picked up an empty plastic bleach bottle from the flotsam washed up along the tideline, shook out the water, and placed it on the corner of the brick embankment over to our left. Then he bent down and picked up a handful of pebbles and stones.

'Hit it from ten paces and I'll give you a quid,' he said.

A quid, I thought. He never gave me a quid; he must be in a good mood. I pictured my favourite toyshop in East Sheen and imagined what I could buy with it: some Subbuteo accessories maybe; a new yo-yo.

He was throwing one of the pebbles up into the air and catching it repeatedly in the palm of his hand.

I marked out ten paces and took a pebble from him. 'Best of three?' I said.

He took out a cigarette, rapped the end of it three times on the box and perched it on his lower lip. 'If you like,' he said out of the corner of his mouth, half smiling. He took out his Ronson cigarette lighter. I liked his lighter a lot. It felt nice in the hand: the leather grip and the chrome burner. Sometimes he'd let me top it up from a small yellow gas cylinder, which hissed as you pushed down on the red spout, and spilled clear fluid that evaporated from your fingers. He lit his cigarette, still looking at me. I sensed he was weighing me up.

I took another two pebbles and lined up the first shot. A riverboat cruised through my eye-line, its lights reflecting in the black steel water. I heard the gentle wash as the river slooshed on to the shore. I pulled back my shoulder, closed one eye, focused on the bottle, opened my eye again and threw the pebble hard. It missed by some distance. I heard it land with a soft pock into the mud.

My dad smiled wryly. 'One down . . .' he said.

'Yes, I know,' I jumped in. 'Two to go.'

I took the second pebble, was about to throw, then switched it for the other one in my hand, then switched back again. The second throw missed. I felt a hot flash in my chest. 'Don't say anything,' I said quickly.

My dad stood there quietly, a low smile on his lips, half affectionate, half entertained. His hair was immaculately parted, a small badger's streak appearing in the swept-back low quiff. He had one hand in his pocket. The other held the cigarette. He took a drag, briefly letting go of it. The orange tip intensified in the fading light like embers caught in a draught. Then he took it again between his fingers and moved it down to his side, and blew the smoke out in a long feathery plume from the corner of his mouth.

The third pebble I just threw quickly. I didn't want to line it up, and make it even worse than it was surely going to be by even trying to get it right. I just wanted to get rid of it.

The pebble sailed through the air and to my astonishment grazed the side of the bottle. For a moment I thought it would fall. I took in a sharp breath. The bottle rocked on the stone wall for what seemed like for ever but then righted itself and didn't fall.

'I hit it. I hit it!'

'So you did. The quid's yours.' He hadn't moved, still the same smile on his lips. 'Tell you what, if *I* can hit it, I'll *double* it.'

I gasped. Two quid. *Two* quid. I thought of the pencils in a row on the gate-leg table and my mum with the tray of tea; it must be good news, whatever it is, I thought. I opened my eyes wide and gazed at him.

He bent over and scooped up a stone. He was two or three paces behind me; that made it at least twelve or thirteen from the bottle. I stepped back. He stubbed out the final third of his cigarette, smearing it into the path with the sole of his shoe. I heard the gravel grind. Then he pulled back his arm. For a moment he didn't look athletic at all. In fact, he looked some-how constricted, and I remembered how he never looked comfortable throwing a tennis ball; often he just threw it underarm. And I thought of how he always pulled out of a tackle if we played football, and couldn't play badminton in the garden without making a jokey shot.

He let fly with the pebble.

As it left his hand I lost it against the background of the huge brick wall of the maltings. It was as though it was a magic trick and he had made it disappear. He used to fool me and pretend he had found a sixpence behind my ear, or had guillo-tined his thumb at the knuckle, and for a moment I wondered if the pebble had vanished. The maltings seemed massive in the thickening dusk, like a huge hole with the pewter sky above it.

The pebble missed by a mile. I didn't know whether I was pleased or disappointed. Part of me had wanted him to smite the bottle into the river like a real dad. Part of me was pleased I had grazed it and he had missed.

He straightened up, and winked. 'The two quid's yours anyway,' he said. 'It's our lucky day.' Then he put his arm round me and we walked back to the car. 'Your father's got a jazz orchestra again,' he said. 'We're back in business.'

6

The door was ajar. Milky April light dropped through the stippled glass of the frosted window at the end of the corridor. It was chilly. The air smelled yeasty. I pushed the door to the flat open into a quilt of dry heat. A whiff of old butter and stale clothes lingered in the hallway. All the lights were on. It was just gone four in the afternoon.

My mum was walking towards me from the sitting room. The TV was on behind her. I could hear the racing commentary. It was Aintree Grand National Day 2002. They had been at the flat for four months. She padded towards me, her purple towelling trousers sagging at the knee, a paper napkin wrapped around two fingers.

'Where is he?' I said.

'In the bathroom, of course.' Her voice was slurred. 'Silly old fool.'

Along the short corridor the bathroom door was open. My dad was lying on the floor. It was a small room; his body seemed to take up all the floor space. He was still in his pyjamas and dressing gown. The dressing gown was unbelted and his pyjama trousers were half unbuttoned. He was lying on his back. Under his head a halo of deep red blood spread out in a thick circle on the grey marble tiles. Some of it had trickled into the grouting like rays of crimson light.

I knelt down. In the calmest, most non-committal voice I could muster I said, 'Dad . . .'

'Mmmm.' He responded to his name but his eyes remained closed.

'You all right?'

'Fine.'

His casual tone surprised me, as though I'd just said lunch would be ready in five minutes. 'The ambulance is on its way,' I said.

'Lovely.' He opened his eyes and blinked at the ceiling. The same brackish sweet smell was on his breath. I felt unnerved. Oddly aggrieved.

My mum was standing behind me in the doorway. She had called me a little more than fifteen minutes before saying he had had a fall. 'Badly?' I'd asked. 'Well, there's blood,' had come the reply. 'Have you called for an ambulance?' There'd been a belch down the phone. 'Can you do it, darling?' she'd said rather flatly. 'Would be so much easier. You know the number and everything.' I'd hung up wondering if she really couldn't remember how to dial 999 before running to find my keys.

'What happened, Dad?'

'No idea.'

'You had a fall?'

He cleared his throat. 'Clearly.' He was still looking up at the ceiling.

'He went for a pee after the race,' my mum said, over-articulating each syllable. 'I heard a crash. I think it was the edge of the bath. He nearly did the same last week.'

I heard footsteps in the hall. I'd left the front door open. It was Jim, the porter from downstairs. He was followed by two paramedics in green jumpsuits.

'You all right, Romany?' Jim said nervously, smoothing his hand across his mat of wiry white hair, his suit rustling. His weak eye seemed to be wobbling a lot.

'Oh, *ye-e-e-s*,' said Mum, extending the 'e' in the word, brushing the moment away with a stiff broom, as though she'd been asked the same question for years and no one ever expected her to say anything other than 'yes' and remain phlegmatically contained in alarming circumstances involving my dad.

'Where is he?' said the first paramedic, pushing past.

I stood up to let him in.

'Oh, deary me. Made a nice mess of your tiles there, Thomas,' he said, crouching down.

'Tommy,' I said.

My dad made to raise his head.

'Just lie still for a moment there, Tommy, and we'll get you sorted out.'

My dad lay still while they tended to him. In his pyjamas, with his little white goatee joined up to his moustache, and that familiar faraway look in his small green eyes, and his red button nose and crimson tributaries on his cheeks, he looked like a little homeless Disney character. The eighth dwarf. Dopey, Grumpy and Tommy, I thought to myself.

Within a few minutes they had him upright and sitting on the edge of the bath.

'Couple of nasty gashes. Not too bad. Seen worse today. Always bleeds a lot, the head. Don't worry,' the paramedic said, as much to me as to my dad.

My mum was back out in the hall.

'Best get you checked over though. You don't want a bang to

the head if you can help it. We'll run you down to St Mary's, Tommy. OK?'

He nodded and blinked.

'Any chance you could make it the Royal Free?' I said. 'It is nearer me and I'm going to be the one dealing with this.'

'Not really supposed to,' said the paramedic. 'We were called out from St Mary's. This is Westminster, isn't it?'

'Borderline,' I said with a beseeching look.

He looked at his colleague, who shrugged. 'Oh, go on, then,' he said. 'But don't mention it if they ask.'

I smiled.

He winked.

A stretcher – more like an orange seaside deckchair mounted on fat pneumatic rubber wheels – was brought in. They dressed his head wound and sat him in the chair, strapping him in. He looked like he was being prepared for an airline safety demonstration.

'Shall I stay here, dear?' my mum said to me. 'Will you be all right without me?'

'Don't you think you ought to go with him in the ambulance, Mum?' I said.

'Really? Do I need to?'

'It might be nice,' I said, opening my eyes wide at her, trying to stir her sympathy. 'For the company, no?' I looked at her: her tipsy expression; her lifeless shoulders. It was as if all her body weight had been transferred to her feet, as though her prevailing exasperation at all of it had snuffed out concern. It wasn't that she didn't love him deep down, I thought. It was that it was getting increasingly hard to dig it out. I sensed the deferral of power blaze in my stomach; everything about them now seemed my responsibility, even attempting to manage their feelings for each other, but as I readied myself, she suddenly spoke up.

'Oh, *all right*,' she sighed testily. 'Where's my bag?' She shuffled off down the hall muttering.

The paramedics were wheeling my dad out of the flat. I said I would bring my mum down, then follow in the car and meet them all at the hospital.

My mum dithered in front of the hall cupboard, peeling off her towelling cardigan, replacing it with a lightweight rainjacket, choosing then rejecting a hat, then choosing another. She searched her handbag for something.

'Will I need to *pay*?' she asked.

'No, Mum. There's been a National Health Service since 1948.'

That seemed to bring the search to an end. She gathered her things and I got her downstairs.

My dad was being hoisted into the ambulance. A man in shorts holding two packed sandwiches was watching from the opposite pavement next to a couple in matching wraparound sunglasses. A vast pink stretch-limousine with blacked-out windows was trying to edge past the ambulance in the narrow road. Up on the steps to the front door of the block of flats I could see Jim the porter watching us, stroking his wiry hair as if it were a cat, his suit probably rustling.

It was a beautiful afternoon. The sunlight ricocheted brilliantly off the white villas on the corner. The trees were leafing. I listened to the steady wind-rush of traffic noise as it ran up from the white tented circus tops of Lord's Cricket Ground. Two black taxis idled in the rank opposite the tube station. I saw the flower-cart and little palm trees, the patchwork of magazines on the news-stand, the people coming and going; I found it alive and comforting. I'd hoped all of it could have brought my parents out of themselves, helped them rise to some last-chance good times in the murmuring city, but as I watched the orange seat disappear, and the door close behind them, and the ambulance slip into the afternoon traffic, they seemed threatened and consumed by it all.

Back up in the flat I fetched a cloth and some water from the kitchen. I mopped up my dad's blood, rinsing it into the basin. There was piss all round the loo and I left it. I walked into the sitting room. All the Venetian blinds were down, but slatted to let in light. It was a decent room to grow old in, I thought. I turned off the dusty TV. Within arm's reach of each of their armchairs – nestled on the side tables, in among the soft peach-coloured paper tissues, the wedges of foil-wrapped Cadbury's Fruit & Nut, the magnifying glasses, the crumbs, the marker pens and jotters – were large tumblers of brandy, not poured as a shot or even a double, but like full glasses of water would be poured. I picked them up and walked into the kitchen. I went to throw them down the sink, then paused. Does this make me look bad? I thought. Too disapproving? The Temperance Society? Why shouldn't they do as they like? I put the tumblers back on the work surface. A hunk of badly wrapped half-dried-out Cheddar sat on a chopping board, the end of it cracked and split like a dry log. Next to it was a loaf of processed white sliced bread flopping out of its packet and some Flora warming with the lid off.

I opened the freezer door above the fridge. Seven frozen Marks & Spencer ready-meals had gathered a heavy frost: the ones I bought them in pairs every weekend to try to make sure they ate something. I closed it and opened the fridge door below. It was almost empty: some parched supermarket ham curling in an unsealed packet, tiny granules of salt crystallising on the darkened dried-out surface of the exposed meat; an opened can of Stella; a bottle of soda water; a gel eye-mask; a brown banana. I shut the door and took the brandy over to the sink and poured it slowly into the waste disposal. It smelled of wood polish and toffee apple. The action suddenly seemed melodramatic and wasteful, but I felt as if I were pouring away risk. Although I still wondered if I had a right to.

I walked back out into the hall to find my dad's wheelchair. I'd driven up the Watford Way to the roundabout near the A1 in Mill Hill to buy it at the 'mobility and independent-living retailer' as soon as they had moved to the flat. I'd circled the shop for ages before hand-picking it. I told myself it was the lightweight functionality that made me choose it, but if I am honest it was just the black metal frame; it made it seem a bit more stylish and less old people-y than the grey institutional-ised design of most of the others in the shop. I was still trying to keep upbeat about the whole thing. The wheelchairs all had names like the Escape, the Breezy, the Getaway. It was like buying a weekend holiday train ticket. I'd weighed up other things in the shop too, and wondered how many I might be returning for at some stage – the wide-head, easy-turn keys for bathroom taps; the heavy-duty ferrules for walking sticks; the handy-reacher-litter-picker; the non-slip bedside rug. Two other women were in the shop. I kept looking at what they were buying. Was their situation better? Worse? At least no one was buying incontinence pants. Onc was asking about a telephone amplifier; that seemed unthreatening. I pictured an elderly relative in tweed and small brown leather shoes settling into a high-backed wing-chair with a nice cup of tea and a copy of *The Field* after a tiring thirty minutes round John Lewis listening to the answerphone messages from her grandchil-dren. The other woman was weighing up the contrasting benefits of 'flange' versus 'chrome' grab rails. All sensible stuff. I paid, dismantled the wheelchair, placed it neatly in the boot of my car with an ease that made me think life was going to be better now, and drove back down the narrow dual-carriageways of Hendon.

My mum had planned to be thrilled by it. She had already earmarked a couple of spots outside the block of flats – 'viewing platforms' she'd called them – where she had imagined she would wheel my dad for sunny afternoons and a bit of fresh air, reading to him from the paper or toying with a crossword clue, as London burbled by. 'Tom's freedom pass,' she'd joked. But when it arrived and she realised how heavy he was in the chair, and how they had argued from the moment he sat in it, it had just stood in the hall.

The wheelchair was beside the front door. A speckled layer of dust was on the armrests. I found the footplates; they were in the coat cupboard. I fitted them back on but had to search in my dad's bedroom for the seat pad. His bed, a single, was unmade as though he could return to it at any minute. The bottom sheet was washed but imprinted where his body had lain and perspired until the cotton had become impregnated with a faint oily shadow. The turquoise pillowcase was freckled with dry skin. There was a screwed-up primrose-yellow tissue on the shiny pine bedside table but that was all – no lamp or clock or water. The blinds were drawn to shut out the day. 'I don't know how he does it,' my mum had said. 'All day in there sometimes. It would drive me mad. Not even a book. Poor sod.'

On the long wooden cabinet against the wall sat his hi-fi system – the same one I'd bought him for his sixtieth in 1985, presented to him somewhat ostentatiously in the dressing room at Hammersmith Odeon after one of our shows. On reflection it had been a clumsy display of power on my part: first I perform the sell-out gig, then I bestow the surprise lavish gift in front of friends and family. Clunky. The golden boy strikes again.

The amplifier had white stickers on some of the buttons, and on them in my mum's handwriting were written in blue felt-tip: *CD, Tape! Not this!* The actual power button was missing, snapped off. A sticker above it said *ON*, and a small hole showed where it should have been. I couldn't help wondering if it had been pushed *inside,* or wrenched away in a confused fury, or knocked off by an unintentional lurch.

His CDs and tapes were neatly laid out – the CDs in flip-front racks, the tapes along the windowsill. They seemed in the same order I had left them. Some of the cassettes were in my faded handwriting on black Memorex tape from when we'd taken possession of a used Sanyo Music Centre from a neighbour in 1977 and I'd shown him how to copy his albums to play in the car. I opened the tray on the CD player wondering what I might find – an old favourite perhaps; Zoot Sims; Bill Evans. But it was empty. It felt as if he hadn't played anything in that room.

I walked back into the hall, dropped the seat pad on to the wheelchair, tidied a few things away in the kitchen, then pushed the wheelchair out of the flat, closing the door behind me.

7

The hospital kept my dad in for two nights. I ran my mum home on the first evening after she realised sitting behind a curtain for several hours in A&E with him 'Nil By Mouth', and her the same, was hardly her idea of a night out. She'd tried to buy a snack from the vending machine but hadn't been able to follow the instructions or work out how to retrieve the coins. I left her at the flat and told her to eat something, drink some water and get some sleep.

It was grey and overcast the morning I collected him, the clouds massed together like lint gathered in the filter of a tumble-drier. 'He's had some painkillers for the bump and we've rehydrated him – should perk him up for a bit,' said the nurse as he was discharged.

The wheelchair was certainly coming into its own, I thought, as we trundled out. He had his few belongings in a blue plastic *Patient Property* carrier bag on his lap. 'They tried to put my teeth in there, stupid fools,' he said, gesturing at the bag. 'Can't greet my public without them – they'll think I'm finished.'

It was a tough push up the steep incline of Pond Street, but we crossed on the zebra, and turned into Hampstead Hill Gardens where I'd parked. 'Lucky you don't weigh a ton,' I said.

'Unlike your mother.'

Same old jokes – it was like nothing had happened. I stopped the wheelchair, and walked round to face him. 'No regrets?' I said, meeting his eye.

'What do you mean?'

'All this. The fall. The hospital. Just going to carry on as before?'

He took one hand off the plastic bag and wiped his fingers back and forth across his brow. 'You're right, Ben. Please accept my apologies. Unacceptable behaviour,' he said. He seemed contrite, but there was something glib in the delivery, an undertow of saying the right thing to please me.

'Have you any idea what the hospital said to me?'

'No, what?'

'Only the extremely obvious: that they thought about admitting you to the "falls clinic" but the reasons were fairly clear to them – chronic breathing difficulties, low oxygen intake, plus alcohol; it's not a great combination for steadiness on the feet, wouldn't you agree?' I waited for a response. He blinked. 'No wonder you fell, and will keep on falling, and I am the one who is going to have to keep picking you up if this carries on.'

He said nothing. He looked down the road, then at the back of his hands. Then he looked up at me. 'Understood, Ben.' He had on his penitent face.

I remembered the day in Oxford a few years earlier when he'd completely surprised me by ending a heated exchange with, 'In this, as in all things going forward from now on, I *defer* to you. And I've told your mother.' I thought he was joking but then I realised he was deadly serious. And with it, a fire had seemed to go out, and over the ensuing months he became more pliant and obliging. But now, I couldn't tell if it was still smouldering, like a dormant volcano.

'Come on then,' I said, moving on. 'Let's get you back. Mum'll be wondering where we are.'

A couple of days later my mum asked me to come over. We sat in the sitting room. They were doing their best impression of being alert. My mum was sitting forward, perched on the front of her chair. 'You'll be glad to hear you father's off the booze,' she said, by way of an introduction. 'Aren't you, darling?'

My dad nodded solemnly from his armchair. He had made the effort to get dressed. An unironed gingham shirt was tucked into a pair of dark blue track pants. His narrow white bare feet looked like fragile seashells resting in his burgundy leather slippers.

'It was all a shock: the ambulance and everything; and we accept we haven't adapted well to the move. I think we have felt, well . . . a little isolated and disorientated, haven't we, darling?' she said, looking at my dad again.

He nodded solemnly again.

'And I didn't tell you, but that was not the first fall,' she said, trying not to look too sheepish.

'I am not totally surprised,' I said. 'How many?'

'A few . . . maybe six. Or seven.'

'Seven!?' I tried to hide too much surprise.

'Yes, the porters have been very helpful.'

'What do you mean the *porters*? They've been up *here*? Into the flat?'

'Yes. They say it is no bother. But let's not dwell, dear. We are *chastened*, aren't we, darling?' she said, turning to my dad again.

'Chastened is the word, Romany,' he said, nodding once as if to cement it into the conversation.

'And *remorseful*,' she added.

'Another good choice of word, Romany,' he said.

They seemed like a double-act. It was hard to tell whether they had selected the words before I arrived, chosen for the effect they hoped they would have on me. I looked at both their faces. They were looking at me expectantly like pets awaiting a treat. I had been here before; the history of my adult relationship with them was benchmarked with promises of abstinence. 'ON WAGON', she wrote to me memorably as I started my second year at university in 1982. 'Dad fell over the saucepans when he came in last night, but apart from this one lapse we have been SCARSDALING without booze in the house since last Monday.'

I looked at both their hopeful faces. Pre-planned or not, I tried to get into the spirit of thinking that a small Rubicon might have been crossed, however temporarily. I smiled. 'Good for you,' I said, trying to muster as much neutral sincerity as possible, but after I'd said it I thought about the oily shadow on my dad's bed, and the hours he was spending there under the landslide of thoughts inside his head, and I knew it was only a matter of time before we were back where we started.

In the kitchen a few minutes later I said to my mum on her own, 'Would he try Prozac, or something similar, do you think?'

'The happy pills? He is resistant, darling. His doctor got him on something like that for a while in Oxford, as you know, but as soon as his mood lifted he stopped. Didn't trust it. Said he felt odd. We are the wrong generation, dear.'

'And you?'

'Oh, you know me, I'll try anything for a quiet life. Maybe now is a good time. I think they work for me. Hard to tell. Have I tried them? I can't remember. I might be already taking them. Pills for this. Pills for that.' She tidied some lists and reminders to herself by the telephone.

I swept some crumbs off the worktop into a dustpan.

'Anyway, it's probably *Alzheimer's*,' she added with a dramatic flourish. 'Doubt you can do much about that. Funny farm only, probably.'

'The hospital made no mention of it, Mum,' I said, refusing to rise. 'They just thought he was drinking too much for a man in his condition.'

'Well, you won't change him now.'

'What's the point in stopping the booze then?'

'Oh, leave it now, please, darling. I can't keep up with you. We're doing our best.'

I put the brush and dustpan back in the cupboard and moved a magnet around on the door of the fridge.

'Sorry for all the fuss,' she said. 'It's all very strange, you know.'

By that summer my Sunday visits to their flat were interleaved with occasional weekday lunches at our house. I found I could wheel my dad from the car along the alley that led to the garden and almost directly into our kitchen. Things seemed to be going quite straightforwardly, although I sensed an underlying note of worry from my mum.

'He was up at three o'clock last night,' she said to me on the phone one morning. 'I heard a noise. He was getting dressed. He said he had an *appointment*. I told him he must have been dreaming. Get back into bed, you silly old fool, I told him. And he keeps thinking we're on holiday. He keeps asking about when we'll be back in Oxford. But he seems all right this morning.'

I said I'd pop round.

I drove to the flat. I took the ticket for the NCP car park under the block, and as the barrier went up, I moved from brilliant August light into darkness. I turned the car tightly past the attendant's booth with its cluster of ghostly TV screens, and past the empty bays of the upper level, each reserved with a single traffic cone. My tyres squealed on the corners as I spiralled down. It was only on the lowest level – four storeys below, and as silent as a mausoleum – that I'd ever found a space, where the ramp stopped up against a dead-end and a chained gate to a darkened generator room, where the only other cars were long since driven, parked in the shadows, shrouded under sheets like long low tombs, thickly caked in dust, spectral and strange.

I parked and got out. The sound of the car door closing bounced off the concrete walls. I thought of my mum moving around in the flat, floors and floors above. It felt miles away. Unnerved, I found the green exit door and climbed the stairs back up to the light. The steps emerged near the front door to the flats. I could see Jim the porter reading his paper. Palms and conifers framed the path as I breathed in the warm fresh air. A chaffinch was singing in the maple above my head.

Upstairs I rang the bell to the flat. Nothing. I rang again. Finally I heard the chain.

'Who is it?' It was my mum's voice behind the door.

'It's me, Mum. Ben.'

She opened the door. In her hand was a frozen Macaroni Cheese – one of the ones I'd bought her from Marks & Spencer.

'Sorry, dear, I was on the sofa with my leg up. I've rather bashed my knee. Nothing serious. Bruise probably.' She held up the ready-meal. 'No peas, so I was using this.'

'Oh, Mum, how?'

'I was trying to plug the TV in and lost my balance.'

'But the TV is always plugged in.'

'Is it? I couldn't get it to work.'

'Where's Dad?'

'In bed.'

'But you said he was OK.'

'He was. But now he isn't, I suppose.'

'Is he taking his paroxetine?'

'No idea.'

'But you said you were pleased he was trying some new tablets.'

'Did I? I can't police everything.'

I made a cup of tea and sat with her for a while.

'He's just switched off,' she said, after a long silence. 'As long as I am here, he is OK, but I daren't go out, not even to the shops, and of course he is not interested in my interests.'

'Was he ever?'

'Oh, don't be cruel, darling.' She looked across the room, lost in thought. 'We have our moments.' She ran her finger across her knee. 'But it's getting worse.'

'What is?'

'Him. His absence.'

'What do you mean?'

'It's like sometimes a piece of him has . . . He's just a little old man. Don't expect too much, dear.'

'I don't, Mum. It's OK.'

'It *must* be Alzheimer's. What else could it be?'

'Well, his chest must be hard to cope with, and he needs his oxygen and everything, but I'll speak to the doctor if it would put your mind at ease.'

'Would you, dear? I would so appreciate it.'

With the two of us sitting there I remembered the after-noons when I was young, when she worked from home as a journalist. She'd let me lie on the floor and draw in the door-way, to be near her, as long as I was quiet. She'd made a new career for herself in the mid-fifties since abandoning hopes of acting amid the havoc of full-time motherhood. ('I was offered an audition for a part in Marlowe's *Edward II*, but was too tired to even read it.') Instead – making use of her first husband Ken's contacts as an author and theatre critic – she'd grabbed an opportunity to write about life with the triplets for the *Daily Express*. The piece went down well. It was sharply observed and drily humorous, and with Ken's help, more select doors opened to the *Evening Standard* and the *Daily Mail* and soon she was writing regular columns. 'No one had written about motherhood as light comedy before,' she once said to me. 'It wasn't just your father who could be funny, you know.' By the early sixties, she was editing the 'Femail' page for the *Daily Mail,* and then *She* magazine came knocking and she was offered the chance to try her hand at some bigger celebrity interviews.

I pictured her tiny study just off the sitting room on the first floor in the house where I grew up. It used to be my room when I was baby. It was barely big enough for the desk and chair that sat in the middle of the room. It had a couple of filing cabinets either side, and piles of papers and cuttings and thick glossy *Spotlight* directories full of thousands of black-and-white publicity photos of endless actors and actresses. The pin-board was covered in clippings and reminders and phone numbers. (*Clear guttering. RING IAN HOLM!!*) She wrote at a small portable Adler typewriter with the phone to hand all the time – a big red GPO 746, with a rotary dial and a deafening ring. She smoked back then – Piccadilly, filter-tipped, the short ones in the wide hard box – and I'd listen to the rat-a-tat of the keys, the ding as she got to the end of the line, and the swoosh of the carriage-return. Suddenly she'd rifle through her address book, then pick up and dial – 'Hello, Peter, darling, it's Romany . . . Listen, I'm sorry to be a *frightful* bore but I'm writing this *dreadful* piece. Need a quick quote . . . you know how it is. Won't keep you. Anyway, do you think *femininity* is *going out of style?*' I'd lie quietly in the doorway to the sitting room with empty paper pulled out of one of her scrapbooks and spend an hour with a ruler and some coloured pens designing my own hand-drawn newspaper, complete with animal stories, TV listings and football results. I enjoyed the eavesdropping. It seemed like the outside world was the place to be.

An hour later, as I was leaving, she said casually, 'I think I'm going to have to find a doctor, you know. Something odd is going on downstairs.'

For a moment I thought she meant something to do with the porters until I saw her face. 'What do you mean?'

'I don't like to bother you with these things, darling, but I have no one else to tell.' She lowered her voice. 'It's like I'm trying to give birth to an *egg*.'

That night I spoke to Tracey.

'Oh, no,' she said. 'Sounds like a prolapse.'

'*Really?*'

'She's had five kids. Three at one time. Women didn't exactly do the exercises back then. Wouldn't be surprised. The womb can no longer be supported. It can *drop*. Poor thing. You'd better call someone.'

Within a couple of days it was clear my mum would need a hysterectomy. Which meant time in hospital. Which meant I had to do something about my dad.

8

'How was the traffic, Tommy?'

My dad looked up across the table at the sound of his name.

We were sitting in a cramped office in a north London care home not far from their new flat. The overhead lights were bright. A geriatric psychiatrist – tall, thin, Irish, in a tweed jacket – was standing on the other side of the table, leafing though some paperwork. My dad looked as if he wasn't sure if the question had been for him. He glanced at the stranger, blinked and said nothing, then looked at the backs of his hands.

'The traffic, Tommy. All right, was it?' said the psychiatrist again, casually. I could tell he was trying to defuse the impression that he was commencing some kind of assessment.

With my mum in hospital for her hysterectomy, my dad had agreed to let me check him into the care home for a few nights. He was OK about it. He knew he couldn't have coped at the flat on his own, and our house was impractical with steep stairs and the clamour of three small kids. I hadn't told him anything about a psychiatric assessment. I'd just told him there'd be a bit of form-filling and registration on arrival.

My dad, now aware he was being addressed, cleared his throat and said, 'Yes, normal traffic.'

'Good. That was lucky. Now then . . .' The psychiatrist sat down and looked at him across the table. 'Mind if I ask a few questions just to get you settled in?'

'Fire away,' said my dad.

'Excellent. Right. Do you know where we are, Tommy?'

'A fine establishment, no doubt. My son has good taste.'

'Indeed. And the name of this "fine establishment"?'

'Search me.'

The bluff charm. I suppressed a smile.

'What day is it, Tommy?'

'Always the weekend for me these days. Has been for years.'

It was hard to tell if my dad knew exactly what was going on and was just being funny to annoy the man in front of him, or was being smart to cover up his own mental deficiencies of which he was only too aware. I remembered how our local vet had once told me a small animal will fight right to the end to hide signs of ill health or weakness, moments after our family gerbil – at death's door – had roused itself from a near coma and fiendishly bitten his hand. I looked at my dad. He didn't look fiendish. He looked isolated and slightly peeved. I flashed a look at the care home manager who was standing silently at the back of the room, but resisted the urge to say anything.

The psychiatrist remained blank. He scribbled something down, then carried on. 'What city are we in, Tommy?'

'London, the last time I checked,' my dad said, a little tightly.

I could sense him getting irate.

'What floor are we on?'

'Oh, for Christ's sake, I don't know . . . *Haberdashery*.' He slapped the palm of his hand on the armrest of his wheelchair. 'I've had enough of this! You'll be asking me the Prime

Minister's name next. Isn't that what you do?' He cast his eyes around the room. He could sense someone else behind him. 'It's like an *inquisition*! Ben, take me away from here, please!'

There was a commotion. Faces appeared at the door. A sheaf of paper was pushed on to the floor, fanning out across the carpet.

Within five minutes we were back out in the lobby and he had calmed down. He was still in his wheelchair. There were apologies and a cup of tea was offered. I felt bad. As though we'd tried to trick a child.

I went up with him to his room in the little lift with the extra handrails. It was a small single with half a view of the garden at the back – better than the front rooms that overlooked the noisy main road, I thought. A care assistant led the way and made himself busy, pulling on the bathroom light, opening and closing the wardrobe door, flicking the light switches on and off, showing us the call button, talking us through it, then left and said he'd be back shortly.

I opened my dad's suitcase and hung up his clothes. 'Got your best stuff, here, Dad,' I said.

'Your mother packed it,' he said, looking straight ahead.

In among his shirts was a photograph of my mum in a frame. I wondered if she'd packed that too. I put it on his bedside table and arranged his travel clock and comb and pocket hand-kerchief around it. I moved them into three or four different positions to try to make them seem more homely, but whatever I did they just sat there like the lone possessions of a sentenced man. I tucked his shoes away against the wall.

He was sitting on the bed. He still had his blazer on and his hair was neatly parted. I glanced around the austere room. It looked like a Travelodge. Or the first day at a modern boarding school.

'You'll be all right?' I said.

He looked up with a dull smile. 'This is all part of it.'

He seemed to be giving me licence to leave. I reached for a platitude as my exit line. 'I'll pop back once you're settled,' I said. It sounded terrible. Shallow and insincere.

Downstairs, I went to sign out.

'Is that your dad's wheelchair?' said the woman on reception, gesturing to the one we'd brought with us.

'Yes.'

'I'd put his name on it if I were you. It's a nice one. They tend to go walkabout. Especially the nice ones.' She handed me some Tipp-Ex.

I painted my dad's name on the frame of the wheelchair with the little white brush. I finished and pushed it into the corner next to the others, where they all looked huddled together like numbered sheep in a pen.

As I put the top back on the Tipp-Ex, it was as though a door was closing.

I walked back to the desk, signed out and left.

My footsteps were muted by soft cushiony oatmeal carpet tiles. The air felt fresh and conditioned. There were star-gazer lilies in a vase on the ledge: the smell of Beverly Hills hotels. Wide windows spread the lush exhaling treetops of Regent's Park and Primrose Hill out before me. There's the zoo; I love the aviary. The city was beyond. If I'm ever ill again, let me be ill in a room like this. It's like a soft shot of proper painkiller. An opiate. No harm can surely come to people in rooms like this. We are in a hidden space at the top of a secluded world: the film set of the ultimate BUPA pamphlet. I turned from the window and ran my fingers over the edges of the crisp freshly laundered bedlinen and cast my eye across the sleek white purring pristine equipment.

In the bed my mum was propped up. Muzzy. Relaxed. I wondered what she made of it. Maybe she thought this was what London was like these days. Maybe she thought this was just the way I did things. I was conscious of the imaginary weight of her and my dad in my arms for a moment. I just hoped the small health insurance policy she had taken out a few years ago using some of her savings ('It was Toby's idea') was going to cover a hysterectomy at the luxurious private Wellington Hospital in the way her doctor had confidently predicted.

My dad was looking at her. He had been given a cup of coffee in some fine white china by a polite and amiable nurse in white hole-punched clogs, at whom he had winked. I'd brought him to see her in his newly Tipp-Exed wheelchair, although I'd hung my jacket over his name as we'd taken the gleaming lift to the top floor.

'You look very at home, Romany,' he said.

My mum smiled graciously.

I pictured her somewhere exotic – Acapulco perhaps. She'd been flown out there in 1968 to interview James Mason and Trevor Howard. Or perhaps on a balcony in Tangier in 1964, or in a cable car riding up to Mons Calpe in 1965, on both occasions with my dad, when Mediterranean cruises were still for dazzling couples who could leave their children behind with nannies and relatives. Maybe she'd be schmoozing with Goldie Hawn in Hollywood as she was in that photograph that used to be on her pin-board. I thought she had always effortlessly taken a glamorous opportunity as if it were some kind of noble right. The spotlight, to her, was warm not harsh. And this room was oddly glamorous . . . I suddenly caught myself daydreaming and reprimanded myself. What am I *thinking*? She's had a serious *operation*. This is a *hospital*, not a hotel. 'You're going to need some looking after, Mum,' I said, approaching the bed, 'after all this silly trouble.' I heard the sound of my own voice; I was overcompensating; it was as if I was speaking to one of my own children.

She turned the corners of her mouth up. It was barely a smile. More a meek 'thank you'. Her face was lightly bleached of colour, like an old framed photograph left out in a sunny spot.

'How about a few days with us? Get you back on your feet. Tracey can make up the spare room. Dad'll be all right on his own for a bit. They're taking good care of him down the road, aren't they, Dad?'

'We're in your hands, my dear lad,' he said.

And there it was. Not exactly a yes. More a set of light regulations to which they were now dutifully adhering. Like kids on a school trip. Their life now felt as much about coercion as anything else, however sweetly and efficiently I was managing it.

9

The sun sparkled on the rooftops and windows of north-west London as I dropped down the steep hill to the main road below. The care home had asked me not to come back for a couple of days. They wanted my dad to settle in and get used to his carers. It was his first week-end in the new place. I'd heard he had been moved to a slightly larger room and I was in good spirits as I went up in the lift, but as I knocked and went in, he was sitting on the edge of the bed in almost exactly the same position as when I had left him in the previous room a few days earlier. For a moment it felt as though he hadn't moved, had had no sleep, had sat upright for three days. On his bedside table was a heap of his things – clock, comb, biro, socks, a tube of toothpaste, all jumbled up and unsorted. It looked as though someone must have dumped them there in a hurry. I glanced in the wardrobe; two shirts had come off their hangers and were crumpled on top of his shoes at the bottom. The room appeared sparsely furnished. Four small indentations in the carpet showed where an armchair should have been.

'No comfy chair, Dad?'

'No.'

'It's a bit of a mess in here. What happened?'

'Was like this when they put me in here.'

'Where have you been sitting?'

'Here.' He gestured to the bed.

'I'll speak to someone on the way down. That's not right. You need a chair.'

'I've seen no one.'

'What do you mean?'

'No one has been here. I slept on the floor last night.'

'*What*? What do you mean?'

'I don't know.'

'Did you fall?'

He looked up and met my eye. 'I dressed myself,' he said. 'Very tiring.'

I had to wait until the morning to speak to the senior manager. She apologised for the missing chair and said it had been replaced, and that my dad had been very confused for a couple of days. She asked me not to read too much into what he said and that appropriate care had been provided on every day since his arrival. I told her there was no sign of his suitcase or his oxygen tank in his new room and that he had no memory of being given any of the medication I had left. She told me it was all in hand. I had no option but to take her at her word. That night I lay awake in my bed and couldn't sleep and stared at the cracks of light at the window and wondered if he was safe and asleep, or awake too, in an unfamiliar room, with unfamiliar cracks of light at an unfamiliar window. I also wondered if he was just lying on the floor.

I rang first thing in the morning. A carer – I didn't recognise his voice – said he had had 'a good night' and had 'eaten a good breakfast'. They were phrases I used to hear the nurses use in hospital to relatives, however unsettled a patient had been. I said I was pleased, and I wanted to believe him.

At home, Tracey made up the spare room: extra cushions and pillows; an armchair with a foot-stool; a tartan travel blanket; a portable television; some family photos; flowers cut from the garden. She was picturing little trips up the stairs during the day: a tray of food; some soup; a pot of tea; a slice of cake; a rerun of *Poirot* on TV.

But my mum was restless the first night. I could hear her turn over in the room upstairs, the soft footfall and faint creak from the floorboards as she went to the window and back. I'd taken her a tray of food in the evening but she had pulled a face. Among her cuttings I once found a light-hearted unpublished magazine feature she'd written about taking days off work, in which she said: 'I was never brought up to be ill . . . I insist on soldiering on, spluttering all over everyone, sighing deeply, and making the family feel thoroughly guilty.'

The next evening, after we'd settled the kids down, she joined us for a meal downstairs but was unable to relax and went up to her room early. A couple of hours later – after I'd left to go out for a gig – Tracey was sitting alone in the kitchen when my mum appeared in the doorway in bare feet wearing only a white nightie with her grey hair down, as if she'd gone to bed but got herself up again. After the briefest of exchanges, she had suddenly made an unexpected grab for the kitchen cupboard, and pulling out a bottle of brandy, snatched out the cork, put the bottle to her lips and swigged with ostentatious insolence, before gruffly returning to her room.

'I was stupefied,' Tracey said. 'It was just weird and embarrassing. I hardly had time to say anything. And you were out. And it was your mother.'

The next night she did the same in front of me.

'What are you doing?' I asked, refusing to rise.

'Well, you won't *offer* me a drink,' she responded crabbily.

'You have just had a *general anaesthetic* and a major operation,' I protested. 'The doctor said take it *easy* for a couple of weeks.'

With her back in her room, I wondered why it all had to be so brilliantly operatic. I wanted to help and sympathise but I resented this engineering of feelings, this melodrama, this intense sense of grievance. I felt estranged. It was a kind of wildness. Disproportionate. Unmanageable. In retrospect I wonder why I didn't put my arms around her, seek more help, but it felt like a storm that could upturn trees, as though I could do no good and I'd be brushed away, and she was the one who needed to change.

As the next couple of days unfolded, she seemed to find her own – and our – company excruciating. If she was unsettled in the room upstairs, she offered little when she came down – just long stares out to the garden, her thumb under her jaw, her index finger pressed against her lips as if she'd shushed her own mouth. The children skirted round her watchfully. She'd take Blake on her lap and read to him from a storybook with big print, but if he wriggled it was an excuse to put him down. The girls grew wary. It was like listening to a silent rage.

'Now what, Mum?' I asked after three nights.

'You tell me.' She seemed adrift and defensive.

'Home?'

'Not yet.'

'Here.'

'No.'

'Some time with Dad?' I suggested. 'At . . . where he's staying now.' (I couldn't say its name.) 'A couple of weeks? Get your strength back.'

She stared at the wall. I could tell she couldn't bring herself to say yes outright. It must have seemed to her like a defeat, the care home a step too far. Then I saw her eyes brighten, as though a thought had come clearly to her.

'Would they let me *visit* like that?' she asked. 'Just for a short time?'

'I'm sure they would,' I said. She could be a 'visitor' if she wanted.

'For *Tom's* sake.'

'For Dad's sake.'

And so she joined him for a couple of weeks. We went via the flat to collect some clothes and belongings, and she chose to wear a smart raincoat knotted at the waist and a mustard woollen beret for her arrival. She was to be invincible. My dad was pleased to see her. He smiled passively as she hovered nervously in the lobby, his trousers held up by his clip-on braces. He had shaving nicks on his face. I thought he looked like an elderly Ernie Wise.

After a week she asked if I would pop back and check up on the flat and bring her a couple of her scrapbooks to show the carers.

'Any in particular?' I asked.

'Make sure you bring the *Burton* one.'

10

I n the summer of 1970, a few weeks before my dad began work writing for his new residency at the Dorchester, my mum interrupted my school holidays with an announcement.

'I'll be away for a few days in August, darling.'

'How many?'

'Five.'

'Five? Where are you going?'

'Mexico.'

If I remember anything about 1970 it's that it was in colour, and it took place largely – as far as I was aware – in sun-soaked Mexico. In June, the FIFA World Cup was beamed into our north-facing little sitting room all the way from Mexico. It was the first World Cup not to be transmitted in black and white. The images glittered and flared. The Brazilian kit looked amazing: iridescent blue shorts; golden shirts. It was like the uniform of gods. The only other colour I could liken it to as an eight-year-old boy was *Jason and the Argonauts*. England wore dazzling all-white. It was like gazing into another lustrous technicolor world. I made my dad buy extra petrol every week from our local Red Lion garage so I could top up my Esso World Cup coin collection. The TV shone. My coins shone. Everything was brilliant.

'Why are you going?' I asked.

'I am going to interview a couple of people for a magazine.'

'Who?'

'A couple of film stars.'

'What are their names?'

'Richard Burton and Elizabeth Taylor.'

'Oh.' I went back to my coin collection.

My mum's scrapbooks and souvenirs are full of notes, inserted scraps of paper, and handwritten annotations underlining the importance of 'Burton' in her own version of her life. Articles and letters are photocopied – sometimes in triplicate. Photographs are marked up with accurate dates and exclamation marks, and in 1985 (a year after his unexpected death at the age of fifty-eight) she wrote a lengthy retrospective story for the *TV Times* called 'The Burton I Loved'. The fuss was not without reason.

She first met him in 1951 at Stratford-upon-Avon, the year after she had acted there herself in the Festival Season of 1950. Her first husband, Ken, better known by his pen name, Richard Findlater, was also friends with Burton and had stayed with him and his first wife, Sybil, in Switzerland. Ken and my mum had travelled up to Stratford to see the young Burton in *Henry V*, taking with them their newly born son – and now my eldest half-brother – Simon. Backstage Burton had greeted them and – as my mum never got tired of recounting – placed his crown over baby Simon's head and shoulders, 'Until,' as she often said, 'it came to rest on his nappy pin.'

'He was just sex in chainmail,' she once confessed to me.

Twelve years later, in May 1963, she was dispatched to Shepperton Film Studios to interview Burton who was playing opposite Peter O'Toole in *Becket*. As they were chatting, the phone rang. It was Liz Taylor calling from the Dorchester where she and Burton were staying in separate suites midway through their affair; it was a year before they were to marry for the first time.

'Can't talk now, love,' said Burton down the phone. 'I've got this wild Welsh Gypsy asking me intimate questions about us.'

After the interview they left the studios together and walked out towards Burton's Rolls-Royce and his awaiting chauffeur. My mum stopped by her scruffy Mini-Traveller and started to say goodbye. 'I've never been in one of these,' Burton said, unflappably, ignoring his Rolls-Royce and running his hand, without a hint of embarrassment, along the wooden trim of the Mini. 'Could I have a go?' Within seconds he had taken the keys, dismissed his chauffeur, and then casually driven my mum all the way home to London. In her own car.

By 1970 he and Taylor were still arguably the world's biggest celebrity couple. Hollywood may have begun to turn its back on them in the wake of low-budget gritty successes like *Easy Rider* and *Midnight Cowboy*, but audiences were still thrilled and repelled by stories of jewels worth three million pounds, the private jet, the yacht, the rows, the inflated fees. Besieged by interview requests, they turned most of them down, but my mum knew Burton was nothing if not loyal to old theatre friends, especially those with a Welsh connection and a sense of humour, so she sent him a telegram:

Have paid for three wheels of our new Renault 5. Please invite me to Mexico and enable us to pay for the fourth.

Burton was tickled. The velvet rope was lifted, and in August my mum was invited to leave rainy London for an enormous world exclusive. Fourteen hours later she found herself in the remote fishing village of San Felipe on the Gulf of Mexico, swimming in the sea with the Burton family surrounded by pelicans.

It was 110 degrees in the shade when she breakfasted with him in his trailer borrowed from John Wayne – the eye-patch from *True Grit* was still hanging on the mirror. He was starring in a desert war movie called *Raid on Rommel* and, striking a chord with my mum, was 'on the wagon'. A photograph by the assignment photographer shows Burton – forty-four – slim, rugged and tanned on the steps of the trailer in beige army fatigues. My mum, forty-six, is in character as the 'wild Welsh Gypsy', and is gazing up at him adoringly, and slightly submissively, leaning back against the trailer dressed in a full-length vibrant orange-and-black kaftan, headscarf, coral necklace and pearl earrings. To say it was a side she didn't get much of a chance to express at home would be putting it mildly; forty-eight hours earlier she'd been collecting school blazers from the dry-cleaner's, washing up dinner plates for seven and lending an understanding ear to my dad's anxieties. It was a transformation. When I was young I didn't recognise her in the official photos that came back from the Mexico trip. I preferred the personal off-duty Polaroid of her in a plain one-piece bathing suit, floppy hat and sunglasses, sitting awkwardly and girlishly on the edge of a blue canoe with her back to the sea on the day she first arrived. In it, she looked just like my mum. The idea that adults could be more than one person – one for the children, one for their partner, one for themselves – did not make sense to me for a long time.

Now, of course, I admire the exuberance and the style, the self-expression that didn't get much of an outlet at home, but I realise she was clever too – she knew it was the side that would get the best from the occasion, especially when allied with her interview style. 'Being ordinary', as she called it, was perhaps one of her greatest assets as a journalist. As an ex-actress she was trusted, and of course had a great deal of sympathy with the stars she interviewed, but, for all the monthly-mag surface fluff, it is clear she succeeded by asking simple well-researched sincere questions that often got to the heart of her subjects' feelings and motivations.

Her style chimed with the times. *Cosmopolitan* had relaunched in the US in 1965 under Helen Gurley Brown – my mum wrote a lead feature on Burton and Taylor for the UK launch issue in 1971 – and 'having it all' and pop-feminism dominated the new driving editorial mantra. Hard work, wily opportunism, lavish indulgences, frankness and liberation could all coexist in an empowering consummate life, where men were smouldering and spellbinding but also malleable and exploitable. Burton and Taylor were perfect triple-page features.

In San Felipe she interviewed Liz Taylor separately. Having been assured in the morning that Taylor was unavailable that day, my mum had sent the outfit she had intended to wear for the occasion to be laundered. Suddenly she found out the interview had been arranged at short notice for the same afternoon, and she was forced to sit down opposite one of the world's most famously beautiful women wearing the only thing she had clean – a tatty towelling beach dress. They met in a deserted café overlooking the ocean. In her notes she writes of Taylor, then thirty-eight: 'She looked stunning, wearing minimal make-up, her dark cloud of hair grey-streaked, as Richard liked it, and her extraordinary kingfisher-blue eyes, fringed with double sets of dark lashes, the envy of all of us.' But my mum's outfit must have struck the right laid-back tone; Taylor was very open and relaxed and revealed a lot about her relationship with Burton. It was, as my mum, said later, 'gold dust', and paid for my upkeep for several years.

Afterwards they both went shopping with Taylor's three children, strolling into San Felipe to walk round the small local supermarket. They bought sandals and jointed wooden snakes for the kids. (My mum brought me one home in her suitcase.) She also bought herself a strap for the wristwatch Taylor had given her the day before – a wind-up watch with a comic picture of Nixon's vice-president Spiro Agnew on the face, dressed in 'Stars and Stripes' shorts and slippers, with gloved Mickey Mouse hands pointing to the numbers. My mum was well prepared; in return she gave Taylor a silk scarf that had belonged to her Romany grandmother; she'd taken it with her to Mexico just in case.

A handwritten letter from Taylor arrived shortly after my mum got back to London:

Dear Romany,

Thank you so much for the fantastic scarf. It was – and still is – my secret ambition to be a Gypsy. (Maybe that's why I so enjoy the way we live.) When I was kid my fantasy was that Gypsies had left me on my mother and father's doorstep and someday they (always a handsome young man on a white, equally handsome horse) would retrieve me – and I would live happily in the magic golden world of my people for ever more.

I have to this day all the fake jewellery, clothes, hairstyles etc etc ever attributed to anyone even resembling a Gypsy. I never thought I'd be so lucky as to have the real article – because I know you're close people – at least according to my lore [or love]. Maybe some of the magic will rub off on me.

Thank you so much,
Love,
Elizabeth

A year later, the Italian magazine *Oggi* carried paparazzi photographs of Burton and Taylor on holiday on the streets of Portofino. Taylor – sporting a variation on the vintage Romany fortune-teller look worn by my mum in San Felipe – is wearing a long pale Paisley kaftan and on her head is my great-grandmother's scarf.

11

'Happy Christmas,' I said, as I helped my dad out towards the car under the overcast afternoon sky.

It was Christmas Day 2002.

My mum had lingered at the care home after her operation but had been back at the flat on her own since the beginning of December, trying out some 'independent living', as the link worker had called it. It was a reprieve from looking after my dad full-time, but she was visiting him every other day. ('Have bus pass. Have stick. Can travel.') On Christmas Eve, my half-brother Toby had taken her over to his house near Esher for a few nights, but my dad hadn't wanted to go. He had insisted on staying put at the care home ('Less fuss, no children') on the condition I took him for 'a seasonal spin in the car' after lunch.

'You all right?' I said, opening the car door.

'All the better for seeing you.'

He had on his double-breasted navy blazer with the gold buttons, and his best tartan trousers. With clip-on braces they were pulled a little too high and I could see his camel-brown socks. On his feet he was wearing his special plum-red leather tassel loafers. Someone must have helped him into them – they needed a shoe-horn to get them on. His care assistant had taken me aside and told me he was up and awake at 2 a.m. The night staff had found him sitting on his bed. 'What are you doing, Tommy?' they'd said. 'Watching out for Santa?' He had got himself completely dressed and had pushed his curtains open and was looking up into the dark silent star-specked Christmas night sky, wakeful and expectant. 'My son's coming,' he'd said quietly. 'We're going for a special drive.' 'He's coming at 2 *p.m.* Not 2 *a.m.*,' they'd had to say. 'It's the middle of the night, Tommy. You've got yourself in a right old muddle.' It had taken them half an hour to convince him. They'd had to get him undressed and back into bed in his pyjamas.

The car was still ticking and clicking.

'I'm not doing this every week for you,' I said jokingly.

'I have no intention of returning.'

I helped him into the car and shut the door.

'Are we off for a spin?' he said. 'Nice car. You've always had good taste.'

His face looked tired and thinner.

'That's what you asked for. OK with you?'

He turned to me in his seat. He had his stick with him. The end of it was down in the footwell between his knees and he was holding the handle with two hands like a little old lady holds a handbag on the bus, or as if he were about to ride a hobby-horse. 'I'd like that very much,' he said.

I smiled at him. 'Where shall we go then?'

He paused for a brief second, then said quite firmly, 'Barnes.'

'Barnes!?' I laughed. 'OK, why not.'

I turned on the ignition, gave him a wink, and swung round and we headed off towards Maida Vale and Westway. We sped down through Swiss Cottage and St John's Wood to Warwick Avenue, my dad gazing out of the window as London flashed by, the shadows of trees and buildings flickering across his pale face. He let out a quiet hum of approval as we passed the lines of brightly painted houseboats moored at Little Venice. All flowerpots and lace curtains. An unexpected yucca.

We passed under the Marylebone flyover and up on to Westway. I have always loved Westway; it is like a futuristic relic from the days when hopeful and expectant planners envisaged central London ringed with an inner motorway. I read recently that it was conceived as part of the London Ringways System and many of the ideas pre-dated the Second World War in the years when issues of environmental impact were not high on the agenda. The plans were ultimately deemed too invasive – and having seen some of them, such as the dramatic flyover from the top of London at Whitestone Pond down over the wilds of Hampstead Heath, I can see why – but two of the three remaining pieces of the expansion programme (the Westway itself, and the dog-legged West Cross Route from White City to the Holland Park roundabout) remain. They are somehow suggestive of a more streamlined and optimistic London, even though the thick monstrosity of their concrete footprints stamps brutally through the old neighbourhoods of Notting Dale and Portobello. Landmarks crouch just visible below its thin hard shoulder: the overground Hammersmith and City Line station of Westbourne Park with its fringed peely-painted white wooden awnings; the voluptuous curves of the old British Rail building that almost touch the guard-rails; the white tent-tops of Portobello Market; Ladbroke Grove awash with colour and noise and the thud of sound systems on Carnival days, when the road above is lined with police vans and aerials and surveillance cameras; the tags and throw-ups of the graffiti writers on the brick walls below on the southern side, which you can't see from the road but you can from a train approaching Paddington Station; and gazing down on it all, still more impressive than the recent office skyscrapers of the Paddington Basin development is Ernö Goldfinger's functionally beautiful Trellick Tower with its patchwork of balconies festooned with drying washing and bicycles. Above us was the wide west London sky, all ancient and modern: a removals-van blanket of flecked grey clouds and fingers of light. It felt like a modish and gracious journey to be taking on Christmas Day.

At Hammersmith Bridge, my dad, who had been largely silent throughout the journey, let out a big sigh, as if it had been in there for a while. Hammersmith Bridge was a gateway on to an old world for both of us. Barnes and south-west London started on the other side. The outspread sweep of the Thames curves in both directions under the bridge, rippling and polished, with the old Harrods repository building peeping over the towpath trees, a once yearly national landmark on Boat Race day. It was also the place I found out recently where my dad proposed to my mum for a second time.

We crossed over and turned right down Lonsdale Road past my old school and the old reservoirs. From the age of eleven I used to ride my bike to school down that road come rain or shine. Neither of my parents ever dreamed of taking me in the car; that would have been far too indulgent. Instead, my mum woke me every school day and I got dressed in my uniform upstairs in my room. She prepared breakfast for me in her nightie and occasionally my dad might appear before I left, but only to stand blearily in his dressing gown at the kitchen sink facing the garden to down a large beer glass of ice cold water from the mains tap – sometimes with an Alka-Seltzer – and then wipe his mouth on the back of his sleeve before turning round and going silently back to bed.

When I was eight, I tagged along with my half-brothers

on the bus, but they were nine years older than me and soon to leave school. Then, until I got a bike, I went on the bus on my own, but secretly hoped for a lift from one of my first-year teachers, Miss Sworder. She drove a beige Mini Clubman and followed the same route as the bus. I'd sometimes catch her at the traffic lights if she saw me. She was elderly, in woollen tights and brown brogues, but her car was warm, and smelled of face powder and lipstick and the papery dust of exercise books. She drove poorly. She ran over a pigeon once on Rocks Lane; it had been winged and was lying flapping in the road. Everyone else was swerving to miss it, but she was oblivious to its plight and just drove straight over it; I felt it burst under the wheel and she didn't bat an eyelid. She once unintentionally put two wheels up on the pavement to squeeze past a lorry near the Red Lion and clipped the handbag of a woman standing at the bus stop. 'We'll be late, late, late,' she always chimed. If anything, we were always early.

I hated cycling in bad weather. I wore a leaking yellow cape with thumb-straps that billowed in the rain. Wind was the worst. It came right off the river and blew pitilessly down the long straight unforgiving road. Many times I pedalled into a fierce headwind, making no progress at all – the massive plane trees waving like wet ghosts above – shouting into the noise with tears streaming down my face, '*Why* can't Mum or Dad take me in the car? *Why* can't I get a lift?' I was regularly passed by my hell-bent wiry chemistry teacher, pedalling scientifically, protected from the elements only by a tightly buttoned tweed jacket and a pair of bicycle clips, and I screamed at him too, into the word-stealing gale.

At the bottom of Lonsdale Road we approached the corner of Barnes High Street and a full view of the Thames across to

Dukes Meadows and the hulking one-hundred-year-old grey railway bridge; I thought it cast a baleful shadow on to the river with its thick riveted iron curves and skinhead graffiti. At low tide I used to go bottle hunting amid the carrier bags, the chunks of polystyrene and shredded nylon rope on the squelchy, putrid mud flat for old clay ginger-beer bottles and transparent sea-green glass bottles of R. White's lemonade with the marble still in the moulded neck; people must have been tossing them over the river wall into the mud and silt at low tide for years from the pubs on the corner. To find an unbroken one made the weekend; you could clean it and keep it, or sell it to one of the little second-hand antiques shops near by for a quid.

'Know where we are, Dad?' I said.

'Not really,' he said.

'Lonsdale Road. Look, that's the Bull's Head on the left, and the Waterman's.'

I was suddenly aware that I was giving him orienteering based on local pubs, not the green promise of Dukes Meadows on the far Chiswick side of the river, or the simple expanse of the glittering tin-foil river we had stood and stared at so often. It struck me that so many of my early memories of my dad were of being with him in pubs.

The Bull's Head was, and still is, an institution on the London jazz scene. A Young's Brewery pub, it was presided over for years by a huge huffing landlord called Albert Tolley. As a boy I only remember the thin voluminous white short-sleeve shirts he wore, outside his trousers, with his string vest showing through from the inside. Short of hair, he combed over the remaining grey strands in a defiant side parting. He was popular amongst the jazz musicians who frequented the place.

'All right, young Tommy?' he used to say to me.

'It's Ben,' I'd say.

'Ha ha ha ha hahhhh,' he'd roar, and ruffle my hair until it hurt.

It became my dad's home from home. A saloon bar man, he was happiest in the company of quick-witted plumbers and fitters, tenor players and drummers. The Sunday lunchtime trips to the Bull's Head became a part of my growing up. The back room was famous for its evening and Sunday lunchtime sessions. My dad drank in the bar, leaving me with a Coke and a bag of crisps on the fire escape by the back door of the music room with only Don the doorman for company. Don slouched on a bar stool in the doorway taking the admission money. He became locally famous for his sandals and socks, which in the sexy seventies was tantamount to wearing your underpants outside your trousers. In honour of the Mel Brooks film, he had been given the nickname 'Blazing Sandals' by someone at the pub; my dad couldn't stop laughing about it, and I laughed too, but mainly because my dad was laughing, as I didn't really know what it meant.

Every now and then he would pop out and ask if I was OK, maybe stand for a moment, pat me on the head, and then slope back into the bar. I can remember thinking that he was to some extent encouraging me to listen and absorb, but I was also conscious of an invisible screen between us when it came to the music, as though it was so much part of his life that transference of something so deep was almost impossible. It seemed he was leaving it up to me, that there was nothing he could impart. I felt awkward and thought I should just stand there and do my best.

Nonetheless, I was transfixed by the jazz room. I was never allowed inside because of my age, but gazed into the darkness of that magical place: the stubby low bar stools; the threadbare fag-butt-burnt carpet; the chalky posters; the portraits of jazz legends; the soft glow of the cigarette machine; the low stage; the microphones and cables; the clink of glasses; the idling exhaust of smoke hanging like low cloud; the murmurs of approval and spontaneous whoops and bursts of applause. It was light outside, yet dark inside the room, and it seemed so rebellious to not turn the lights on and see what you were doing in the middle of the day. It was a secret world – not like Sundays at all.

As a kid who had seen Marc Bolan and Sweet on TV, I thought how unremarkable jazz musicians were in their appearance, and wondered if they had just got out of bed; many of them probably had. The resident trio of Tony Lee, Tony Archer and Martin Drew seemed so gloomy. It only took a couple of choruses before Tony Lee's shiny bald head was glistening and his huge hands were striding across the piano, but his face and Zapata moustache remained a picture of despondency. Tony Archer on double bass wore loud Hawaiian shirts unbuttoned uninvitingly to the chest; I thought this was a bit off-putting on an old man, although he was probably only in his thirties. When the soloists played I was transfixed. I loved Bobby Wellins's tone when he played the slow ones; it was a sad, warm, resigned-but-resilient sound that spoke to me even as a boy. When I first heard Don Weller play – a vast vagabond of a man with a dishevelled beard and a tenor saxophone that spat splinters – I thought he must make a frightening dad.

I found the jazz I heard mysterious and difficult and gripping, played by unfamiliar people who were often quite scary, people it would not be easy to get to know. Although I couldn't articulate it at the time, I sensed it was like a secret society: language-less men with so much to say, who came alive through music, who understood each other and revealed so much through beats and notes, each with a common hinterland. When a session ended and the lights came up, it was as if a spell were broken, and as they packed away their instruments they returned to being just quiet, unexceptional men: self-protective; self-effacing; internalised. I don't think I ever quite shook this off. Maybe it informed my relationship with my dad.

After the Sunday session was all over, I was allowed into the room and stepped up on to the stage and touched the piano, which I thought was a very daring thing to do. The grand piano was like a holy relic. When they replaced it with an upright they took the covers off to increase its volume in the room, and I adored its skeletal appearance, the rows of felted hammers, the thick wound strings. Very occasionally my dad played the piano after everyone had gone home, and the glasses were being cleared away and the ashtrays emptied, and even though a few of the regulars stood in the doorway and whistled a bit and shouted, 'Yeah, Tommy,' his playing made me think he was lonely inside.

'What are you thinking, Dad?' I said, as we turned into Barnes High Street.

'It was all a long time ago,' he said.

'Good memories, though?'

'I can't remember.'

I wondered what exactly he couldn't remember. Just the faces? Or was much of it now just rubbed out?

Back then, he bristled with confidence. He insisted on driving to the pub and driving back several hours later. He assured my mum that the car 'knew its way home' and that negotiating the dark tree-canopied roads by the ill-lit common, keeping a steady thirty miles per hour past the front door to Barnes Police Station before driving in a straight line over the two

consecutive railway level crossings, and swinging in between
the extremely narrow concrete gateposts leading to the car-port
at home presented absolutely no problem to a man of his intui-
tive driving skills, however many he had drunk; and to his
arguable credit he pulled it off, week after week. Then one day
in the early seventies my mum insisted enough was enough; if
he didn't end up in a ditch by the side of the common, then
they'd lose a gatepost they could ill afford to replace. She said
that he must take up *cycling*.

The shed at the end of the alley down the side of the house
was tidied in readiness and two headlamps, a yellow reflective
belt and a fashionable 'space-frame' racing-green Moulton
bicycle with small white tyres and a high saddle appeared. She
was rather pleased with my dad's ready acceptance of the new
routine; I even overheard unexpected light talk of a new fitness
regime too. In fact, she called me over to the sitting-room
window and we waved him off to the pub at eight o'clock on a
mild April evening on the first 'trial night' (as it was referred
to), and a little later we retired to bed.

The alley down the side of the house in those days benefited
in winter months from a warm orange glow that spilled over
the wooden fence and was cast by the outside light above our
neighbour's back door. As soon as the clocks went forward,
however, our neighbour was in the habit of turning it off.

We were woken at around midnight by a colossal clanging
racket. By the time I was out of bed and at the window I could
see lights on in other houses in the road.

It turned out that after three hours of steady drinking in
the pub, my dad had successfully managed to put on his
reflective belt the right way round; he'd illuminated both of
his lamps correctly, negotiated two roundabouts, the darkened common, two sets of level crossings *and* our narrow

gateposts, but – flummoxed by the unexpected absence of the warm glow from our neighbour's back-door light – had lost control of the bike down the side of the house and ploughed straight into three large metal dustbins and a garden rake, injuring his elbow and, for good measure, writing off the bike.

My mum was incandescent with suppressed rage at breakfast the next morning as I got ready for school.

'Look on the bright side, Romany,' he said the next evening. 'At least the gateposts are still standing.'

I turned to look at him in the car. He was ageing so quickly – such a small man, somehow shrunken. He seemed to be growing more and more like his own soft-edged mother. The backs of his hands were bruised, as if stained with purple ink. He was tapping his feet up and down on the black foot mat to an imaginary beat. It was exactly what his mother used to do, only she would accompany it with a dry toneless whistle to the tune of an imaginary Scottish tattoo that used to drive us all round the bend.

'There's Barnes Pond, Dad, and the Sun Inn, look,' I said. (Another pub, I thought.)

'No swans,' he said.

'What?'

'No swans on the pond. Used to be. We had swans on the river that came right up to the house in Oxford. Very majestic creatures.'

He turned and glanced at the pub and rubbed the full face of his index finger right across the closed top lid of one eye.

'You and Mum used to go there a lot,' I said.

'Did we now?' he said in a measured tone.

It was an odd turn of phrase. It came out sounding as if he was tired of being shown pubs, and that he was sensing something disingenuous in my voice – castigatory even – as though he thought I was trying to prompt him into an admission of some kind. But then the thought receded and I wondered if I had merely projected my own feelings on to him, and he could quite possibly just not remember.

We turned right at the pond and down towards the abandoned police station, and right along by the common.

'Do you remember Colin Welland's house, Dad? The playwright. Just back there.'

'Do I?'

'Of course you do! You did some decorating for him.'

'That's right. I did. You're right,' he said, suddenly brightening. 'Well, I'll be blowed. You have got a good memory, Ben.' We turned into Vine Road. 'Never much liked him though. Very full of himself.'

We drove along under the beautiful arch of lolling and embracing winter-bare trees, and on up towards the old pale blue railway signal box, now derelict. The gates were open. We trundled over the level crossing, down the short dip with the recreation ground on our right, and up to the second set of gates. The signal box that used to stand there had been knocked down.

Back then, I could see right up into it if I was waiting for a train. On hot days, the signalman kept the door open and I could see the rows of gleaming polished levers and machinery used to operate the points. You had to be strong. Young lads often got the job, and in the summer holidays, they'd be wearing cap-sleeve T-shirts and handkerchiefs round their necks like roadies for Rod Stewart, and teenage girls gathered under the box to watch and giggle as the latest sweating recruit worked the levers; he would be loving every minute of it. Sitting there on my bike waiting for the gates to open in my school uniform I thought it was one of the coolest jobs in the world.

We drove up and over the line and down the other side, past the scruffy green open space where I used to play football until it was dark on Sunday afternoons with anyone who wanted a game, or sneak under the rope – draped by the Council to protect the cricket square – to bowl on a real wicket.

At the pillar box we turned right. I drove quietly down the dead-end road and stopped outside number 15.

'There you go, Dad,' I said.

It was our old house.

12

With the car windows down I could imagine the wind rustling in the huge twin copper beech trees that had stood outside the house – one at the front, one at the back – for as long as I could remember. They were so tall that they were higher than the house itself and their mahogany leaves changed colour as the months passed – old gold, henna, ginger, burnt orange – gathering in the front garden and alley-way in autumn like the sweepings of broken and torn pieces of dark parchment. I used to ride my bike through them, listening to them crunch under the thin tyres.

The house seemed smaller. Semi-detached. Quite squat. But still quiet and insulated from the world. No passing traffic. A coveted dead-end road on the edge of Barnes Common. Christmas lights were on in the downstairs front room. So different to how I remembered it: the darkened bedroom of my ancient grandmother. The house was converted and divided back then. A self-contained flat at street level. It was the only way my mum and dad could afford it back in 1962: they bought the top two floors; my grandmother paid for the ground floor. We all used the front entrance, but we had to go upstairs to our flat door, while my grandmother's door was right there in the hall.

I was a baby in a cot in that room above the porch. Born in the December of the brutal winter of 1962–63. Thick fog on the night I was delivered. I wasn't allowed outside for three months. There'd be ice on the inside of the window in the morning. I glanced up at the single dormer window in the slate roof and pictured the old temporary partition walls in the top-floor bedrooms, put up when everyone first moved in in order that my half-brothers and my half-sister could all sleep up there.

Looking again at the first-floor window above the porch I thought back to the late autumn of 1970 after it had been turned into my mum's little office. I would have been almost eight. I pictured her typing energetically, basking in the glow of success after her trip to Mexico to interview Burton and Taylor, my dad in the back bedroom feverishly writing arrangements for his new jazz orchestra residency at the Dorchester in the coming new year. It must have been a good time, each of them with a sense of purpose, the relationship balanced, twin layers of lightning.

It can't have been easy for a few years before that; their careers were going at different speeds. Her acting ambitions long gone – and with the older children more independent – my mum had been writing showbiz features mainly for *She* magazine since 1963. She used to love recounting her favourites, the 'goodies', as she called them: a young ambitious David Frost at the Waldorf; a badly hung-over Richard Harris slumped before her horizontally, dressed only in a shortie silk dressing gown and a pair of tennis socks; a nervous Michael Caine on the eve of stardom in *The Ipcress File* in 1964 in his flash new flat at Marble Arch with its freshly hung Japanese grass wallpaper, Dino storage units designed by Zeev Aram in the sitting room, and pristine navy-and-chocolate curtains in the bedroom. 'I've only brought an electric razor and a teaspoon from my last place. I've already spent three grand on this flat,' he said. 'I've gone for just a five-year lease, as I reckon I'm either going to be rich enough to live here, or so poor that's all I'll be able to afford. So five years is about right. If the film flops, I'll not go out; I'll sit here on my own till the rent runs out.' By 1969 she was doing ten major feature interviews a year. She meticulously collected the published versions in her scrapbooks, among them, Rod Steiger, Glenda Jackson, Anthony Hopkins, Goldie Hawn, Woody Allen.

In contrast, my dad had not had any decent work in over four years, and you could say nothing serious in almost eight. Unwilling to compromise his musical principles, he had watched the wave of pop music that came in the wake of The Beatles wash many of his dreams away. Interest in big band jazz faded. Ironically he was asked by George Martin at Parlophone to work on the Beatles project as an arranger right at the beginning but, sticking to his guns, said no. In the event, his days leading and composing for a big swinging successful jazz orchestra stuttered to a halt in the mid-sixties. While my mum was working in town three days a week – sometimes not getting home until ten – and travelling abroad on assignments three or four times a year, he had managed to fill the ensuing gap with only a couple of years as a jobbing arranger for the BBC and a false start writing for the difficult early months of London Weekend Television. With four teenage stepchildren and me, he had been forced to accept an unexpected role as house-husband. I am sure it isn't how he imagined it would turn out, at the peak of his powers when he first met my mum.

The role reversal is captured in a photograph from the time. It was taken for a magazine article in 1969 about modern working mothers called 'He's So Nice to Come Home to'. I was six. My mum's desk has been pulled from her little study into the doorway of the sitting room to fit it into the shot. I remember thinking it was stupid because it didn't live there, and no one could get in and out of the room. The whole family is in the picture. It felt unreal; I could sense it even though I was young. I knew my half-brothers and half-sister wouldn't be doing the things the photographer told them to do for the picture in real life – not all together at the same time, and not without shouting at each other. Simon, aged eighteen, is in the background, sitting on the back of the sofa beside my dad's turntable in a tangerine nylon polo-neck and straw hat pretending to read the sleeve notes on a vinyl LP. Jennie, aged fifteen, is next to him, resting her elbows on the back of the same sofa while pretending to read a book. Roly and Toby, also fifteen, are lounging on the sofa pretending to chat, while I am on the floor in front in a black roll-neck jumper pretending to play a ukelele. I can remember feeling cross and idiotic. In the foreground, my mum is at her desk in the role of the modern working mother, her hands poised over her typewriter, a stubbed-out ciggy in the ashtray, a press release for the Spinners to hand – the text artificially turned to the camera to make it easier to read. She is pointing out something she has just pretended to write to my dad, who is standing over her shoulder in a lilac shirt, hand under his chin pretending to think, while wearing a striped French apron and pretending to offer her a cup of coffee.

Although my dad says in the accompanying article – which, with no heed paid to impartiality, was written *by my mum* about 'four very helpful husbands' who take over the 'domestic chores' while their wives go out to work – 'I enjoy running the house very much', I am sure sitting at the piano writing for thirteen hard-blowing brass players, a pianist, a drummer and a bass player and then steaming up to the West End to lead them until the small hours of the morning would have been preferable.

In February 1971, the Dorchester residency finally started. All that hard work writing in the bedroom was going to pay off. The musicians' charts – one hundred and twenty-eight of them, each for one of nine players – arrived home in time for the opening night in individually bound leather folders, tied with ribbon and embossed with gold lettering: *Tommy Watt Orchestra*. They were the same ones that that tumbled out of the suitcase on the day they moved into the new London flat in 2001. The Dorchester was clearly pushing the boat out. Apple-green flyers appeared: *DINE and DANCE in the Terrace Restaurant to the Music of TOMMY WATT AND HIS ORCHES-TRA from 8 p.m. – 1 a.m. (every weekday evening).* He had personally selected the band; he had always been very fussy about that; nothing but the best. And I remember seeing him standing in the kitchen window polishing his shoes on the opening night – one of his favourite rituals. (I'd sometimes come down for school in the morning and find he had polished *my* shoes after he had got in from a late night out and left them gleaming on the kitchen floor for me. He was big on shoes.) His freshly dry-cleaned black-wool dinner jacket and cummerbund were hanging in clear plastic in the hall. I never understood what a cummerbund was for and wondered if it might be an apron, but why you needed an apron to play the piano I hadn't yet worked out. I liked the silk braid down the side of his trousers though; I thought it made him look a bit like a soldier. My mum said he looked handsome in a bow tie.

In retrospect, it seems so obvious that he was being naive to think it could be a success in the way he imagined – a throwback to the heyday of the fifties, or the start of a jazz big band revival. Maybe he secretly suspected it at the time, but suppressed it in the hope he might be wrong, but whatever was in his mind, the residency was a crushing disappointment. The clientele who arrived to dine and dance in the Terrace Restaurant had very little interest in the music of Tommy Watt, or his band. It wasn't that the people who came didn't want to dine and dance, it's that they were largely elderly nostalgic couples from the suburbs, who had grown up with the softer melancholy sound of Glenn Miller and wanted two courses and then a quiet waltz before catching the last tube home. Most nights the place was virtually empty by 11 p.m.

A photograph shows him – aged forty-five – seated at the Dorchester's grand piano not long after the opening, the band behind him in black tie, playing from padded leather lecterns in front of marbled columns and velvet drapes, and on his face is simply an unalloyed look of innocent boyish hurt, as though bigger boys had come and stolen his baton. On the piano lid is a stack of charts, the same charts I had heard him painstakingly write day after day – 'Turn the telly down for your father, darling. Master at work!' – many of which must never even have got looked at. Within a few weeks the management cut their losses, pulled the plug and it was all over.

He tried not to let it get to him. I found a draft for a press release written in the aftermath, in my dad's handwriting with some corrections of the grammar and punctuation by my mum:

Brilliant arranger and pianist, Tommy Watt, has formed a hand-picked nine-piece band for both dancing and listening. Personally responsible for scoring the band's library – which includes standard tunes, hit-parade toppers of the last ten years and the latest bossa novas – Tommy has just completed a season at the Dorchester Hotel, and has been featured on the BBC.

It is the 'and has been featured on the BBC' tacked on the end that smells of desperation. The phone didn't ring. Weeks passed. By June, in need of work, he had accepted a booking to play piano in a pit band at the Bournemouth Winter Gardens for the summer season's 'pre-season' run. He wasn't needed for the main attraction. He was playing on middle-of-the-road arrangements for the Beverley Sisters and listening to comic turns from Arthur Askey and Hope and Keen in half-full houses before the main season started with Bruce Forsyth in *Here Comes Brucie!*

I visited him with my mum. We stayed in a bed and breakfast together. My dad was in digs. We went down to the seafront one afternoon and they had a big row in public near the crazy golf. Then my mum walked off, and my dad took me for sausage and beans in the theatre canteen, and I ate while he smoked and stared out of the window.

13

'They've made a nice job of it.'

My dad was looking up at the house through the car window.

'Very smart,' he went on. 'Nice paintwork.' He nodded to himself. 'Good workmanship.'

The old front wall and gateposts had been partially demolished and replaced by neatly pointed yellow-stock London bricks with elegant York coping stones. Small ornamental box hedges marked out the path to the front door. A young honeysuckle had been allowed to run up and loop itself through the holes of the first-floor balustrade. There was only one doorbell. It looked like a proper family house.

'They've cut down that tree too.'

'Which one?' I said.

'The little one by the porch. Pointless tree it was anyway.'

There was barely a breeze from outside. It felt so mild. The temperature gauge on the dashboard read thirteen degrees.

'It doesn't feel very Christmassy, does it?' I said.

'Why should it?' he said, still looking at the house.

'Because it's Christmas Day, Dad!'

He turned and looked straight ahead through the wind-screen and down the road. 'Is it?' He blinked a couple of times, then turned his head back to the house. 'Was that garage always there?'

'No, Dad. We only had a car-port, remember.'

'Did we? Your mother was always tight-fisted.'

A man marched past us on the pavement in shirt-sleeves, walking an eager dog wearing a collar laced with tinsel. All the houses seemed so smart now: white louvred plantation shutters; German cars; clipped hedges; curtain swags.

'Do you remember the porch, Dad . . . when you painted those moulded faces that sat at the top of the brick columns? I think they were originally meant to be cherubs or Greek gods or something.'

'Did I?'

'Yes, don't you remember? Most of the road painted them in a neutral colour to blend in with the brickwork, but one of them had its cheeks puffed out to represent the god of wind or something, and you painted it black, to look like Dizzy Gillespie?'

'Did I? Was it a good likeness? Your mother never liked jazz. Pretended to.'

'Mum was mortified; she thought someone would complain; but then one of the neighbours suggested we painted all four the same to make up his quartet.'

'Oh, it was a very progressive road, you know,' he said, whip-smart.

On the way back I took a different route – along Queen's Ride and the Lower Richmond Road, past Putney Common, where the fair came every bank holiday weekend. I used to win goldfish and carry them home across the common in a plastic freezer bag half filled with water, then tip them into a bowl and top it up from the tap. I'd feed them with fish-flakes that left a carpet on the surface like tiny leaves after a storm. A few mornings later I'd come down and the fish would be dead, floating on the surface, with a bulging eye, or worse just lying on the bottom amid wet uneaten fish-food. No one ever told me what I did wrong. My dad used to shrug and ask me what I expected from a fairground.

'Why did you stop playing?' I asked after a few minutes of silence.

He said nothing for a moment and I thought he hadn't heard me, but then he said, 'What do you mean?'

'Jazz. What made you give up?'

He was looking out of the window. 'I had nothing left to say.'

I had heard this answer for years. It was like a stock rebuff. A flat bat. Back down the track. 'Didn't you miss it?'

'Lovely finish on this dashboard,' he said, running his hand above the glove-box.

I tried again. 'Didn't you regret giving up?'

'Nope.'

There was something in the way he said 'Nope' instead of 'No' that sounded defensive, a little irritated. I'd learned to accept the jazz big band sound had been his one and only voice; he'd always told me it was how he had wanted to express himself, and perhaps it was true . . . perhaps he honestly felt that he'd said everything he'd meant to say, which is why he stopped so early. But as I grew older I suspected there was something he had never admitted, because if he'd loved it so much he might have found a way to keep going, even on a small scale, even when his sound was driven on to the side-lines in the sixties. And that's when I realised that was the problem right there: small-scale was not his style. He didn't want to play with *any* jazz orchestra; it had to be *the* jazz orchestra; an orchestra with a stirring, irresistible contemporary sound of which he was the mastermind, leading dynamically from the piano. *That* was what he wanted. Which was exactly what he hadn't been allowed to have since the early sixties. In fact, he had only had it for about five years. From 1957 to 1962. Five years. In a whole lifetime. Did that make his decision to give up a bit more shallow?

'You never played at the Bull when I was growing up. Well, a bit maybe – after everyone had gone home – but never properly,' I said.

'That's right.'

'Why?'

'They never asked me.'

I found it hard to believe. I sometimes wonder if it was because he'd seen himself as a writer and arranger, not a soloist or member of a trio or quartet, which meant he'd never pushed for it – even though his piano playing was often praised by his peers – or whether he'd made too many enemies along the way, or worse, his confidence had just deserted him. It happens in jazz; the courage goes. 'Why did he stop?' you can ask a jazz musician about another player. 'Some do,' is often the reply.

'Not once?' I asked.

'A few times maybe. Sitting in for someone. I can't bring it to mind any more.'

Maybe, in the end, it was because it lacked glamour, and only reminded him of something that was no longer there. An intimation of a lost past. Honest, grafting jazz was not for him. He didn't need that side of it enough.

I remember being told by my mum that the death of Tubby Hayes hit him hard and wondered if that gave him a final chance to walk away. I was only ten, but I remember my dad telling me about it suddenly one evening a few years later when I was in my late teens, and turning away from me in the kitchen and wiping quickly at the corner of his eye with his back to me. They had been great friends. The event itself seemed to signal a particularly resonant death knell on the British scene at the time, and for my dad it came only two years after his own personal calamity at the Dorchester. Hayes (or just 'Tubby' as everyone called him) was only thirty-eight when he died in 1973. He was perhaps the greatest British jazz musician of his era in the fifties and early sixties, a true Titan to compete with the Americans. He played tenor on all of my dad's early jazz orchestra sessions from the late fifties onwards. He used to share a flat in Barnes with the drummer Phil Seamen – another pioneer – and fell into a hard drug-fuelled hedonistic life in the mid-sixties as rock pushed British jazz aside. When Tubby sorted himself out and made his comeback in the early seventies following open-heart surgery, many wondered whether he would have modified his sound to compete with the vast changes that had gone on in jazz in the interim, but he returned with an approach that was something of a throwback to his heyday. In spite of the excitement that surrounded his return, perhaps it seemed to signal a fading of a light. Miles Davis had recorded *In a Silent Way* by then, and the world was transfixed by the cacophonous rule-breaking freedom of players like Ornette Coleman.

We crossed the river at Putney. Illuminated bunting was threaded between the lamp-posts. There was hardly any traffic. I saw the darkened floodlights of Fulham football ground where we used to stand when I was a boy on the windy open terrace overlooking Bishops Park. My dad was never a hardy football fan; there was nothing doughty about him when it came to the weather. If it was cold, we went home. If it was wet, we didn't even leave the house. Neither of us were even Fulham fans – I was Chelsea as a boy (following in Roly's footsteps) and my dad was Charlton from his days living in Blackheath after the war – but it was nearer and more easygoing at Fulham, and that was enough for my dad. We were there when Alan Mullery scored *Match of the Day*'s 'Goal of the Season' with an unstoppable volley from outside the penalty area against Leicester on a freezing winter afternoon in 1974, and as the crowd went crazy, my dad merely shrugged and said, 'Not bad. Fancy a Wagon Wheel? And then we should think about getting back.' I liked his company and the silly jokes he made on the way to the games, pointing out people's quirks and mannerisms, but I sometimes wished we could make it last longer.

At World's End we took the chicane into the heart of the King's Road. Flurries of spray-can snow were trapped inside the corners of the shop windows. I saw an enormous suspended Christmas cracker, a reindeer in a space helmet, a red straw heart hanging from a front door, two snowmen in top hats, little birds wrapped in gold foil, pendant stars, silver pine cones and stacks of empty gift boxes. It was like snapshots and footage of wistfulness. We swung around Sloane Square and up towards Hyde Park Corner.

'Heading towards civilisation,' my dad said after a spell of silence.

As soon as he'd said it, I sensed the tug of a magnet, the flutter of anticipation, the suburbs giving way to the West End, and I could see myself very young standing next to him in a central London street reaching up and feeding sixpences into a parking meter, and then following him down some narrow basement steps, and in through a darkened door and along a narrow poorly lit corridor, and into a small smoky room with a bar and bottles and optics, where he was greeted warmly by other confident men and women, and his suit looked smart and his oiled hair shone in the low light; and then I was playing on the carpet in the corridor, making shapes with corks and beer mats, and the door swung open and hit me on the head and I burst into tears, and my dad came and picked me up and took me into the bar in his arms and people made a fuss of me. He introduced me to the woman who had opened the door. She wanted to apologise. She put her face near mine – an arresting black face with big eyes, and she smiled and cooed through big white teeth with conspicuous gaps – and I didn't understand, and I burst into tears again. One night, a while later, I was watching *Top of the Pops* in the sitting room in our flat and the same face appeared on the TV screen and started singing into the camera, and my dad happened to come in and see her, and said she was the woman who was sorry for opening the door on to me at the Buckstone Club, and it confirmed in my mind that he went to interesting secret places and knew startling mysterious people.

The light was thickening. There were more cars, their brake-lights lush red in the gentle violet winter twilight. Along Piccadilly miniature Christmas trees twinkled in the windows of Korean Air and Aeroflot.

'The Ritz!' said my dad. 'Now we're talking.' There was a twang of energy and approval in his voice.

'Good times?'

'The *best* times,' he said crisply.

It was in 1955 that my dad walked into Levy's Sound Studios on New Bond Street and recorded and conducted his first ever arrangement with a hand-picked jazz big band. Located above the Bunch of Grapes pub and built into a large old forty by forty foot art gallery, Levy's was one of the few top independent recording facilities not run by any of the major record labels at the time. Aspiring artists could cut a professionally recorded demo straight to acetate disc using high quality equipment and walk out with it under their arm the same day.

The session was paid for and organised by the actor-manager Brian Rix. Brian was a big jazz fan and had made friends with my dad eleven years earlier on their first day in the RAF together, when they were called up as eighteen-year-old air cadets to the Air Crew Receiving Centre in Scarborough in 1944. The only two in the room with long hair, they hit it off right away, and were soon staging concerts in the hotel where they were stationed. 'He was a tough little bugger,' Brian told me recently over lunch, recalling their first meeting, 'but a brilliant pianist.'

When they met up again in London in the early fifties, following the first of Brian's string of comedy successes at the Whitehall Theatre, it was a perfect match: Brian had some spare money and had always wanted to produce his own big band; my dad, then still just the pianist with Harry Roy's orchestra at the Café de Paris, had been sharpening his skills studying part-time at the Guildhall during the day, and had always been eager to write for one. 'I saw Woody Herman's band while on pilot officer training in Canada in 1945,' he once told me. 'I knew the sound I wanted. I just needed the chance.'

The version of 'A Slow Boat to China' that was recorded live that morning at Levy's in 1955 was a key to a door at the BBC. Armed with the acetate, Brian set up a meeting with a couple of the station's producers and within weeks the Tommy Watt Orchestra had elbowed its way on to radio with a crisp swinging sound and was broadcasting at lunchtimes from the Paris Theatre on Lower Regent Street. It was an audacious and auspicious beginning, but some of the bigger, more established bands objected. Who was this upstart who seemed to have come from nowhere? Competition for air-time was fierce. There were eighteen working big bands touring and appearing on radio at the time; everyone needed exposure; there were established musicians to pay, reputations to enhance. To make it worse, my dad was borrowing their best players but had none of the additional overheads of running a band on the road.

Forced off the air for a few months while the arguments raged, he and Brian simply turned to George Martin at Parlophone Records, an imprint of EMI, who promptly paid for a single to be recorded ('Grasshopper Jump') and offered my dad a two-album deal. When the single was picked up as a sound-bed for various American radio shows, word got back to London, and some British radio producers thought – from the impressive sound – that the band must be American.

'That's Quaglino's down there,' I said, passing the turning for Bury Street.

'Ahhh . . . Quags . . . A good little band that was . . . Always packed.'

'Did you know it reopened recently, Dad?'

'Did it?' He looked astonished. It had been closed since the early seventies.

'Yes, Terence Conran relaunched it.'

'Well, I never! A decent band?'

'Just a restaurant now,' I said. I imagined the modern version: wall-to-wall tables full of cosmetic dentists and hedge fund managers on their mobile phones.

'Ah, too bad,' he said.

We slowed for a red light.

Back then, in the mid-fifties, he'd realised that to fully push the door open at the BBC he had to be not just an occasional arranger-conductor on radio, but a respected leading nightclub bandleader. The opportunity arose to become one at the old Quaglino's with the departure of the Tim Clayton Orchestra in late 1956. Quaglino's was at the centre of the London social scene at the time. It had a cocktail lounge and dining room and dance floor, and buzzed with aristocrats and actors, socialites and stars. It was the perfect place to get noticed. London was still gripped by austerity. Food rationing had only ended eighteen months earlier in the summer of 1954. Quaglino's was a gleaming bauble of sumptuous high living.

Initially booked as the pianist for the new incoming slimmed-down in-house quintet, he saw that it was a chance too good to miss, and convinced the management with compelling force of character that he should lead the band under his own name. 'What did you tell them?' I asked him when I was growing up. 'I told them,' he replied, without a trace of self-consciousness, 'that they needed *the new sound* and I was the one who could give it to them.'

And so, on 30 December 1956 the Tommy Watt Quintet was launched; it made the front cover of *Melody Maker*. My dad was thirty-one and suddenly the youngest bandleader in London. It was just the spark that was needed; within a year he had recorded his debut album for Parlophone (*It Might as Well Be Swing*) and was booked to go back to the Paris Theatre with a twenty-piece orchestra for his own forty-minute lunchtime radio show (*Time for Watt*) on the BBC.

We swung round under the animated neon hoardings of Piccadilly Circus and into Regent Street, and up above us the Christmas lights hung thrillingly white and glittering as far as we could see: snow crystals; stars; necklaces and bracelets;

cascades of illuminated raindrops above the shop-fronts; crescent moons and icicles. It was like a magical guard of honour. I thought of all the streets he must have confidently walked down back then – streets we were passing – suit pressed, shirt laundered, shoes buffed, owning every pavement, every corner, never imagining anything could ever end or change; knowing the doormen, cracking jokes, taking stairs two at a time. And I turned and looked at him, and there he was, back in the same West End, on his former stomping ground, perhaps for one of the last times, now a little old man buckled in under his seat belt, the world flowing past him unstoppably, and his face was bathed in a mirror-ball of shimmering reflected light.

14

My mum lasted a few days at Toby's over that Christmas ('She was just prowling around after the booze') before she went back to the London flat on her own. I couldn't tell if she wanted my dad back for good or not. She'd take a taxi from the rank outside her flat to the care home, then afterwards catch a bus straight back down the road on the way home. The journey became puzzling in spite of its direct simplicity. Twice she overshot the bus stop and once ended up disorientated at Baker Street, where she had to ask a newspaper vendor the way back – although not before confusing him by being unable to resist pointing out she used to write for the very evening paper he was selling.

It reminded me of the last time they ever tried travelling abroad together. It was 1993. I was performing in Brussels with Tracey and – with some covert help from our tour manager – they had arranged to secretly fly over and surprise us, but they had nearly missed the flight. After collecting their boarding passes, my mum – then sixty-nine, and a little rusty at travelling – had crisply asked the check-in staff for directions, not to Departures or Passport Control, but Customs. As a result, they had been sent to a small remote office in the far corner of the terminal that dealt with all those things we all know there is no point ever trying to take with us on an aeroplane, like snails or soil or exotic plants. It was a good half a mile from where they should have been going. By the time they finally got back near the flight's actual departure gate, hot and exhausted and out of breath, they weren't speaking to each other, and my dad – hearing their names for the third time over the public address system – saw red and encamped himself sulkily in the duty-free shop, refusing to budge another inch, while my mum pressed on and stoically got on the plane without him. A search party was sent by the ground crew to collect him and they had to talk him into boarding the flight.

I tried to picture my mum on her own at the flat. I saw her restive and ill at ease, spending the first forty-eight hours moving photo frames around, smoothing and re-smoothing a shawl across the back of the sofa, squinting at a Final Reminder, huffing and sighing and looking out of a window, absent-mindedly waiting for the sound of my dad to clear his throat in another room, but I couldn't picture her cooking for herself or listening contentedly to Radio 4 or taking her tablets every day at the right time or even enjoying her own company for very long – doing anything that might actually qualify as 'independent living'.

When I think of her eating on her own it is always cold food – half a quiche, cottage cheese on Ryvita, a bowl of Alpen, a banana, a biscuit. A kind of deprivation. She drank half-cups of sweetened black coffee, but she used sweetener (Hermesetas) not sugar, even though she hated the aftertaste. She had always been conflicted about food: disgusted by waste; never indulgent. Cold scraps were put in the fridge after every meal, covered by a side plate. Even cold vegetables. They would stay in there for a couple of days until it was clear no one in the family in their right mind would touch them, and then she would finish them off in a show of dreadful self-sacrifice. As a child, I once saw her open the fridge at seven in the morning in her dressing gown, and bitterly eat a coagulated spoonful of cold Brussels sprouts and cheese sauce before throwing the remainder in the bin with disapproval and revulsion. 'I grew up in a manse,' she said, mid-mouthful. 'What do you expect?'

It was true. She was born in Carlisle in 1924, the daughter of an itinerant Methodist minister. Her mother was a Welsh Wesleyan too. After a brief stop in Huddersfield, she was five when they moved for most of her childhood to Halifax, where the first manse they occupied was set in the grounds of a cemetery on Skircoat Moor. 'It was like a dark barn,' she said, 'and funeral processions regularly pulled up outside our front door.' The graveyard didn't bother her as a child. She played hide-and-seek around the tombstones with her best friend, Joan, collecting discarded flowers left by the visitors. 'We ran our own imaginary florist just for ourselves,' she said. 'A little table with all the wilting posies on it.'

On the edge of the cemetery – now overgrown – was a vast deserted octagonal brick tower, two hundred and fifty feet high, that still stands imperiously and incongruously over the Calderdale countryside. It used to creak in the howling wind at night. Sparrow hawks nested in its empty abandoned galleries. Her mother hated it. It was built as a chimney in the 1870s to take fumes from the old abandoned Washer Lane dye-works factory using an underground pipe, but in the end was never used. The owner, a rich Victorian magnate – John Wainhouse – had paid for it. Determined that it shouldn't be an eyesore, he had spent a fortune on its design, including its four hundred and three interior steps and double viewing platforms.

Wainhouse's Folly, the locals called it. A colossus in the coun-tryside. At night my mum sometimes thought it would fall on the house if she'd been bad.

When she was eight they moved to a new house on Rothwell Road with outhouses and a croft and a paddock, where her mother felt less oppressed by the surroundings. She went to a local school on the moor for a couple of years before being sent to a Methodist boarding school in Arnside, near Grange-over-Sands, and from there she went to another – Hunmanby Hall near Filey. 'Life was very spartan,' she told me, 'bordering on the puritanical.'

Her father was not only a minister, but Romany on his mother's side. Born in Hull, a nephew to the celebrated Chris-tian evangelist Rodney 'Gipsy' Smith, he grew up with a consuming love of wildlife and the countryside, and for eleven years of my mum's childhood the family spent summer holi-days touring the country lanes around Whitby in a reconditioned horse-drawn vardo – the Romany name for a caravan. It was a proper barrel-roofed wooden wagon with casement windows, locker seats and a split door, bought from Brough Hill Fair in the Eden Valley for seventy-five pounds by her father three years before she was born. It sounds romantic but it was tough for a child: living frugally and walking the hedgerows for hours during the day, always in regimented single file with her older brother, much of it in silence in case they should disturb their father's self-absorbed bird-watching or charcoal sketch-ing; camping out under leaky canvas at night, spooked by the ants and the moths. If they weren't out in the countryside they'd be parked up for weeks on end on the edge of wind-swept Eskdaleside in a farmyard near Hard Struggle Cottages with little to do except run races and swing on gates.

* * *

I dropped round one afternoon in the new year to see her at the flat. She'd left a short message on my voicemail: *Could you bring me some cheese?* When I arrived she was in the lobby with her coat on.

'Oh, I thought you weren't coming,' she said. 'I'm just stumbling out to the shops.'

'I came as quickly as I could. If you still want to go, I'll come with you.'

She smiled as if to say that would be lovely.

We pushed open the glass swing door. Outside, with her on my arm, life seemed to speed up suddenly. A motorbike courier was remonstrating with a cyclist. A group of tourists blocked the pavement, herding round an *A-Z* street map and pointing the wrong way towards Abbey Road. She gripped my arm and we walked gingerly down the steps. That same oaky sweet smell was on her breath.

'The air is nice, darling,' she said. 'So stuffy in that flat some days.'

'You should open a window.'

'They're all sealed up.'

'No, they're not. They're double-glazed but they all slide open.'

'*Do* they? You'll have to show me.'

'Again,' I teased.

We walked along the pavement to the corner and turned and walked to the end of the block. The supermarket was on the opposite side.

'What kind of cheese, Mum?'

'Oh, forget it. I've got plenty really.'

'Really?'

'Yes, you know me. I'll eat any old leftovers.'

'If you're sure.'

'Let's just go once round the block. It's nice like this.'
She squeezed my arm.

I remembered being with her in a wheat field in Sussex near the Walberton cottage where we used to stay in the late sixties. I was almost seven. I could see her edging through a thicket and an iron kissing gate, and suddenly we were out the other side and the sky above our heads was streaked with tattered white clouds. The path cut down the side of the field. We ran our fingers through the outermost line of the blond crop – rough and smooth, rough and smooth – the heads craning and stretching away to the rise in the field, the leaf blades and stems nicking at my fingers. And then she was calling up ahead, 'Come and look, come and look! Cow parsley and yarrow.' I loved to hear the names – convolvulus, knapweed, lords and ladies, rosebay willow-herb. The sleeves of her smock were pulled high over her elbows, her crow-black hair pushed back over her forehead, her skin tanned. And at the end of the field we scuttled down the steep slope and over the sedge to the brook. She held my hand across the little wooden bridge. The clear water was puckered like seersucker by the rushes in the shallows, the pebbles on the bottom shining like toffees.

'Why is it called the rife?' I asked.

'It's an old word for river. A country word. It may look small now, but in the olden days, it was a big river and the tide would sweep right up here carrying boats with food and people on board.'

'Where is the river now?'

'It's gone back to the sea.'

We started to climb up the other side.

'Let's recite a poem to get us to the top,' she said, pushing on ahead. And I could hear her voice, strong and articulate:

> 'I went out to the a hazel wood,
> Because a fire was in my head,
> And cut and peeled a hazel wand,
> And hooked a berry to a thread;
>
> And when white moths were on the wing,
> And moth-like stars were flickering out,
> I dropped the berry in a stream . . .'

'"And caught a little silver TROUT"!' I shouted.
'Yeats!' she shouted back.

I loved the rich evocative words and was frightened of the white moths and the dark hazel wood, and then we were at the top of the hill and we stopped and sat down and looked back to the brook below and the wheat field beyond. A breeze disturbed the hedgerow. The leaves shivered. A cluster of finches darted down the track.

'Finches love the hedgerow and the crops,' she said. 'We might see linnets and buntings this week too.'

The old small church was at the top of the rise. I half looked at it, half hid my eyes. It was frightening and beautiful. We'd walked there once in winter when the track was as hard as bones, flecked with snow, and the fields were empty, in a huffling wind, and I wouldn't look up. The bell-tower was black in my imagination. And then my mum had taken me to the graveyard wall and *made* me look, and when I opened my eyes the ground was a carpet of glistening frosted snowdrops and it was like something from a fairy story.

The cottage where we stayed smelled of woodsmoke and books. The front door opened directly into the small living room. There was no central heating. The downstairs was heated only by a small open fire. The staircase to the two bedrooms above and the short passage to the kitchen had latched doors to stop the draughts. When they creaked it made me want to hide my head under the bedclothes. The passage to the kitchen was piled high with old newspapers. Dried mud clung to the coir matting. At mealtimes we huddled round the kitchen table under a huge poster of a snowy owl with yellow shining eyes with yet more newspapers piled up beside us. Often it was so cold the steam from the food looked like smoke.

Two steps down from the kitchen was a bedroom with more books and pictures of clowns on the wall, and I wasn't allowed to play in there, as the man who lived in the cottage most of the time had 'his things' in there.

Upstairs there was a bedroom for grown-ups above the sitting room with a double bed, and another room with bunk beds and orange nylon sleeping bags, where I slept beside a smelly paraffin heater. The cold bathroom had a dark cupboard full of cobwebs and a tank full of water that spluttered and groaned. I used to scare myself by opening it and leaning inside.

Outside the back door there were three small gardens, inter-linked by high hedges with fat shiny leaves. It was all unkempt and overgrown and gave me itchy legs. There was a knotted and crinkly fruit tree that hurt my knees if I tried to climb it, and tall grasses grew at the back. ('Don't go in there. There are tigers.')

If you scraped away the undergrowth you could find big iron rings embedded in the ground. My dad told me they were 'Sinbad's buried treasure' and that he had landed at Climping and dragged his haul of jewels to the garden and buried it, but no one had had the strength to prise it out, and I tried not to believe him, but I wanted to, and it was only when my mum told me the place used to be a blacksmith's forge and the rings were for the horses that I stopped looking at them, and was annoyed at my dad for lying to me.

In the furthest garden was an outbuilding, a small barn. Downstairs had been made into two bedrooms and my half-brothers sometimes slept in there. My eldest half-brother, Simon, was eighteen by then and had one of the rooms to himself and burned sandalwood joss sticks and played Roy Harper and Beach Boys records. He had cut out the face and shoulders of Roy Orbison from the front of a vinyl record sleeve and pinned it to the window ledge, and made a small hole where his mouth was and would dangle a lit joss stick from Roy Orbison's lips. I thought it was a dangerous thing to do but also strange and lovely – like the altar at the end of a church where the cross stands. Simon used to walk across the fields on his own to the church some days and play songs on the organ when no one was there.

Above the bedrooms was a huge dark loft full of long strips and sheets of polystyrene; I never knew why they were up there. A rusted iron ladder was propped up outside against the gabled end, half hidden in an unruly thorny pyracantha bush. It scratched my legs, but I could get to the top and swing the loft door open, and turn round and sit in the doorway, and look out over the wheat field where I walked with my mum.

'Who owns this cottage?' I would say to her. I often asked the same question several times if I felt the answer I got the first time didn't make sense, or to test whether I would get the same answer twice, and therefore it was more likely to be true.

'Uncle Ken rents it from a nice man in the village.'

'And who is "Uncle Ken" again?'

'He is your brothers' and sister's father. And I was married to him once.'

'Why aren't you married to him now?'

'Because I am married to your father.'

'Is he your brother?'

'No.'

'Then why is he called *Uncle* Ken?'

'We just call him that, darling.'

'Why does Simon light joss sticks?'

'It's his room and he can do what he likes. Now run along.'

I think being unsure of Ken's identity made the cottage even more special and secret.

We walked on slowly. The pavement was uneven. Padlocked to a lamp-post was a bicycle frame with no wheels. A police siren wailed near by and I felt my mum flinch. I filled the moments with chatter about the kids.

At the traffic lights she said suddenly, 'Do you think I could have him back?'

I watched a plane disappear behind a cloud. For a moment I couldn't think what she was talking about and then realised she meant my dad. 'What makes you say that?' I said.

'He makes such a fuss now when I leave. I can't bear it.'

I thought of them without me there at the care home: just a couple; still the little shifts in dominance; moments of beseeching; the things we do and the roles we play when we are sure no one is watching. 'And how will you cope?'

'Like I always have done, dear.'

We stood at the crossroads. I watched a car slow down, climb up on to the raised speed-table, then ease itself down the other side. I wondered how it was having to ask your children for help, knowing that some things can no longer be done without them – lifting things, organising things. Was it a little degrading, having to wait on the authorisation of someone who once relied on you so completely? As the traffic lights changed I asked myself if all this was easier in other people's lives – *these* people, the ones in front of me in their cars criss-crossing in a matrix of dropping off, picking up, going home, leaving town. Was it the same for everyone? Life as a slow journey of negotiations. Back and forth. I pictured my mum and dad back at the flat. It was not much more than a year since they'd first moved in. I saw myself unpacking their things, making it nice, mapping it out, feeling I could make a difference. And suddenly I was conscious that I might make *no* difference, that I could help them *do* something but not influence its outcome, as if I had simply been invited in to view it all at close quarters, made to witness something, and it was going to unfold inexorably, whether I liked it or not, whatever I said, and it was something I just had to get through.

15

On a busy stretch of the Finchley Road, a few doors down from the Secrets table- and pole-dancing club, and the Thai Siam health and beauty bar, stands a large boarded-up sports bar called the 3one7. It was once a three-storey Victorian pub called the Carney Arms and at weekends – before it folded in the wake of an under-age drinking scandal – it doubled as a pre-club evening nightspot with DJs playing funky 'sexy' house music for buff lads on the pull, and girls on their way 'up West'. There were pool tables and big-screen broadcasts, although during the week most of the sixteen satellite TV screens scattered around the venue were blank, the upstairs and basement roped off, and the clientele corralled on the ground floor in the mid-afternoons would change to companionless off-shift waiters on their way to the bookie's and a few unaccompanied professional drinkers. It was here, on a January lunchtime in 2003, that my dad, accompanied by a blind man and a chef – both from the same care home where he was staying – escaped for a celebratory drink to mark the new year.

The exit doors at the care home needed a manually entered key-code before they would open on to a narrow brick driveway set back about ten feet from the pavement. My dad didn't know the code and I don't suppose the blind man did, but I'm sure the chef could do it in his sleep. The section of the Finchley Road outside the door is a 'red route': double red lines; no stopping at any time. The noise can be quite startling when it's busy: four car lanes and two bus lanes of delivery lorries, skip-hire trucks, double-deckers, cars, coaches and white transits all jostling like jockeys in the final furlong for that extra yard of space.

The 3one7 is about two hundred yards away from the care home. It sounds near, but my dad, with his bad lungs, had been finding a short walk up and down the corridor was about enough most mornings; not only that, but the bar is situated on the other side of the road, across a box junction and a couple of pot-holes, where the pelican crossings need smart decision-making once the pedestrian signal flashes green.

By the time the three of them arrived, my dad was gulping for air. He made it through the front door, took a few tottering steps and then collapsed on the carpet.

You might have thought that at this point the chef – an employee at a care home, after all – would have realised how reckless he had been and sprinted back for help, but no; instead, he and a member of the bar staff propped my dad up against a fruit machine, and gave him a glass of whisky to revive him. The effect on his brain, already dangerously short of oxygen, must have been nothing short of psychedelic, but – more by luck than judgement – his heart didn't stop, and they got him upright and seated on a bar stool. My dad, to his credit, composed himself and got his breath back. Everyone cracked a couple of jokes, and then, quite remarkably, they all got to the front door and somehow managed to walk back.

I suppose you have to have some sympathy for my dad. As a persistent drinker he must have found the enforced sobriety at the care home – unless you count the evening sherry – hard to bear. The drop in blood-alcohol levels must, at the very least, have brought on mild withdrawal symptoms and cravings, and with no emergency sugar substitutes readily to hand – the Coca-Cola, the bars of chocolate, the dried fruit – it must have all got too much, especially when a young companionable chef was rolling back the years before him.

Of course when I found out I confronted the care home and expressed my outrage in the strongest possible terms, and there were unstinting apologies, but apart from moving him somewhere else – which in itself would have been even more disruptive for him – I realised there was little else I could do; I had no legal charge over him; he was still a grown-up; the care home had adequate security measures in place on the front door, which were circumvented in extremely unusual circumstances; and I could no more control events than I could stop him going back to bed all day. Perhaps I should have insisted on the chef's dismissal, but that seemed overly hysterical, and anyway I considered that was up to them.

When it all blew over I realised I actually secretly admired my dad for the sheer audacity of his escape; and it occurred to me that I had felt many things for him over the years – admiration, respect, anger, disdain – but overarching all of it was a long indecipherable allegiance.

'So you tunnelled out then?' I said to him a few days later. We were sitting in the lobby of the care home just inside the doors to the outside world.

'What?'

'You and the chef. The bid for freedom.' I nodded towards the doors.

'Do you know the chef as well?' he said, looking at me as though we'd found a mutual acquaintance. 'Nice fella.'

I couldn't tell if he was deliberately avoiding the subject or had clean forgotten. 'No, not personally,' I said.

'Good sense of humour.'

That was the stamp of approval. I remembered coming home from school one day and riding my bike down to the shed at the end of the alley and seeing a huge extendable ladder propped up against the back of the house. At the top of the ladder – which was flexing under the weight – and about six feet below the guttering, almost on the top rung, was a man. He must have been about thirty or forty feet off the ground. But what made me gasp was the fact that *another* man was standing on his shoulders and reaching up *over* the guttering. They seemed unfeasibly high – as if performing a reckless circus trick. My dad was at the bottom looking up. I'm not sure if he was meant to be helping to stabilise the ladder, but he was leaning on it nonchalantly with one hand, smoking. He saw me and gestured to the spectacle above. 'That'll be our Chris Kerrigan up there,' he said. 'Fine roofer. Good sense of humour.'

I smiled at him sitting there, his hands mottled and creased, planted on his knees, the rumble of traffic kept at bay by the glass doors. 'Glad to hear it. You're getting on all right then?'

'You've got to get me out of here, Ben, you know,' he said, turning to me.

'Why?'

'I'm not cut out for it.'

I tried to think of an answer. I knew if I answered firmly and logically he would accept it, as the deferral of power was in place, and I was now in charge, but before I could find the words he carried on.

'They've asked me to play the piano, you know.'

It seemed unlikely. He hadn't played for years. I looked at his stiff white fingers. Was he imagining it? Had he been telling jazz stories to impress them? 'That's nice of them,' I said, for want of anything better to say.

'You must be joking. They're all potty.'

One of the staff passed us, carrying a bag of linen. 'Feeling better this afternoon, Tommy?' she called out.

My dad flashed a compliant smile.

'All at sixes and sevens this morning, weren't we?' she said loudly. 'But we're all here for you, that's all that matters.'

I smiled at her too. She winked at me. I didn't ask what had happened. She carried on towards the lift.

We sat in silence for a moment. I wished I knew the best course of action. I wished there was a sign. One minute everything was normal – by which I meant the same as a recognisable and non-frightening past – the next, everything was strange and alarming. Then words came out of my mouth, as if from nowhere: 'Mum's doing much better. Feeling stronger. She's been thinking of getting you back to the flat with her.'

He immediately took my hand. His palm felt cold. I was aware of his bony fingers as they squeezed mine, and the power I seemed to be wielding.

'Thank you,' he said. 'Thank you.'

16

n May 1971 my dad's father – my grandpa – died in hospital following a car crash. He was seventy-one. He held the steering wheel with the same white matchwood hands. I was in the car when we crashed, together with my grandma. My recollection of it is as vivid now as when I described it in *Patient*. We were on our way to the swimming pool in Dumbarton in my grandpa's bottle-green Mini. My grandpa was driving. My grandma was in the back. I was in the front passenger seat, my feet up on the dashboard, my trunks rolled up in a towel held across my chest. We approached the traffic lights at the big crossroads. The lights were red but my grandpa just seemed to accelerate rather than brake. Behind me I heard my grandma shout, 'Will!' When I came round, there was a crowd around the car. A tiny trickle of blood was on my ear. I touched it with my fingers. Hundreds of small crystals of glass like transparent cane sugar were all over my lap. The car wasn't in the middle of the junction – as it would have been if we had continued in a straight line – but pushed over as though we'd turned left but sideways. There was a double-decker bus stopped too. My grandpa wasn't speaking. He was still in his seat but he looked floppy and awkward, like a discarded puppet. The bus had hit his side of the car on the junction, side on, and pushed us some distance. The steering wheel was very near me, touching my leg; it seemed odd to have the steering wheel that close to me, as though it had been positioned in the middle of the dashboard for use by either the driver or the passenger. My grandma was lying on her side on the back seat. She was saying something to me. Her shoulder seemed tucked behind her back. An egg yolk was dripping off the seat and there were peas on the floor. I couldn't tell how much time had passed. It felt like a minute but it must have been a while for the ambulance to have already got there. A woman I'd never seen before helped me out with an ambulance man. I was barely marked. My grandma had dislocated her shoulder. We had to wait while they cut my grandpa out. The sparks cascaded into the grey afternoon light. In the ambulance, he opened his eyes for a second and said everything would be all right, but then he closed them again. He was very pale. The liver spots on his balding head stood out. His fine wispy white hair was messed up like he had been sleeping on it. He didn't have his glasses on any more which made him look less like him. I didn't see him again after that.

I remember the phone call several days later when I was back home in London and the hospital said my grandpa had died. They said the cause of death was pneumonia and a broken ribcage. I wasn't sure what a ribcage looked like; I wondered if it was like a bird-cage. Every Sunday morning my dad used to shut himself in my mum's study just before 11.30 a.m. and a couple of minutes later my grandma called on the dot of the half-hour for the week's news. Their chats usually only lasted about five or ten minutes and started with my grandma saying – as my dad often impersonated, purring his 'r's in a comic

Glaswegian accent – 'Anything fresh to report from south of the border, Tom?' but I remember after my grandpa died there were a couple of weekends when my dad was in there talking for a long time.

I think my dad felt guilty. I'd been only eight, alone on holiday with my grandparents when the accident happened, four hundred miles away, while he was in London still licking his wounds in the weeks after the Dorchester. Even while my grandpa was in Intensive Care I heard my dad criticising his driving one night and referring to him as a 'stupid old man'. I worried about why he didn't like him.

We had been up to stay with them in their retirement bungalow in Milngavie on the outskirts of Glasgow the previous year. They had only recently moved in. It was on a long curving residential drive high up overlooking the small town, silent except for the wind that got in behind the brick and whistled long hollow sighs. It felt very remote even though there were houses all around. Concrete steps led up to a yellow front door that swelled in the rain and was only ever used for visitors. The sitting room had a bay window that looked north. On a clear day, with my grandpa's binoculars, I could stand on a chair and see across the town and beyond Craigmaddie Reservoir as far as the ruined Mugdock Castle. It was the first thing I wanted to see when I arrived.

'Who lives there, Grandpa?'

'No one, it's a ruin. Just ghosts.'

When he said the words 'ruin' and 'ghosts' he sounded like Private Fraser in *Dad's Army* and it made me shiver and I always asked him to say it again.

The furniture seemed plain and strange. A dark oak sideboard with carved mouldings stood behind the door laid out with a spider plant in a jade-green fruit bowl, a small set of leather-bound books and a Chinese teapot. Next to it stood a folding cake stand; I had to ask what it was. I couldn't imagine my grandma serving cake on a cake stand, but my dad told me they used to run a little guest house after my grandpa had retired. I wanted to ask what a guest house was, and maybe even what 'retired' meant, but I thought that was one too many questions.

On the wall above was a small oval glass mirror and two prints of Buenos Aires brought back by my grandma's brother-in-law, Harry, who was a merchant seaman. There was an oak dining table in the window that never seemed to be used. (I got the feeling my grandma wanted to lay it with nice crockery when we stayed, but my dad insisted we made less of a fuss, so instead we all had to cluster round the tiny drop-leaf Formica table in the kitchen, while my grandma made a simple tea of potato scones.) A velour three-piece suite with tan vinyl armrests was grouped around a gas fire and a black-and-white TV. Behind one of the chairs was a glass display cabinet with eight sets of china. I used to try and count the teacups without opening the doors. 'Do you drink a lot of tea then, Grandma?' I once asked.

I sat there with my dad and watch him stiffen. It was unlike him; he was usually loose and relaxed. He seemed uncomfortable, getting up from time to time and pacing around. Once I found him shivering on the back step smoking, the dank sky shrouding the huddled rows of back gardens and pebble-dashed garages. While I saw fascinating curiosities, he just saw a suffocating asceticism.

His father was born in the mill town of Strathaven in Lanarkshire south of Glasgow in 1899. Some typewritten references left among my grandma's belongings show he got an apprenticeship at fourteen as an engineer and fitter at the vast Dalzeel Steel and Iron Works in Motherwell. He travelled to New York in 1923 on a steam ship on a work visa to make his fortune, but came back within a year and married my grandma, then Jean Cairns, a baker's clerk from Partick, in February 1925. She was born Jane, but everyone called her Jean. He was born William, but everyone called him Billy. On their wedding day he was twenty-five, she was twenty-three, and nine months later, almost to the day, my dad was born. After years of factory life where he rose to become a foreman, my grandpa was forced to take early retirement through intermittent ill-health but they moved out of the city and he helped Jean set up a seven-roomed guest house in the market town of Crieff – fifty miles north of Glasgow. They had most of the year to themselves but each summer they rented out the rooms, taking on a girl to help with the serving and cleaning. In the back garden was a vast rock that rose out of the lawn. It gave the house its name – Rockearn – and my grandma told me in the old days an auctioneer used to climb on to it on market day and the rock was surrounded by a sea of farmers and animals. They had looked forward to their retirement in Milngavie but within a couple of years of moving in there was the car crash and everything changed. Jean was widowed at sixty-nine.

One night when I was little older, maybe fourteen, I was standing with my dad leaning on the rail at the Ship Inn as a big black barge crossed slowly in front of us sending ripples of water slapping against the brick pier below, and he said out of nowhere, 'We could see the canal from Banner Road.'

'What canal?'

'It's not there now. I was four when we moved. Knights-wood. My mother and father were so proud. It was only a little two-up, two-down, but it was *Knightswood*.'

On the way back in the car he told me his father had worked all hours to improve his trade and became a machinist – a tool-maker – so they could move again, and at sixteen they transferred to another house in Knightswood, this time with a garden.

'I was at school,' he said. 'I wore a Mackenzie kilt! I can remember cycling home and finding Mother in the new house – it was marvellous.'

Knightswood was one of the major garden suburb develop-ments of the twenties and thirties in Glasgow after the city's slum clearance schemes. Working-class families who were moved into the smart new-built semi-detached houses and cottage flats were hand-picked, and expected to be principled and hard-working. Everyone paid their rents on time, and there was little or no crime. Probity and godliness were bywords in many of the households but it could lead to a biting austerity in the battle for respectability. 'My parents scrimped every penny,' my dad said to me, 'but it never brought them a moment's joy.' Rectitude must have mixed powerfully with the politics of the factory floor. His father came home at night only to lecture on how avarice and capitalism were nothing short of punishable sins. 'He was a textbook *Christian* Socialist,' my dad added scathingly. 'And a *Freemason* – that took the biscuit.'

His mother, meanwhile, dreamed of a university place for her teenage son or a job in the Corporation. School results were the focus of great attention, but, as my dad said, 'I just wanted to play the piano.' His precociousness was apparent even as a schoolboy. His old schoolfriend, Eric Monteith Hamilton – who went on to become a jazz archivist and owner of one of

Glasgow's most famous hi-fi shops – sent me an email in 2009, at the age of eighty-seven, about their growing up in Knightswood. He had tracked me down and wanted me to know, before he died, what an influence my dad had had on him – a life-changing influence:

> He was very popular, and did things most of us were scared to do. And I must tell you, that while most of us were very clean with nice clothes, Tommy was always immaculate, with nice-cut clothes and smart ties; he always looked good. This was unusual at this time. As you know, he was a good-looking boy, and attractive to the girls. We were not so lucky, as we did not have his assured ways.
>
> When we walked up from school he would beat out rhythms to me. 'Is this a quickstep, a slow or fast foxtrot, or modern waltz?' I had to answer, and I tried and tried, until I got it.
>
> When we reached his home we would get a drink from his mum, then [we'd go] up to the piano, for a concert. I lived in Cedric Road, which was only about three minutes away.
>
> Then I started record collecting in 1940, I heard Glenn Miller, and was struck, but Tommy was moving on. He wanted to buy a 12" disc of Bunny Berigan's 'I Can't Get Started', so he sold his old records to me. We were both so keen.
>
> I was very lucky to meet Tommy, and while he did not know it, he shaped my life in music.

To their credit, my dad's parents gave over an entire room on the first floor at the front of their Knightswood house on Arrowsmith Avenue for his ambitions. He studied hard

– classical music initially – and at weekends he was allowed to take the bus into the city to Buchanan Street to Paterson, Sons & Co. where they sold all the leading pianos and player-pianos and organs, and he was allowed to play on all the top brands 'to keep them warm'.

After he finished school in 1941 at the age of sixteen he got a gig playing piano for the Jack Chapman band ('I couldn't really play at all at that stage') at the Albert Dance Hall in Bath Street. He'd volunteered for the RAF but was given a deferral because of his age. There were places in several bands up for grabs; many of the best players had gone to war. The opportunity was unique and the money was incredible for a teenager – up to ten pounds per week – while most men in Knightswood were taking home three, factory managers maybe five. His parents were very proud – Jack Chapman was regarded in local circles as 'such a nice man' – and they were impressed by an advertisement in the local paper that ran: *The Albert Dance Hall. For Select Dancing.*

One night, not long after starting, he ran into a homesick Glaswegian pianist called John McCormack who was touring with one of the hottest bands at the time, run by the Trinidadian clarinettist Carl Barriteau. In a piece of unshrinking opportunism, my dad suggested that they simply swapped gigs. Before he knew it, it was all agreed, and McCormack had joined Jack Chapman and my dad had left home and was based at the Belle Vue in Manchester with Barriteau, earning twenty pounds per week and flying by the seat of his pants. For eighteen months before call-up to the RAF, he found himself touring the country in the best band around, learning fast and walking on air.

I remember waking in the morning after he told me about his Knightswood childhood and saying to him, 'You know that photograph of that young man on the dresser in Grandma's bedroom?'

'Yes,' he replied.

'Grandma said it was you before you ever left Glasgow.'

'Did she now?'

'Yes, she did. Is it really you, Dad?'

'No. It's who I was.'

17

For the rest of the summer of 1971 the lid of the piano at home stayed shut. Back from the Bournemouth Winter Gardens my dad would cook an evening meal, and then just as my mum and I were getting ready to join him in the kitchen, we'd hear the jingle of the keys, and he'd have slipped out to the pub leaving all the food in the warming drawer, with no indication he was coming back.

My mum flew to Rome for her second big syndicated interview with Richard Burton and Elizabeth Taylor, and a couple of days later my dad said we were going to drive out to Heathrow Airport to collect her. Her return flight was landing that afternoon, but he seemed subdued. I remember being allowed to have the sunroof open on the Renault 5 and thinking the whole thing – Heathrow, my mum home, sunroof – was all incredibly exciting, but my dad didn't say much the whole journey.

That night they had a row in the kitchen just before we were about to eat. My mum told me to go upstairs. I heard my dad raising his voice to her. He never shouted, just seemed to increase the pressure and tension in his voice, until it was insistent and intimidating. Even through the door I heard him say, 'You're just an *embarrassment*, Romany.' He said it twice. It sounded wrong. Even though I wasn't totally sure what it meant, it sounded like a bad thing to say.

Then I heard something big crash, and then the kitchen door open, and then the sound of car keys being lifted off the hook, and the flat door open and close, and then the front door open and close. I heard the car leave the car-port and then I heard the flat door open and close again, and I thought my dad must have gone to the pub and my mum followed him down the street. I crept downstairs from my bedroom. My heart was beating like a drum. I pushed open the kitchen door. A sauce-pan was lying on the floor near the radiator. There was a dent in the wall and little bits of green paint and white plaster were on the linoleum tiles below. I stood and listened for a minute. All I could hear was the blood beating in my ears and the hiss of the gas-ring that was still burning on the stove. I went to the window and I saw my mum down in the garden. It made me jump. She was just standing still near one of the flowerbeds, at a slight angle, not fully facing the lawn or the few scant roses that grew along the fence. She had her arms tightly folded and her back to me. I wished one of my older half-brothers was home but everyone was away.

The months passed and the work dried up for my dad. There was still a bit of library music on offer, but the royalties from his own compositions started to dwindle as they got played less and less on the radio, and the films for which he'd written music – a few farces for his old friend Brian Rix – were repeated more infrequently. To compensate, my mum had started doing additional travel writing for newspapers and magazines. It partially covered the cost of a holiday too, as the travel and accommodation were often thrown in if a commission came up. My half-brothers and half-sister were too old for family holidays by then, so the three of us – plus a schoolfriend I was allowed to take with me for company – drove all the way to Wales for a week over Easter in 1972 so she could write a lightweight 'family feature' on the Butlin's holiday resort at Pwllheli.

We arrived in driving rain. There were people asleep in our chalet. A man found us another one but it was right next to a generator that chugged and thrummed all through the night. My dad lasted forty-eight hours, then knocked the hinges out of the door frame slamming it in a rage, and we all drove home. 'The walls were so thin you could hear someone fart in the chalet next door,' he had said in the car on the way back. I was only nine. I thought it was funny but also a bit scary. I caught my friend's eye. I think he thought the same.

That summer I went with my parents to Majorca when it was still pronounced with a 'j'. It was my first time abroad and my first time away with just my mum and dad. We went to the Pontinental Village at Cala Mesquida. Again my mum had been commissioned to write about it for a magazine. My dad kept saying how at least Pontin's was a step up from Butlin's although I didn't understand what he meant.

I played crazy golf with other families, bought ice creams from the Sundae Bar and watched English films in the communal day rooms when it was too hot in the afternoons. I wore a yellow sombrero all day long and had a scuba-diving lesson in the shallow end of the pool. My mum and dad mostly just sat on sun-loungers, my mum with a book, my dad with a hangover. The travel company gave us a complimentary Fiat 126 to 'explore the island'. We used it once to go into the nearby town before my dad dismissed it as a 'joke car' and didn't set foot in it again. At the hotel he mocked everyone behind their backs.

The only people he didn't belittle were the local Spanish wait-ers and the housekeeping maids. Photographs were taken of all of them – more than anything else. He drank with the waiters and chefs after they knocked off work, sometimes staying up late and playing cards with them, and I would hear him come back into the room in the darkness, stumbling into a chair, cursing under his breath, pulling his trousers off, and falling into bed next to my mum.

There are other photographs from the holiday of me stand-ing with a fishing rod on the rocky coastline below the hotel. My dad is in the pictures too, in a black-and-white-checked shirt and blue cotton shorts and espadrilles, with a denim fish-ing hat and gold-rimmed sunglasses. In one, he has his arm round my shoulders. My mum must have taken them – she has even managed to get herself in the foreground of one or two – but when I look at them I don't remember them feeling very real; they strike me as something set up to look like a touching holiday photograph. I can remember my dad's face in the mornings on that holiday – fixed and pale and distant like a waning moon – and that is more the impression the photo-graphs leave me with.

A year later, on another of my mum's press trips, we went to the Pontinental Hotel Pineta Beach at Platamona in Sardinia. We had a chalet in a small pine forest, but I was mostly distracted from the friction between my mum and dad as two players from the Chelsea football team (Peter Osgood and Ron Harris) plus the team manager, Dave Sexton, were staying at the hotel with their families. As a fan, I was overcome with excitement.

One afternoon I saw Osgood – as close to a demi-god as it got for me at the time – standing up to his waist in the sea on his own. It was too good an opportunity to miss, and swallowing down my nerves, I swam out towards him underwater and surfaced near by. It all came out in an excited garble.

'Hello, Mr Peter . . . Mr Osgood . . . I think you're really good and I love Chelsea and I watched you win the FA Cup . . . and the Cup Winners' Cup . . . and I think you're really good . . .'

He stood looking at me. He was bronzed and muscular with an unashamedly thick covering of manly chest hair.

'Oh, yeah?' he said economically.

I waited for a moment. Then I realised that was all he had to say, so I pressed on. 'And I've got a proper shirt . . . a blue Chelsea one . . . with number 9 on the back . . . that's your number . . . well, you know that . . . and my mum even got me a pillowcase with your face printed on it . . . and I sleep with it every night . . . and I think you're really, really . . . talented.'

He scooped some water up over his arms. 'Oh, yeah?' He glanced at me, then looked up the coastline the other way.

I was undeterred. 'And that diving header in the replay against Leeds . . . when you won the cup . . . was just the greatest goal . . . and I stayed up and watched it . . . and like I said, I love Chelsea and all of it . . . and you, and the winning the cup . . . and your face on my pillow . . . and I'm here and you're here . . . and I like football . . . and you like footb . . .'

I ran out of steam. I looked back at the beach. My dad was standing taking a photo of us. I felt I ought to go. 'OK. Bye then,' I said.

He wiped seawater out of his chest hair. 'See ya.'

I swam back to the shore. I was disheartened, as though I had made a fool of myself. I didn't understand how an adult could be so offhand when I was trying so hard and telling him how much I liked him. I told my dad what had happened. He couldn't stop laughing. He thought it was all just hilarious and said Osgood was 'a clown', and later that evening, whenever I asked for something at the dinner table in the restaurant, he just winked at me and said in a mock affectless tone, 'Oh, yeah?'

As on most nights, we then walked back to the chalet in the dark and my dad smoked a cigarette on the verandah on his own, looking out into the shadows over the wooden balustrade before sloping back to the hotel bar without a word. 'Your father has always needed stimulating company,' my mum offered in explanation. And then I would walk out with her between the chalets into the pine forest listening to the cicadas, feeling the dry needles crunching under my flip-flops, the scent rising under the spindly canopy, and out towards the deep indigo sky studded with stars, talking quietly, collecting little pine cones. One night we heard an owl, and although we crept right beneath the tree in which it sat, and heard it clear and loud, and strained our eyes, we couldn't see it.

18

I t was February 2003 and a blast of unexpected fresh air cut across the hall of the flat.

'I managed to open a couple of windows,' said my mum, greeting me, 'but I can't shut them, and now there is a gale force wind threatening to blow us back to Oxford.'

I laughed and went into the sitting room and slid the window shut. A newspaper was strewn across the floor. I gathered it up and placed it back on the sofa. 'You've made it nice for Dad's return,' I said, walking back into the hall.

'He'll probably go straight to bed,' she said mordantly. 'But I shall stay accommodating if it kills me.'

I followed her into her little study. 'Been tidying in here too, I see.'

'Yes, if you *must* know.'

A box of papers was open on the desk.

'I'm going to make a small coffee. Do you want one?' she said.

'Not for me, thanks.'

'Please yourself.' She went out to the kitchen.

I sat at the desk. It was the same box containing her Stratford souvenirs that I'd looked through on the day they moved in. To the side was a large certificate. The thick paper crackled as I opened it. *Royal Academy of Dramatic Art, London. This Diploma is awarded to Romany Evens as a special recognition of talent. April, 1947.* Next to it were two theatre programmes I hadn't noticed before. I flicked one open. *The West of England Theatre Company.* Dear Brutus *by J. M. Barrie. December 1947. In the part of Lady Caroline Laney – Romany Evens.* I smiled. The whole cast had signed the programme. The tour was a tightly routed journey through Exmouth, Yeovil, Chard, Bridport and Sidmouth, and several more towns of the South-West.

She came back in with the coffee.

'You must have done this between RADA and Stratford,' I said, holding up the programme.

'What?' she said waspishly, anticipating provocation. She peered at me. 'You know I can't *see* it from here.'

'J. M. Barrie. *Dear Brutus.* West of England Theatre Company.'

'Oh, that.' She lightened. 'Probably all nonsense.'

'Don't be silly. It's great. Sounds like fun. How long were you in rep before Stratford?'

'A couple of years, I think.' She huffed. 'You must have heard all this. Why are you asking again?' she said suspiciously.

'I *like* hearing about it. You must have gone to RADA right after the war, yes?'

She put her coffee down. 'Yes, I would have gone sooner but Mother wouldn't let me. She thought a doodlebug would fall on my head if I went up to London during the war.'

I remembered how – after the information was declassified – she'd told me about her time in the Women's Royal Naval Service and her work on the fringes of Ultra signal intelligence, playing a small part in the decryption of the German ciphers and the breaking of the Enigma codes. She'd finished her education at Cheltenham Ladies' College and joined in 1943. She was posted initially to the empty Gayhurst Manor, a huge Elizabethan house in acres of parkland less than ten miles from the main centre of operations at Bletchley Park. A hundred and fifty Wrens were stationed there. Some were out in the woods, some in the house itself. Bunks were thrown up in the grand ballroom. New arrivals often had to construct their own beds out of reclaimed bed-frames. Doors were left unlocked to rooms stacked with priceless antique furniture, paintings and china.

The round-the-clock working conditions in the Nissen huts out in the woods were hot, noisy and smelly, the air rank with the stench of oil from the decoding machines. The shift work was stressful and tedious. At night, exhausted, they'd walk back through the looming darkness to the house, under the canopy of trees, picking their way between the tiny headstones of an overgrown dog cemetery by moonlight. Towards the end of winter, the woods were filled with a carpet of snowdrops. There was a chapel in the grounds, and a beautiful dovecote and turreted stables, and out in the parkland war planes were draped in camouflage waiting to be pressed into service. During the late-autumn weeks, as the light drew in, the walk to the huts was accompanied by the unsettling throaty sound of roaring stags and the clash of antlers.

Later she moved to the base at Eastcote, where she made the most of her time off and proximity to London by helping to organise entertainments, putting on dances and concerts and amateur dramatics, keeping everyone's spirits up, and dreaming of the day she could get away and do it for real.

For years, before she was allowed to talk about it, she could only hint at her involvement. 'What did you do in the war?' I'd ask both my parents when I was young. 'I helped sink the *Bismarck*, darling', was all she would say, to which my dad once responded, in front of the whole family, 'Yes, she *sat* on it!' It became a family joke for years until its underlying heartless-ness made me stop laughing when I was older. 'And what about you, Dad?' I'd ask. 'I flew around in Tiger Moths and played the piano,' was always the nonchalant reply.

'So you had to wait before you could enrol at RADA?' I said, as she picked up her coffee again.

'When the war ended I went straight there. I was still in uniform.'

'Did your mother know?'

'Yes. She knew she couldn't stop me. Not that she would have done. And Dad had just died. It was all I ever wanted to do,' she said, shuffling some papers together.

Her first experience of acting came in 1938 when she was fourteen. Her father, the Reverend G. Bramwell Evens – while still a Methodist minister – had become a radio star among children in the north of England, since accepting an invitation from the BBC in 1932 to write and deliver a couple of five-minute stories drawn from his abiding passion for wildlife and the countryside. They went out on *Children's Hour*, broadcast from Manchester. His anecdotes and soothing unflustered style proved popular and soon led to a regular weekly half-hour programme called *Out with Romany* that followed him ('Romany') on a nature ramble accompanied by two children and a dog. The programmes gave the illusion of a country walk complete with Romany's impromptu descriptions of plants and animals and their habits, but were all scripted with sound effects and made entirely in the studio, much to most of the listening public's surprise when the techniques were exposed some years later; even the two children – Muriel and Doris – were actually two grown-up actresses putting on children's voices. My mum's mother, Eunice, helped with the script editing, and my mum herself was written into a few episodes as a young girl, and was even give a little time off school to perform.

Her father was a gifted communicator, bringing nature to life through people's wireless sets, with a style of programme that would blossom at the BBC under later broadcasters such as David Bellamy and Sir David Attenborough. He refused to rehearse the scripts in order to give them a natural informality, and at the programme's height, during the war, it provided the perfect escape from the blackouts and the bombs, and an estimated thirteen million listeners – adults and children alike – tuned in to its prime time slot half an hour before the six o'clock news.

My mum once told me she had dreamed of being an actress since before her radio debut, but admitted the moment the red light first went on was 'utterly thrilling'. Yet I have often also wondered how she felt to have her father pinch her name when she was only nine years old, and then become a star with it. He had previously written articles for newspapers and magazines under the pen-name 'The Tramp', and it is said the idea to change it came to him on the spur of the moment, when put on the spot moments before he first went on air. Admittedly she had always been known as a child by her middle name, June, and loved the extra attention she got at school when her father became famous with her *first* given name, but I doubt it was ever fully explained, and I wonder if she sometimes felt as though a piece of her had been taken away.

It was perhaps symptomatic of her father's self-absorption. A gifted public communicator maybe – he also went on to write a string of children's books based on the radio programmes – but he was reportedly hopeless domestically, and happiest alone in the field: traits that are dutifully, and perhaps too easily, forgiven in his wife Eunice's 1946 memoir, published shortly after his death, *Through the Years with Romany*.

Reflecting on their childhood in a letter to my mum in the seventies her older brother Glyn – then in his sixties – described their father as 'fundamentally a nice, honest, Wordsworthian sort of man, who should never have had children'. Sent away to boarding school in London as a child, Glyn describes how he only ever remembered his parents visiting him once in six years; they were too parsimonious and wrapped up in their own world of radio fame, he thought. Even at half-term his father refused to pay his train fare back home to the South Pennines. He had to spend long lonely days, 'bitterly unhappy', wandering the playground and playing fields of an empty school, fed by the caretaker or a resident housemaster, too proud and hurt to complain, while all his friends went home to their families. Eleven years older than my mum, he was too old to be very close to her, a restless teenage brother, who teased and goaded his little sister in frustration. Of their childhood caravanning holidays he remembered mainly 'intolerable boredom, punctuated only by visits to the Spa Ballroom in Whitby', and endless futile hours spent throwing darts against the stable door. In a car journey to Whitby as a boy he claims to have spoken out, calling their father a 'petty domestic tyrant', and was ordered out of the car and left in the road while his mother burst into tears but didn't have the courage to call him back. 'You were lucky to come second,' he wrote to my mum, 'as I had won all your battles for you.'

Among my mum's cuttings and souvenirs is a comprehensive archive of her father's career – pages of newspaper articles and photocopies, obituaries and fan letters, all carefully filed and labelled. In 1996 she was asked to help relaunch the Romany Society, a small organisation dedicated to preserving his name and works, that had been dormant for thirty years. Celebrity fans were unearthed who had been captivated by the original *Out with Romany* programmes as a child (including Sir David Attenborough). Terry Waite – at the time famous for his years as a hostage in Lebanon – became their patron. Money was raised to recondition her father's vardo that until its recent move to the Bradford Industrial Museum had stood in a small memorial park in Wilmslow, the town where he died suddenly from a heart condition in 1943 at the age of fifty-nine. His death caused widespread sorrow among many schoolchildren in the north. Local papers carried the news on their front pages and some schools even had to close for a day of mourning.

My mum must have been only nineteen when he died – it was during wartime and she would have been away from home, hearing the news unexpectedly – and I can't help thinking in all of her industrious archiving is still the little girl with the shared name, trailing silently behind her father in the fields, voiceless, uncertain of his approval, still seeking his approbation.

19

'No reoffending, Tommy. We don't want to see you back in here any time soon,' said the carer, as he helped my dad out of the lift and into the lobby. 'You've done your time. Going straight now, aren't we?'

My dad was smiling.

There can't be many people they check in, then actually get the opportunity to check out again, I thought. We made our goodbyes and the glass doors opened and I helped him out to the car.

'Not a bad bunch,' he said, as I reached over him to clip in his seat belt. 'I've met worse.'

I was half relieved, half anxious to be taking him back to the flat but I tried not to show it. 'You're still alive, at least.'

'*Just.*'

'You'll get visits from the link worker once you're back,' I said, injecting a serious tone. 'Help you get yourself sorted. Mum's looking forward to seeing you.'

'Don't know what we'd do without you, Ben,' he said. He had on his sincere face.

I shut his door and went to put his wheelchair in the boot. Parked in front was a white van with the side door slid open. A man in white dungarees was wiping a paintbrush on a rag, the inside of the van a jumble of pots and buckets and mastic guns.

As we set off back to the flat, my dad said, 'Very satisfying, decorating.'

I pictured him in his old whites. 'You always liked it, didn't you?'

'A sense of achievement.'

We slowed behind a grid of traffic.

It was in the early seventies that he sidestepped all of us by announcing he was quitting music for good to become a painter-decorator. He'd always been handy with a brush around the flat, and had taught his skills to my half-brothers when they were looking for work to supplement their university grants. He'd even decorated for a neighbour in the road. But it was still a surprise when he said he'd arranged to take up 'an apprenticeship' (his words) at the small local decorating firm based in East Sheen where he used to shop for supplies. When the day came, he'd bought himself a white boiler suit and a new set of brushes, and when he turned up to work the firm greeted him affectionately as 'Young Tommy' even though he was nearly fifty.

After buffing up his expertise, he set up on his own, and began shopping for paint at a little decorator's shop in Barnes called Gaytrends and I heard him use phrases I'd never heard before like 'feathering', 'laying off' and 'cutting in'. It coincided with his passport renewal and he joked he might change his listed occupation on the form from *Musician* to *Musician and painter*. Most of all, I became aware of how much more settled he and my mum were for a while. My mum started cooking again in the evenings; they'd watch a little television, have one drink, not several, and both be in bed by 10.30. I'd even see him for breakfast in the mornings before school, as he'd be up at 7.15 and out of the house by 8.30. It was a huge change for him: for most of his working life he'd played until the small hours and not got up until lunchtime, but he seemed content to be earning an honest wage for an honest day's work, earning some 'walking-around-money' while my mum forged on as a showbiz feature writer earning the 'paying-the-bills-money'.

If my mum was out working late, he knocked off early to be at home when I got in from school. He used to buy my favourite loaf of bread – a poppy-seeded bloomer – and some freshly sliced garlic sausage from the high street on his way back. I'd burst into the flat and shout 'Yes!' if I spied them on the counter – much to his quiet delight – and would eagerly make myself a sandwich, full of stories from school, while he stood smiling at the kitchen window with a cup of tea, his face freckled with paint.

The summer I was twelve he was decorating in a flat above a local shop and I was allowed to meet him on a sunny lunchtime during school half-term. We walked from his workplace to Macarthur's – my favourite hamburger restaurant at the time – for a special treat for 'no reason in particular'. The doors were folded back and we sat in the window in warm sunshine, sharing crinkle-cut chips and sweetcorn sauce and a slice of blackcurrant cheesecake, until it was time for him to go back to work, and he seemed relaxed and there was light in his green eyes, and I was aware that I was pleased that he had somewhere to go where he was needed. I thought it made him happier.

In the evenings my mum came home from work. Sometimes she brought me an autograph or – if I was in luck – an extravagant signed publicity photograph from her latest assignment. I wasn't choosy; everyone seemed exotic and cosmopolitan. My prized collection included Noel Edmonds (then the BBC Radio 1 *Breakfast Show* DJ), Wings (*To Ben, love from Linda and hubby, Paul McCartney*) and James Galway (*To Ben, from The Man With The Golden Flute*). My dad's work benefited from my mum's contacts too. Interviewing a young rising actor in their new unfurnished flat, or a celebrity in their recently acquired period house, usually threw up a moment for her to drop in a neatly placed recommendation, and within a fortnight my dad was round with his brushes. For several years afterwards, evenings at home in front of the TV were punctuated with my mum saying things like, 'Oh, look, Tom, Honor Blackman: you made a nice job of her downstairs loo.'

At weekends, my dad's whites were folded up neatly in the hall on top of a pair of paint-flecked moccasins ready for the following week. When he was working and sober he was very approachable, even first thing in the morning. I loved it if he was in a good mood. As a boy I remember standing in the doorway after breakfast on Saturdays and listening to the slow, steady buzz of the electric razor as he shaved while humming jazz phrases to himself in the bathroom mirror. He fastidiously towelled himself down after his shower – in between the toes, the crack of the arse, the inside of the foreskin ('Always dry the old fella well') – and then liberally dusted his bollocks and armpits with a cloud of medicated talc, until the bathmats looked as if they had been dusted with icing sugar. He never cared if I was there; he carried on happily, making jokes, passing comments. Dropping his small stainless-steel plate of false front teeth into a glass of effervescing Steradent he used to catch my eye in the mirror and wink, before turning round and saluting with a stupid toothless grin, and exclaiming something like, 'Aha, Jim-lad! I'll make 'e walk the plank, that I will!' He then vigorously brushed his teeth and and his gums and his tongue, and rounded it all off with a furious gargling of mouthwash. It was all done for laughs. With a flourish he then popped his teeth back in, hung up the towel, coughed, and – if the coast was clear – casually strolled across the flat stark naked ('Oh, Tom!' from my mum) to get dressed.

It was jockey briefs first, and vest tucked in, which struck me as a bit unmanly, and then some exercises that passed for keeping fit. He touched his toes (or almost) ten times, rotated his upper body at the waist with his hands on his hips, then tucked his hands under his chin with his elbows raised out sideways and flung his arms open once or twice with a groan, before finishing with five (sometimes three) press-ups. It was all a bit desultory, and a leftover, I suspected, from the RAF.

As for his clothes, the fashions changed over the years, but the peacock's instinct didn't. I was too young to remember much about his sharp hand-made Savile Row suits from the early sixties when he was a bandleader, although I used to finger them where they hung at the far left of his built-in bedroom wardrobe for years afterwards, admiring the buttons, the slanted ticket pockets, the racy silk linings; some of them were still in polythene from the dry-cleaner's, but the fronts would be slashed to 'let them air'.

The first thing I can visualise him in is relaxed but expensive open-neck cotton shirts in pale purple or dusty pink – we're talking late sixties – with the sleeves immaculately turned up to the forearm. These gave way to fishermen's smocks and tunic shirts in the mid-seventies, and then – in the early eighties – he went back to collared shirts in understated bird's-eye checks, worn with cravats (purple chiffon, gold cotton) and a silver woggle, straightened with a dainty dapper precision, and topped off with a tan suede – or perhaps a bottle-green-leather – bomber jacket.

He was not a tall man. Five foot six. Shirt-sleeves needed metal elasticated armbands worn at the biceps. After the suit era, his trousers became neutral low-rise slacks worn below his little paunch with a Spanish leather belt. His feet were small and beautifully pedicured, not professionally, but by himself with clippers and files. Fresh socks went on with a comic grunt – a short 'Ooh' and a stifled 'Ahh' – his calves and hamstrings stretching under the effort, until finally he'd cry, 'Success!' and standing up, smile and proclaim, 'Ta-da!' with a look of satisfaction and relief. If it was chilly perhaps he'd reach for one of his V-neck lambswool sweaters; they were invariably dry-cleaned at the first sign of an oil spot or ash mark. Everything was well laundered, well ironed. In fact, whenever I think of him – from the tailored suits and thin knitted ties of my earliest childhood memories to the open-neck shirts and woggles of his fifties – it was always Era-Appropriate Jazz Gear.

On the middle shelf in the wardrobe he kept white handkerchiefs and a cream-leather box of cufflinks emblazoned with a vintage Bugatti. It was embossed with his name and the title of one of the Brian Rix productions for which he'd written music: *T.M. Watt*, Simple Spymen *1960*. His wore a Longines watch – gold trim, delicate hands, champagne face, black-leather or chocolate-brown-metal stretch strap – and at night he left it on a sea-blue oval glass dish with some loose change from his pockets. At the back of the shelf were the duty-free packs of cigarettes; over the years Gold Flake gave way to Three Castles (green pack), then Camel. On the top and bottom shelves were piles of his jazz orchestra arrangements, some loose, some stacked freely in ring-binders.

After he had picked his outfit for the day and was fully dressed, he applied a streak of concealer to the drinker's veins on his nose, squirted a blast of Goldspot bad-breath spray on to his tongue, added a splash of cologne to his neck and cheeks (Acqua di Selva in the sixties, Aramis in the seventies), and he was ready for the day. Sauntering to wherever my mum was in the flat, he'd stand in the doorway, and wait for her to look up and deliver an approving comment – 'Lovely, darling' or maybe 'Look at your father! What a handsome man and smelling all fragrant' – and if he swaggered slightly, he also seemed to earnestly covet her assent; the one was always accompanied by the other; it was masculine yet somehow needful.

I sometimes wonder what he was thinking in those overcast years following the failure at the Dorchester, as he came to terms with the end of the career he wanted, and made the decision about what to replace it with. If anyone were to have guessed what was in his mind, I am not sure they would have come up with painter-decorator. On reflection, however, he was clearly too proud to take the obvious route other contemporaries took: moving into pop orchestration, or into television and becoming a light-entertainment musical director.

In spite of one memorable season in Scarborough in 1969 directing the pit orchestra for the comedian Tommy Cooper ('the funniest three months of my life') he often derided the music he would have been expected to work with. He used to scoff at Ronnie Hazlehurst – the king of BBC light-entertainment musical direction at the time – whenever he came on TV, especially when he did that humble awkward turn and bowed to the camera, dainty white baton in hand, headphones on. It was a symbolic image in my dad's mind – an image of acquiescing, of submission. The night Hazlehurst popped up unexpectedly on our TV during the Eurovision Song Contest of 1977 as musical director for the singers Lynsey de Paul and Mike Moran, wearing a bowler hat, holding a morning newspaper and shamelessly conducting the orchestra with a rolled-up umbrella, I thought my dad would explode with ridicule and contempt.

How did he become such a well-groomed and fastidious yet aggressively principled man? It certainly lost him as much work as it earned him. In November 1960 – following his hot streak with Parlophone – the BBC's Head of Programme Contracts wrote to him to discuss the possibility of his engagement as Conductor of the BBC Northern Dance Orchestra to replace the outgoing and exceptionally successful Alyn Ainsworth. The band broadcast from Manchester and had gained a reputation across Europe for being one of the best ensembles on radio. It was an auspicious opportunity, and although restrictions were placed on how much work he could do elsewhere – something that had caused several other prospective conductors to turn the job down – within a week he had accepted the appointment. He decamped to Manchester, only to find himself almost immediately at loggerheads with the producers. 'I wanted the NDO to sound as good as Basie,' he once told me curtly. 'They didn't.'

Refusing to compromise, he was eased out of the job at the end of the six-month trial period by a management who were intent on moving with the times as *they* saw it, not as *he* saw it. He was replaced by the amenable flautist Bernard Herrmann, who was to lead the band in newly created TV vehicles that indicated quite clearly the commercial direction in which my dad had been expected to go. The titles speak for themselves: *Here We Go with the NDO!* and *Pop North*.

I think it would be easy to romanticise his stance as that of a man who would not compromise, who stood by his jazz principles and his own sense of integrity, but I have to ask myself how much of it was just sheer bloody-mindedness. As his old friend and partner Brian Rix said when we met recently, 'Back then your father was principled, yes, but sometimes he was just an obstreperous Glaswegian, who liked getting his own way. And the whisky didn't help.'

Whether he liked it or not, I think my dad's own father's moral rigour left an indelible mark on him. While he may have violently rejected his father's religious and Masonic convictions, he was affected by his socialist beliefs and denunciatory judgements on an increasingly commercialised world, and used them just as vigorously and parochially in his own life and against his own targets.

Of course there were high points – the three years at Quaglino's which brought the final big breakthrough at the BBC, the recordings for George Martin at Parlophone, and the Ivor Novello Award he went on to win in 1957 for his own composition 'Overdrive' – but he battled with commercial expectations. He downplayed the Parlophone albums, saying the choice of tracks and style of approach were compromised and mediated by the record company, so perhaps it was unsurprising that the moment he considered the pinnacle of his jazz life was the moment he was allowed to do exactly as he liked.

It came about in unexpected circumstances.

In September 1960 at the Trades Union Congress at Douglas on the Isle of Man, a resolution – number forty-two on the day's agenda – was passed that said trade unions should play a bigger and more active role in the promotion and encouragement of the arts. A number of writers and theatre directors on the political left responded positively and the upshot was the formation of Centre 42 in 1961 under the direction of playwright Arnold Wesker. A grant of ten thousand pounds was provided by the Gulbenkian Foundation. The Trades Council of Wellingborough was the first to embrace the initiative, and later that year, with the help of Centre 42, staged an arts festival aimed at finding a popular audience and a boost to its membership. Five more councils followed suit (Nottingham, Birmingham, Leicester, Bristol, and Hayes & Southall) and a travelling festival programme was planned based on the initial Wellingborough success; it included a production of Stravinsky's *The Soldier's Tale*, a new work by Wesker himself, music by the English composer Wilfred Josephs, a National Youth Theatre production of *Hamlet*, a new play by Bernard Kops, and many other fringe events including folk song concerts, poetry and jazz, art installations and readings in factory canteens. Every night would then climax with a festival dance, where the music was provided for the delegates and attendees by a crack big band – the Forty-Two Jazz Band. Its leader and director was my dad.

With no commercial constraints he put together the finest British jazz big band he could think of. In a review of their first Wellingborough performance, the jazz critic Benny Green said in *Scene* magazine: 'It may well turn out to be the most outstanding big band this country has ever possessed.' A month later, he wrote in the *Daily Telegraph*: 'Rhythmically the orchestra, unimpeded by complexity, has an impressive impact, sweeping dancers into action and pleasing the jazz-lover with an ensemble sound so rare in this country today as to have the appeal of nostalgia.' On first reading it seems like a compliment, but on second it seems to damn with faint praise; it would certainly suggest that in the band's approach were also the seeds of its own demise. To make things worse, Green also noted: 'There is nothing experimental about Watt's writing.' At the music's heart, he pointed out, was a 'harmonic conservatism'.

It was impossible to get away from the fact that not only was the jazz big band being barged into the past by rock 'n' roll but many commentators thought if it were to survive it would have to adapt and move in a new, more musically adventurous and slimmed-down direction. Some critics, it's fair to say, praised the Forty-Two Jazz Band's hard-swinging exuberant directness. Others sympathised with the low turnouts for some of the events, pointing to odd venue choices and snobbery among British audiences, who had always told themselves 'American jazz is better'. Yet in spite of my dad's best intentions, it all just seemed – in one way or another – too little too late. The band stayed together for six months before the money and the impetus ran out. After a concert for the National Union of Tailors and Garment Workers at Shoreditch Town Hall, they ended with a final string of appearances at the TUC headquarters in Great Russell Street in March 1963.

At the outset, my dad had said to Benny Green after the debut Wellingborough show: 'I feel sure that if we could get this band on record and on radio, people MUST like it. Maybe this is the time to start a big band revival.' In the end, in spite of the shifting sands, four recordings *did* actually get made; Norrie Paramor from Columbia Records saw the band at the closing TUC event and signed two singles. The four tracks that made up the four sides were always what my dad would direct me to when I asked about his music. 'That was what I *meant*,' he once said to me. Listening to them now, they are muscular, uninhibited and joyful – dynamic, smart, swinging renditions of four classics: 'St. Louis Blues', 'Tuxedo Junction', Woody Herman's 'Woodchopper's Ball' and Duke Ellington's 'C-Jam Blues'. The playing on all of them is outstanding. The recordings remain thrilling examples of a sound that was destined to come to nothing.

A socialist all his life, my dad had stood up and announced at the final Centre 42 event, 'We dedicate this tune to the TUC and all it stands for: "Time And Three-Quarters".' Perhaps I shouldn't be surprised that when he finally ran out of road in the early seventies as a musician, he took the noblest, least reproachable route he could think of, and that by becoming a painter-decorator he became something of which the TUC, and his own father, would also have been proud: a 'working man'.

20

'Oh, for *crying out loud*, look away!'

It was the summer of 1974 and I was sitting on a beach towel, aged eleven, looking out across the ink-spill of emerald and malachite greens and cobalt blues in the wide waters of the bay. Two small fishing boats were anchored off the shore, their paintwork blistered and blanched, yellow nets piled up like seaweed, the wooden rudders lolling in the shallows. Under the parasol, I could still feel the sun through the stretched cotton panels. The sand was so hot a man was sprinting across it to the water's edge.

The voice was my dad's. I swung round just in time to see him turn back from looking over his shoulder and resume reading his book. His tanned front was glistening with sweat. I looked up in the direction of where he had been looking. The village of Lindos rose up: whitewashed houses jumbled on the parched mountainside; the crenellated battlements of the acropolis above silhouetted against the hot sky.

'What is it?' I said, narrowing my eyes in the brilliant noon-day light.

'Who do you *think*?' he snorted without looking up. He cracked the spine on his book. I still wasn't sure why he was reading something called *Nunaga: Ten Years Among the Eskimos* on a sweltering summer holiday on a Greek island. Maybe it was deliberate.

I shaded my eyes with my hands and peered again. A rough track was cut into the hillside down to the beach from the village. Halfway along it, and heading our way, was a man leading a small donkey with a load on its back. My eyes were still refocusing from looking out at the glimmering sea, so I squinted and could see the load was a person. Little puffs of dust rose from the track. I recognised the shape on the back of the donkey immediately; it was my mum. Beyond her, further up the track, a couple were ambling down ordinarily with rolled-up bamboo mats under their arms. We had been on holiday for a week and although I'd seen donkeys taking people up to the acropolis I had never seen anyone on the beach path on a donkey until now.

When they were directly above the beach, not far over our heads, my mum cried out fulsomely, '*Hallooo* down there! *Kalimerrrra!*'

'Jesus,' said my dad under his breath, still fixed on his book.

A few people on the beach turned to look. I could see someone say something to the person next to them, cupping their hand to hide their mouth, then smirking.

The donkey slowed. My mum was sitting side-saddle in a startling scoop-neck orange smock with puff sleeves; the colour screamed against the weathered, matt terrain. A dark blue pleated straw hat was tied down and secured under her chin with a black silk spotted scarf, so that the sides of the hat were pressed unflatteringly against her cheeks. All I could see of her face were big sunglasses and a grin. Her legs were covered in an ankle-length brown cotton skirt, her feet sported pop socks and sandals, and over her shoulder was a bulging lilac floral beach bag.

My dad snatched a look over his shoulder and turned back. 'What a state,' he muttered.

I had never seen him like this before. He seemed ashamed.

'Darling, *woo hoo*,' she cried from the path. 'Have you got a few *drachma* for the man? I've stupidly brought no *money*. I've paid for the ride, just not enough for a *tip*.'

I saw my dad close his eyelids slowly and open them again. His face was like thunder. He levered himself out of his deck-chair, reached underneath, fumbled in the front pocket of his shirt, took out his wallet and made his way up the beach. I watched as the donkey man helped my mum down and she let out a shrill laugh that cut through the torpid heat. It made several people look up again. I watched my dad with fascination. I felt I was seeing something new. It was as though a little cold sustained undercurrent of dislike was being allowed to rise to the surface in front of me.

In retrospect – over the weeks and months that followed – everything about that moment seemed to have triggered an attempt by my dad to start a new alliance between the two of us. I became aware of his disrespectful jokey remarks about my mum on a more regular basis – her class, her background, her friends, her appearance – in exchanges during which I was often encouraged to laugh and be complicit. Perhaps such enmity had been in there longer than I understood – and I was certainly too young to fully understand it – but whatever caused it, I began to notice it manifesting itself in streaks of jealousy and distaste that were negative and subversive.

In contrast, the family was encouraged to think that my dad had adapted successfully to his new life as a decorator and house-husband, that he was content in his middle age, and much of the time, it's fair to say, he kept his own counsel, and cut a laid-back and imperturbable figure. If he did get drunk and confrontational it was 'just Tom', and I was not old enough to ask why. Yet, with hindsight, it is clear that some things still nettled him greatly, and if he was ever intimidated by my mum's ongoing buoyant career and idiosyncratic tastes, he also struggled to reconcile the continued successes and choices of his old partner, Brian Rix.

In 1977, Brian was the subject of the popular biographical TV documentary *This Is Your Life* with presenter Eamonn Andrews. It was one of the biggest shows on television at the time, conferring star status on its special guests. Millions watched. My dad was secretly invited to appear as one of Brian's oldest friends. It can't have been easy for him, especially as it was the *second* time Brian had been picked to appear.

My dad dealt with it the only way he knew how. With the cameras rolling, Andrews turned to the famous onstage sliding doors with the words, 'Your old friend, Tommy Watt.' The doors slid back and my dad stumbled out drunk into the TV lights. His prearranged anecdote came out as a slurred jumble of incomprehensible nonsense before Andrews managed to usher him decorously to one of the guest seats at the side of the stage.

Fortunately for all concerned, the show – while presented in front of a live theatre audience – was being prerecorded, and was not live on TV. At the edit, my dad's entire performance was unsalvageable. When the programme was finally broadcast, he was seen coming through the doors, but that was it – they cut to the next guest. The rest was left on the cutting-room floor.

They were once so close, he and Brian. Brian had been made my godfather. But after the show was screened he barely spoke to my dad again.

21

n 1976, my mother's mother, Eunice, died. She had lived on in Wilmslow for several years following her husband's death in 1943, before selling up most of her possessions and moving down to London in the early fifties to be near her daughter and grandchildren. By the time I was aware of her, it was the late sixties and she was already over eighty and living in the flat downstairs. I never knew her as Eunice; none of the children ever did, as none of them could pronounce it. Instead she had become 'Nunu'.

I used to let myself in from school and even on the brightest days the entrance to her flat was darkened. She left her door on the latch. I was half afraid to go in, but the ground-floor front room was her bedroom, and she left me out a square of milk chocolate with a Rowntree's Fruit Pastille perched on top on the corner of her chest of drawers just behind the door. The room smelled of mothballs. Her wide single bed in the corner was covered in a lime-green eider-down and the sturdy elm legs at the end were raised up on silver biscuit tins, which, together with the magnet she left on the bottom sheet near her feet, supposedly 'helped her rheumatism' (whatever that was). There was a photograph of an old man on the mantelpiece and a barley-twist bedside table. The tumbler of water and the plastic protector around her hardback library book made me think of illness and spilling things, and the empty black wooden dressing table in the window made me think of death.

I knew the sweets were part of an unspoken bargain: if I took them I was expected to say hello, but often I didn't want to go and find her, and have to look at her baggy stockings or her dry hands; for one thing, they made me think of discarded snakeskin. So in the end I usually took the sweets, ran out quickly and then felt guilty for a bit. But the guilt passed – quite rapidly in fact – so much so, that by the age of twelve I was rummaging around in her knicker drawer among the elastic supports to find the tin where she kept the chocolate and the Pastilles to help myself to a bit more.

It was not just me. Even when they were older my half-brothers slipped in to ponce cigarettes and ten-shilling notes from her purse under the guise of a quick hello. And in general, everyone popped in and out unannounced to collect tools or light bulbs or ripening apples from the shared cupboards in her hallway. In the evenings her flat door was open to a steady stream of emergency darning, school shoes that needed polishing, or a child who needed supervising for an hour. Mostly me. I was forever urged to 'go and see how Nunu is'.

She lived most of the time in the kitchen at the back overlooking the garden, although she had turned it into more of a sitting room. It was sparsely furnished. She smoked forty Player's Navy Cut cigarettes a day and ate at a green baize card table. There was an armchair, a dinner wagon, a small oak desk with green tomatoes in the bottom drawer and stamps in the top, an electric fire and a huge black-and-white television set in the corner.

Off the room was a pantry, no bigger than a broom cupboard, fitted out with a small gas stove, a cream flat-fronted Formica dresser and a cold shelf against the exterior wall faced with fly-mesh where she kept Cheddar cheese. She had no fridge; she kept haddock and milk in our fridge upstairs – bread too sometimes. I knew if anything was hers because she put an elastic band around it.

A shared house was never going to be easy, but from the outset Eunice was keen to be involved in life upstairs. She'd slip through the flat door like a ghost – perhaps for the fourth or fifth time that day – and the first anyone heard of her was the slow scuff of slipper on carpet, and the sound of her nails tapping on the hollow kitchen door. It was not so much a knock, as the sound of my mum's conscience arriving. Not unreasonably Eunice felt if the children were allowed to play downstairs any time it suited my parents, and a little house-keeping and mending was expected of her, then she had just as much right to come up, but discretion and timing were never her strong points. 'Your husband out at the pub again, dear?' would be a typical provocative opener for my mum, who knew only too well that the opportunity to come upstairs had been presented by the first sound of the key in the ignition from the car-port. It might be followed by a shuffle to the stove and a comment such as, 'Why do you always have to have *two* vegetables?'

As my mum said, in a funny and honest portrait she drew of her in *Woman* magazine following her death at the age of eighty-seven:

She was courageous, stoic, independent, and puritanical as only a Methodist minister's widow could be. She was also self-opinionated, dogmatic, tactless and devoid of charm.

She had no small talk, grew increasingly deaf and said what she thought at all times.

Many of Eunice's views and criticisms were contained in long, articulate, often outraged, letters and notes addressed to my mum, left dauntingly on the hall table in her spidery longhand. My mum kept the best and worst of them bundled together in a box for a kind of masochistic posterity. Clearly Eunice didn't see herself as nosy and meddlesome in the slightest. She felt she was used when it suited everyone, but criticised when it didn't.

A new baby (me) in the house sharpened her interest in family affairs and gave her an excuse to be seen. She was suspicious of the stream of Austrian and German home-helps and nannies that passed through our flat, all charged with marshalling an infant and four siblings under twelve. If my parents were out at work or the pub, she would appear at mealtimes or bedtime, ostensibly a familiar face with a familiar voice. She would then catalogue her inevitable consternation to my mum in writing later that day: cot blankets were too damp; portions were too large; competence was in question.

She found it hard to embrace my parents' new lifestyle. She was disgruntled by my dad's social life: the trips to the pub; the trail of musicians he brought home who stayed until three in the morning. It was so different to her previous son-in-law Ken's life of literary friends and dinner parties. She thought it set a bad example to the children, especially when my mum was involved too. 'Where's Mummy?' she is said to have asked me one Sunday when I was six. 'At the pub,' I am reported to have said cheerfully. She saw it all as a waste and a wilful diminishing of her daughter's intellect. Years of opening nights at the theatre with Ken were being replaced by mindless boozy nights at the local pub with my dad.

That's not to say Eunice didn't find fault with Ken. In spite of his intellect, she considered him cold and aloof and self-absorbed. Yet she reserved her strongest feelings for Tom. She soon saw him as fundamentally a poorly-educated layabout sponging off my mum, a man-child whose affection for his wife atoned for much, but not enough. She deplored his 'ungovernable temper' and couldn't forgive him for throwing a pair of garden shears across the lawn 'in front of SIMON'. When he traded in his car for a brand new model – not long after moving into the house they had all scraped the money together to buy – Eunice thought it 'extravagant' and vulgar, and bemoaned the unnecessary financial burden it placed on her daughter. When he dared suggest it was my mum's idea, it made him something far worse in her eyes – 'untruthful'. If she and Tom argued, she vigorously denounced his subsequent one-sided 'duplicitous' reporting of events back upstairs.

My dad was unnerved. Just when he thought he could settle down with my mum, he found himself confronted by a fearsome adversary, and what was worse, it was a throwback to what he had run away from in Glasgow: a harsh, moralising, judgemental voice, snobbish and unsentimental. He often simply didn't have the articulacy to battle back. 'Mind your own business!' he would shout at her in the garden, as she tried to intervene while he was hanging out nappies to dry. 'You're an old meddler! A wicked old woman!' If he stormed out or hid behind my mum's protection, Eunice called him 'cowardly'. In fact, in her view, everything Tom did was designed to weaken her position with her own daughter, and the consequence, as she coldly wrote to her, was 'undermining the little affection you have left for me'.

Forced to choose, my mum of course stood by my dad; she'd endured so much to secure him. Yet no one likes to be the pig in the middle. The upshot was a fifteen-year running battle in which Eunice was regularly banned from the flat. Of course she retaliated in kind: children were banned from hers. I remember being told to ring the bell before collecting a bicycle pump from the tool cupboard. 'Never forget', she wrote to my mum icily, 'that you alone are responsible for our living in the same house, that you told the [estate] agent you'd buy the house without even asking me or letting me see it. I was very happy in my cosy small house [in East Sheen] and hated the flat on sight.' It was typical of many of her comments: if it contained some truth, it also contained a good measure of psychological manipulation. She had been peppery and opinionated all her life, wherever she had lived.

In August 1970 I went on holiday with my mum and dad to Sussex, and Eunice was astonished to find herself locked out of the upstairs flat. I overheard my dad say in the car on the way down that he was fed up with her 'snooping around'. With my half-brothers and half-sister away too, Eunice wrote two letters to my mum at the cottage where we were staying – holiday or no holiday – itemising her indignation. She pointed out sniffily that the cat had been cruelly locked *in*, that her *sole* loaf of bread was unretrievable from the upstairs fridge, that she'd had to walk to the shops *before breakfast* to replace it, that the window cleaner had been forced to leave the upper glazing dirty, that the family carpets would have to remain un-vacuumed, and that the stain in the sitting room would have to remain untouched. Now it seems comical, a textbook version of guilt-inducement, half fact, half fiction. The stain was something neither of my parents could picture. The flat had only just been hoovered the day before they left. And the cat had been quickly released by Roly on a mercy mission – although he was told to carefully lock up again afterwards. But it was all symptomatic of Eunice's dogmatic staying power and compulsive reluctance to let anyone enjoy themselves. She ends the second letter in a melodramatic flourish that could have been written by my own mum at any stage in her later years. 'Even now,' she writes, 'as I've no stamp, I doubt if you'll get this. Love, Mother. P.S. The weather this weekend has been ghastly. Cold. And gales.'

'A born martyr,' my mum has scribbled on the envelope of one letter among the several she kept, and Eunice allowed little room for others' sympathy. Even approaching the end, she snuffed out any chance of a sentimental reconciliation. She wrote in her unsteady handwriting shortly before her death:

> I want the quietest, quickest, cheapest funeral possible. No mourners, no flowers, no cars. With recollections of the hundreds of funerals conducted by your father and the way the funeral directors took advantage of emotionally upset relatives to persuade them to have expensive coffins with *brass* handles, I want the *cheapest*. I recall being embarrassed by piles of wreaths lying outside the crematorium when your father was cremated so simply; these I discovered afterwards remained there from one funeral to another. And no urn. I want my ashes left at the crematorium.

Under my dad's influence, I grew up learning to mock and disparage her, and yet, with hindsight, it is of course impossible not to feel sorry for her, in spite of her sourness and pugnacity. It shouldn't be forgotten that her husband died suddenly at fifty-nine, taking with him not only their companionship but her small cherished role in the limelight too, and that she left Cheshire for London to live in a city where she had barely any friends. As she confessed to my mum in one letter: 'I often go up to your flat because I feel I shall scream if, having been deprived of the interests I used to have I can't talk to someone.' In another: 'There have been times when life seemed so empty and living on so pointless that I could have committed suicide. But suicide is a cowardly business and you may have to tolerate me for some time.' More manipulative melodrama maybe, but it makes for uneasy reading.

Fourteen years after her death, my mum must have reread them all and come to the same conclusion, as she has inserted a sheet with a few words:

> 1990: Looking at these distressing letters and notes I really don't know why I have kept them. They show the fearful stresses we all lived under at Woodlands Road. I feel terribly sorry for Mother . . . but what other course was open to me? Poor, poor Mother.

It would be wrong, however, not to remember Eunice's eccentricities in her old age too, and how they lent an absurdist edge to the cantankerous drama that was being played out – stories that made us all laugh, and carried her legend long into family folklore. As my mum wrote in her 1976 portrait of her after her death:

> Age did not deter her in the very least. I found her (at eighty) one morning balanced on top of a chair on a table painting her kitchen ceiling. The following year, when we came back from a holiday, she had just painted half her sitting-room walls bright green because she could not reach any higher.
>
> At eighty-four, she was still mowing the lawn regularly, burning mattresses in the two-foot incinerator, and wreaking her will on our garden. She transplanted bushes while

in full bloom, and woe betide any poor plant that failed to flower within its first six months of life. She just whipped it out. Our compost heap was a picture all year round, but you could usually count the blooms in the beds on one hand.

She repegged all my washing on the line each week 'so that it would dry better'. She aired brand new football boots, best jerseys and plastic gloves on top of her electric fire. She stowed away ashtrays and dinner plates 'because we did not need so many'.

She cut all my king-size bath towels in half 'because they are too big for normal people', sliced a third off a hand-knitted scarf belonging to my son 'because it was too long' and once sent a perfectly good suit of my husband's to the jumble 'because he never wore it'.

As a boy I have strong memories of the notes she left on the hall table. I passed them on my way to and from school, or in and out of the garden. The serious ones to my mum were in small brown sealed manila envelopes with *Private: June* written ominously on them. The rest were scribbled out on whatever came to hand – the inside of a fag packet, a torn-out page from the *Radio Times*. A few have been kept. Some were just shopping lists:

40 Players
40 Silk Cut
4 Wombles Milk Choc Bars
2 large Rowntree Fruit Pastilles
6 Fish fingers
½ Cheddar Cheese
2 qrtrs Typhoo

Others were simply designed to make everyone feel bad: *Roly and Toby, Could each of you deny yourself a night's pay at the pub to play badminton with Ben . . .* or: *I've taken my last codeine.* ('If only,' my dad is reported to have said.) Some were unintentionally comic. Preparing to make soup she warned those who might be using the garden: *I've hung my old bones on the line.* A favourite was the day she placed a handwritten note under the windscreen wiper of a builder's van parked across our drive: *Please don't block our entrance again. We have had to park down the road. You evidently don't know the rules of the road. Perhaps you are a beginner.* I came home from school to find the van gone and the note posted back through our letterbox. On the bottom, in pencil, was scrawled *Bollox.*

For me, she has also been immortalised in the song my dad wrote the evening after she thought she had lost her dentures in bed one night, only to find them forty-eight hours later inside her spare slippers under the bed. He jumped on to the piano stool, and to a perfectly wrought twelve-bar blues – that I can still recite – sang:

'Nunu has swallowed her teeth
Nunu has swallowed her teeth
Nunu has swallowed them, don't try and follow them
They have slipped right down beneath
Nunu has swallowed her pegs
They're probably down by her legs
Will she get rid of them, don't bet a quid on them
Better call up the police
Oh, poor old Nunu's lost her 'ampstead 'eath.'

22

The hot summer months of 2003 wrapped my mum and dad's flat in a somnolence that slowed the days down to a near standstill. Flies zigzagged between the rooms. I notched the fridge thermostat up a digit or two. The sports commentators on the television chugged away, filling the background to the afternoons with a soft and comforting burble of statistics and truisms, while the dazzling blue skies beyond the wraparound windows of their second-floor St John's Wood sitting room were marked only by occasional thin silvery plane trails, high up, like long deliberate key scratches along the side of an expensive shining car.

Care workers and link workers occasionally looked in but my dad was too proud or low-spirited to talk to them, retiring to his room at the first sound of them in the hall, leaving my mum to make small talk for ten minutes and then send them away. They were much more interested in the little visits from Luis, the porter, who would pop out to the corner shop for a half-bottle of emergency Scotch or brandy; they had had him in their pocket pretty quickly.

And then one day in September, not long after the heatwave, following a routine check-up at the local health centre, and less than twelve months since having her womb removed, my mum was told she had a lump in her breast. Immediate surgery was recommended, and this time the procedure was to take place on the NHS. My dad would have to go back to the care home.

I took her to St Mary's Hospital behind Paddington Station for a preparatory meeting. We went up in a black London taxi.

'This is nice, dear,' she said, as we passed through Baker Street.

'You *know* where we're going, Mum?' I said. Had she grasped how important this was?

'Yes, yes,' she said irritatedly. 'Message received.'

At the meeting a female doctor patiently went over the planned lumpectomy: right-hand side; small incision; less than two centimetres; take tissue from the lymph gland; check the left side at the same time; out of action for four to five days if lucky, possibly seven to ten; radiotherapy starts after two months; side effects include fatigue, sunburn. I kept glancing at my mum. She was nodding but her eyes were roving. She looked like a distracted child being lectured by a primary school teacher.

We left. She looked exhausted.

It wasn't long before I had the bed manager's direct line and the name of the ward. It was all going to happen.

She went into the hospital the night before the operation. She was quiet on the way, but then, as I was leaving, she was momentarily galvanised and asked if I could bring her in a couple of shawls, and post a letter she had left in the kitchen, and give Luis ten pounds she owed him.

It's often struck me that people who have endured something serious in hospital have a unique look about them. In contrast to outpatients – who see themselves in a permanent state of passing through, who perch and fidget and sigh, look at their watches, return to the front desk to check on the delays to their busy day, stop a nurse in the corridor, worry they might be catching something off the vinyl upholstery – the proper in-patient seems to have sensed their immobility and the seriousness of an unexpected procedure in one heavy blow, knocking out any idea that they might be somehow able to influence or effect change on their bad luck. And with it, they quickly become a part of the actual fabric of the hospital. A component part. Attached to it. A parked-up vehicle to be worked on. A service that is due. And so it was with my mum when I visited her after the operation.

She was on a big recovery ward up on the second floor. As I approached the bed, I knew something unforeseen had happened. It seemed her whole body had melted on to her bedclothes. She was propped up, her ashen hair streaked across the pale pillow behind her, but the muscle-tone seemed absent in her arms, her shoulders forming one long continu-ous contour on a relief map of creased sheets and crumpled blanket. Her face was gaunt and waxy, but for the gentle woozy softness to her pearly blue-grey eyes brought on by synthetic opiates.

On the operating table the lumpectomy *had* got more seri-ous. By the time they moved her back down on to the ward, she'd had both breasts removed in a double mastectomy.

'We had little choice,' the doctor told me straightforwardly. 'It was worse than we'd been led to believe. But the good news is we feel it was quite contained. She won't need radiotherapy. Not unless anything shows up in the check-ups. Unfortunate, yes, but hopefully all over in one fell swoop.'

Another car successfully serviced, I thought.

I looked at her, ragged and serene on the pillow, and wondered how much she knew. First her womb. Then her breasts. I told myself it was just terrible bad luck and perhaps not even that uncommon in women of her age, and I thought of Eunice her mother, who battled her way to the very end – still on her hands and knees reseeding the bald patch on the lawn just before she died – and I thought about the belief in forbearance and endurance that was part of my mum's Methodist upbringing, and wondered if it was any solace to her now, or whether it was just bloody awful.

The tough Methodist strain in my mum's family dates back to my great-great-grandfather Cornelius Smith. Born in 1835 he was a Romany, one of the Smiths of Epping Forest, who along with the Boswells and the Loveridges make up three of the biggest Romany families in England. In and out of prison, a horse-dealer and clothes-peg maker, known for deer-stealing and occasional violence, he was twenty-nine and travelling with his family in their horse-drawn vardo outside Baldock in Hertfordshire when his eldest daughter Emily fell ill. They called the local doctor, who wouldn't enter the wagon, but called the girl to the door and announced that she had smallpox. He told the family they couldn't drive to the town as she was contagious; they would have to park up in a lane in the countryside.

Even though it was March, the snow was on the ground and it was bitterly cold. Cornelius pulled the wagon over on Norton Lane, one and a half miles away, and pitched a tent for his wife and his four other children under an overhanging hawthorn tree. He then took the wagon two hundred yards up the road and parked it by a chalk pit in view of the tent to be the sick room.

Cornelius's wife, Polly (born Mary), was heavily pregnant, but made a three-mile round trip into Baldock for provisions while Cornelius tended to Emily in the wagon, but it wasn't long before Emily's brother Ezekiel fell sick too, and the doctor, on returning, insisted he join his sister in quarantine.

A month of fetching and carrying and nursing followed. Polly left food on a stone halfway between the tent and wagon, in order to avoid contact with the infected. Some days Cornelius was so busy nursing that the food gathered a crust of snow before it could be collected. As the days passed Polly could not resist recklessly edging nearer and nearer the wagon to catch a glimpse of her children, but with an awful inevitability it wasn't long before she too fell ill. Cornelius was almost distracted. He had no choice but to gather everyone together back in the tent and hope for the best. Polly gave birth, while gravely sick, and died a day later in Cornelius's arms. Emily and Ezekiel survived and rejoined their siblings.

The health authorities – mindful that they were Romanies – ordered that the funeral take place after dark at the dead of night. In preparation, Polly's coffin was laid out between two chairs outside the tent and Cornelius made a bonfire for the infected clothes, but a kettle overturned and the tent caught fire and all their belongings were lost, although the coffin was untouched.

My great-great-uncle Rodney – who went on to become a famous evangelist preacher – was one of the surviving children. He takes up the story in his 1901 autobiography:

And now darkness fell, and with it came to us an old farmer's cart. Mother's coffin was placed in the vehicle, and between ten and eleven o'clock my father, the only mourner, followed her to the grave by a lantern light. She lies resting in Norton churchyard, near Baldock. When my father came back to us it was midnight, and his grief was very great. He went into a plantation behind his van, and throwing himself on his face, promised God to be good, to take care of his children, and to keep the promise that he had made to his wife. A fortnight after, the little baby died and was placed at her mother's side. If you go to Norton churchyard now and inquire for the gipsies' graves they will be pointed out to you. My mother and her last born lie side by side in that portion of the graveyard where are interred the remains of the poor, the unknown, and the forsaken.

After his wife's death, the grief-stricken Cornelius packed up and made his way with the children to Cambridge where he ran into his brothers, Bartholomew and Woodlock. They were heading to a service at the Primitive Methodist Chapel in Fitzroy Street. Cornelius and his children joined them. When the preacher asked if he was saved, Cornelius is said to have cried out in anguish, 'No, but that is what I *want*.'

Returning to Epping Forest, and still heavy-hearted, he joined his brothers on their way to another prayer meeting, this time in a chapel in Notting Hill built and run by a charismatic businessman-turned-preacher named Henry Varley. The congregation were surprised by the arrival of Romanies – who were frowned upon as untrustworthy outsiders – but the new revivalist movement of the time was opening its doors to all-comers from all classes and the brothers were admitted. By the end of the meeting the three brothers were 'converted'. Cornelius is said to have collapsed hysterically to the floor, frightening his own children, before rising to his feet and telling the congregation he felt so light that, had the floor been covered in eggshells, he could have walked across and not broken one.

Like her brother Rodney, Cornelius's daughter Tilly also became an evangelist. By the age of seventeen she was

singing and preaching at Salvation Army meetings in
Carlisle. In 1885 she married a Wesleyan from Plymouth,
George Evens, and while campaigning on a Methodist
mission in Hull, gave birth to my mother's father, Bram, on
Anlaby Road – and not in a vardo, as Bram was to romantic-
ally depict his beginnings for his *Out with Romany* listeners
when he became a radio star.

In 1931, Rodney's extraordinary fame as the globe-trotting
evangelist 'Gipsy' Smith helped pay for a new Methodist
church in Letchworth near Baldock, and it wasn't long before
the remains of both Cornelius and Polly were moved from
paupers' graves and into the grounds of the churchyard in
Norton with a smart new shared headstone.

My dad paid lip-service to all this backstory for several years.
In spite of his vehement atheism he allowed my mum to have
me christened at the Methodist church in Barnes when I was
four – in her words – 'just in case'. There is a photograph
commemorating the day. I am standing holding my dad's hand
in the front garden of our house in Barnes beside the spindly
weeping silver birch. My dad unsurprisingly looks good in a
lightweight navy safari jacket with four matching sporty
flapped patch pockets, slicked hair, white shirt, black knitted
tie and grey slacks. Unfortunately I am dressed not quite so
stylishly in knee-length black socks, little grey shorts, turquoise
blazer and a *top hat*. Just for good measure I am also carrying a
large pink rose. I look like a precocious child-ringmaster. The
Romany fortune-teller whom my mum consulted when I was
born insisted I would become a priest or an entertainer. The
casual reader who knows anything about me may gasp at the
accuracy of this prediction, but one look at the occupations of

most members of my extended family will show it wasn't exactly a risky guess.

Yet as the years passed, my dad became less and less tolerant of her religious side. He was being deliberately provocative when he suggested Rodney was only in it for the money and the girls, eagerly pointing out how he was thrown out of the Salvation Army for accepting an inscribed watch from his congregation when he was young, how he travelled first class on the *Queen Mary* to his multiple engagements in America, and how he married his twenty-seven-year-old secretary at the age of seventy-eight after the death of his first wife. 'Showbiz religion,' my dad called it, 'from a randy old man.'

Although remembered for his common touch and reputed indifference to material wealth, Rodney was certainly rich. I remember when his second wife, Mary-Alice, died in the mid-eighties. I visited her little mansion flat on Exhibition Road in South Kensington with my mum and Tracey, and we found a jaw-dropping treasure trove of jewels and silk and lavish gifts, many doubtless amassed from the offertories of his congregations, but others clearly bought as dazzling souvenirs and presents from his travels: pearl-inlaid make-up compacts; hand-tooled leather shaving cases and manuscript folders; drawers of silk underclothes; crocodile-skin suitcases; white kid gloves; solid silver photo frames and hand mirrors.

If provoked, my dad even lashed out at my mum's father's reputation, suggesting he was an ambitious man bewitched by fame and not the humble Methodist minister in the field that he portrayed. 'Own up!' was one of my dad's battle cries. He spared no one's feelings once his blood was up, and tore down anyone he considered dishonest in their intentions, or caught playing a double game, however much pain and controversy he might leave in his wake.

But for all his attacks, my mum dug in, and for all her reservations about her upbringing and leanings towards agnosticism, she could never quite shrug off her own history. On the day she heard of her mother's death she instinctively got into her car and just started driving, and didn't stop until she was miles out into the countryside, beside an anonymous plain village church, where she slipped inside and offered up a prayer.

Years later, in Oxford, she befriended the local clergyman. ('Invited to the next-door vicar for mince pies and a glass of wain [*sic*] tonight. Don't expect I shall be accompanied. Have a peaceful Xmas,' she faxed in 1997). Even at the flat in St John's Wood, when she tried living on her own for a few weeks after my dad first went into the care home, she made an effort to visit the local parish church at the foot of the high street, only to be deflected by its grand Regency-style portico, and white and gold ionic columns. 'Too High Church for me,' she said.

I looked at her in the bed – remote, weakened, ruthlessly stripped of any last vestige of her sexuality, uncertain of her faith, mocked yet loved by her husband, her memory fading – and I wanted to well up, to feel some surge of emotion that would make me instinctively embrace her and touch her soft grey hair and whisper in her ear, but instead I leaned back and looked into her drowsy eyes from the chair in which I sat, and she looked back at me, a momentary smile across her lips, and then just eye contact again. I reached out and took her hand. And she seemed unbowed. Enduring. Flinty.

I wondered if she could have had her life all over again what she would have done differently. Could she have left my dad in the late seventies when it all got vicious and spiteful? She would only have been in her mid-fifties. She could have found some room to be herself again – uncriticised. She could have renewed old theatre friends, carried on writing, basked in the reflected glory of her children's successes, gone bird-watching, indulged her Romany roots and collection of vintage postcards, raised money for her favourite local charity projects – all without fear of withering reprisals from her own husband. Or did the guilt of her own remarriage pin her down? Would it have been too shameful to admit defeat again? Maybe she feared it would be perceived as a reflection only of her selfishness and lack of stickability. I wondered too if there was a side to her that was bored by herself. Was my dad *still* a way out? Even in the bad years? Sharp, acerbic, still exotic. Worth withstanding. Still forgivable. Or like any of us, maybe she just needed the company, and they kept the battle going as it was the only battle they had. It was an empty house after everyone left home.

> Home is so sad. It stays as it was left,
> Shaped to the comfort of the last to go
> As if to win them back. Instead, bereft
> Of anyone to please, it withers so,
> Having no heart to put aside the theft
>
> And turn again to what it started as,
> A joyous shot at how things ought to be,
> Long fallen wide. You can see how it was:
> Look at the pictures and the cutlery.
> The music in the piano stool. That vase.
>
> 'Home Is So Sad' by Philip Larkin
> (pinned above my mum's desk, 1978)

23

One night in 1978, my mum was woken at around midnight by the sound of my dad coming home from the pub. She heard the click of the flat door, the tinkle of keys and the sound of hushed voices. This wasn't unusual. In the sixties a procession of musicians came through the flat in the small hours to listen to jazz and smoke and play poker in the sitting room across the landing from her bedroom. More recently, since my dad had taken up decorating, his friends had changed. Instead of drummers and trumpet players, it was now more often fitters and roofers. She was used to them in the flat. After a few drinks at lunchtime he might bring one of them home to do some odd jobs. 'Skipper' was a regular visitor with his doleful bloodhound face and rough cracked hands. It was said he could take on most things, which was never entirely clear from his work: he put in a new shower that ran only hot *or* cold for three weeks, then laid a floor in the kitchen only to hammer a nail straight through a central heating pipe causing a leak that brought down the ceiling in Eunice's coat cupboard in the flat below. But there was something about the voices that night that made her sit up: one of them sounded higher than usual.

She pulled on a dressing gown and blearily stepped out on to the landing. The voices were now in the sitting room. A seam of light was under the door. She pushed it open to see my dad fixing two drinks. Perched on the sofa was a young woman in heels. She worked as a barmaid at the pub.

I didn't hear about it until a few days later. I overheard my mum telling someone on the phone, and saying things like she wouldn't stand for it, but then I heard her crying quietly after she'd put the receiver down. Quite what my dad's full intentions were I've never been sure. An offensive snub to my mum, no doubt. A humiliation in her own home, yes. Perhaps it was just an obnoxious show of virility. I was fifteen. His purpose was puzzling to me, but I knew it was a serious and cruel thing even then.

A couple of weeks later, the three of us were all set to return to Lindos where we had been in 1974. At the last minute my mum had to back out as an opportunity to interview Richard Burton again had come up unexpectedly. He was staying at the Dorchester for the release of a new blockbuster war movie, *The Wild Geese*, and there was a star-laden party to attend as well. With my dad's decorating income intermittent and his royalties all but dried up, she needed the money. Instead of us pulling out of the holiday altogether it was agreed I would go with my dad. He teased me in the days running up to it. 'A chance to dip the old wick,' he leered quietly in the kitchen, the night before we left.

At Gatwick Airport the next morning we sat in the busy departures lounge waiting for our flight to be called. He said he needed cigarettes and I should wait for him to come back. He disappeared in the direction of the bar. A family sat down next to me with two teenage daughters. Five minutes later I saw him coming back. As he approached it was clear he had something in his hand; I thought it was a packet of cigarettes. When he was about ten feet away he tossed it at me like a Frisbee. I went to catch it but fumbled it and it bounced off my leg and landed in my lap. I looked down. It was a box of condoms. He was standing over me now. 'You'll be needing those,' he said quietly, with a wink. I didn't dare look round at the family next to me.

On the plane I wouldn't talk to him. I wanted to go home. He tried to order me a beer from the air hostess. I didn't like beer. 'Please yourself,' he said. Three miniatures of gin were lined up on the tray-table in front of him.

In Lindos, we had adjoining village rooms. He was matey during the day but encouraged me to 'do my own thing' after dark. The village was unthreatening. He said I could find him in the popular Socrates Bar. I would wander down to the village's only discothèque and sit on the wall and watch a handful of people dancing to Wild Cherry's 'Play That Funky Music' and Santana's 'Black Magic Woman' on the tiny open-air dance floor, and thought how I was too young to impress anyone. Instead I hoped I might see one of Pink Floyd; it was said he owned one of the big captain's houses in the village. I watched other families eating late in the restaurants and wished my mum was there.

Back at Socrates Bar I'd find my dad, garrulous, telling stories to whoever would listen. A photo of Jim Morrison hung above the cocktail mixers and bottles of spirits on the rear counter. People sat on upturned logs under the dark starry night sky. Wicker lanterns hung in the trees. I watched him try to dazzle everyone, seeking out people younger than himself. He'd give me the key and tell me to let myself into the room and promise he wouldn't be long, but I'd be woken from sleep when I'd finally hear him blunder in. In the mornings he'd have an ouzo 'to settle the stomach' and then I'd watch him skip breakfast. There was something demeaning about it all. He was fifty-two. I threw the condoms away.

The days weren't so bad. After he'd shrugged off his hangover, we'd make a few jokes and walk down to the quieter of the two beaches, and go snorkelling off the rocks among the sponges and black spiny sea urchins and the shoals of damsel fish, looking out for eels and rays, or pointing out the dogfish, both of us hovering wide-eyed on the surface of an astonishing translucent otherness; and for an hour or two we would be lifted out of our lives and exhilarated, communicating only in sign language. It felt easier.

Back home the following week the atmosphere was jumpy. Each day my dad tidied the house and did the shopping, but there was no work of his own to return to and he didn't say much. I kept myself to myself. My mum was out at work. ('I felt like the opposite of other people. I seemed to relax when I *left* home,' she said, reflecting on it years later. 'I'd tense up on the walk back across the common from the station after work, not knowing if I'd find him home or not.')

The third night back she tried to tell him about the Richard Burton party she had attended while we were away in Lindos. He'd been skulking in the kitchen making some food for them. With the dishes stowed in the warming drawer he suddenly started up. I heard him from the sitting room. It began as a long monologue but it slowly turned into a tirade, sweeping up the multinationals, the CIA, the bourgeoisie, the Catholic Church, the Pope, and then inevitably her mother, her father, his stepchildren, her ex-husband, Richard Burton, *everything* into one huge desolate bonfire. It wasn't the first time I had heard him sound off, but not for a while. My mum was in there with him. I knew he was never physically violent towards her but I didn't hear her voice, and I could picture her in there not moving, absorbing it silently. Towards the end I went outside, not wanting to listen, and sat on the front wall, and then walked to the end of the road, and when I got back the car was gone and my mum was red-eyed in the silent flat and I didn't know how to speak to her, let alone console her.

'He told me I was an embarrassment to his friends,' she said. 'He called me a snob, not fit for the pub. A joke figure. That can't be right, can it?'

I didn't know what to say. I felt young and tongue-tied. I tried to be grown-up about it and my mum thanked me for listening ('I don't have anyone else to tell some days') but I went up to my room and opened the window on to the garden, and listened to the wind in the tall copper beech and watched the string of planes in the cool night air with their beads of lights heading into Heathrow.

He tried it out on me a few times when I was growing up. He'd put a plate of food down in front of me in the evening and then start talking from the sink. It would start with good-natured if somewhat stern lessons in socialism and the Trade Union movement. But then one night – it must have been 1973 – after a couple of drinks he wound himself up about the death of the Chilean socialist leader, Salvador Allende. He said Nixon – whom I took to be the US president – and the CIA – who he said were like MI5 'only much worse' – were behind an internal armed coup that had led to Allende's death. He went into detail about a 'fake suicide cover-up' and the installation of a military junta (whatever that was), and he said I should know about it and not 'take any shit from any teachers' who told it otherwise. I was sitting at the table eating shepherd's pie. I quite liked my teachers. I couldn't imagine a Chilean military junta coming up in class. I felt like the lone member of a harangued congregation. When it was time for me to speak I said yes, I understood, and then asked if I could be allowed to go and watch *A Question of Sport* with David Vine.

In such moods, he struck me as a sullen cornered animal, and not like the dad who went to football with me or showed me chords or told funny stories. I'd hear him complain to my mum about my half-brothers and half-sister too. They were as good as grown-up, no longer malleable, one or two maybe even resentful. And in return I think he resented their youthfulness, their sloppy manners, their use of the flat as a hotel when it suited them.

Not long after the tirade against my mum – in part an effort to heal simmering family disaffection – a Christmas was planned at Ken's new cottage in the countryside, out past Burford. Everyone assembled on Christmas Eve – my mum and dad, and me, and Simon, Toby, Roly, Jennie, who were all now in their twenties. It was an achievement getting everyone together. Ken was going to join us on Christmas morning. But as the evening wore on and alcohol began loosening everyone's tongues, and the guards came down, and we were all cramped into the low-ceilinged cottage sitting room, the recriminations started.

It was late. I'd been sent to bed. I heard the arguing begin downstairs. I could hear my dad's voice and Toby's voice rising. And then Roly came upstairs and told me to go to sleep and it would all be all right, and silently climbed into his bed beyond me and pulled the covers up over him. And then there was shouting, and I crept out of my bed and sat at the top of the stairs and peeked through the banisters in my pyjamas to see my dad saying something disparaging about Ken and belittling his achievements as a father, and Toby standing up to him and then pulling back his arm and throwing a wild punch and my dad stumbling backwards, tripping over presents, grasping at something to keep his balance, but only finding the tree and pulling it down on top of him in a heap on the floor, the baubles tinkling and breaking. And then I watched as, without a word, he pushed the tree aside – the branches dislodging cards on the mantelpiece causing them to fall into the fireplace – and staggered to his feet with everyone just staring, and, reaching for his jacket while brushing shreds of tinsel from his hair, he opened the front door and – closing it behind him – blundered out into the cold night.

Toby's face was smudged with tears. I heard the car engine start up, and watched Simon leap to his feet and fling the door open and rush out, slamming it shut. It was a treacherous night. The lanes were icy. My dad then drove all the way back to London with Simon beside him making sure he didn't run the car off the road.

24

With my mum in hospital again, my dad was back in the care home on the Finchley Road. I drove him there. He was very good about it. They gave him a room with a garden view. I think everyone thought – although no one likes to voice these things – that it might be for the last time. Living at the flat suddenly seemed impossible, and it was clear my mum would have to join him to convalesce after she was discharged. I couldn't picture her going back home as though nothing had happened. She'd been through enough. Twice. Inside a year. Someone else needed to be in charge now. The next afternoon I started to think about how to sell the flat and what to do next. They'd barely been in it two years. And then the phone rang.

'Mr Watt?'

'Yes.'

'It's the care home here. It's about your father, Thomas.'

'Tommy, yes, what is it?'

As I said it, something small boomed in my chest. I had an image of him at the bottom of a set of stairs, a big pool of blood under his head, or wheezing helplessly in the back of an ambulance, his hair dishevelled, a paramedic pulling up his upper lid and shining a light into his eye. Or just dead in his bed after an afternoon nap. An easy exit. Still warm. His arms across his chest, his little feet crossed. Not so bad in the end.

'We think he's . . .' There was a moment's silence. ' . . . escaped.'

I glanced round the room repeating the words to myself as I thought I might have misheard them, and a voice in my head shouted, 'AGAIN?' but I didn't recognise the person on the end of the phone, and I stayed calm. 'Right, OK. What do you mean?' My heart was pounding. It was as if a mains switch had been flicked and a current of strong voltage was running down my arms and legs; it made me think of the time our burglar alarm went off in the middle of the night, and I had to bolt out of bed, groping for the light switch, still half-asleep in the dreadful cacophony. And then I could only picture the front doors to the care home. I could see them opening. Only ten feet from the road. I could see a National Express coach thundering recklessly along the bus lane.

'We can't find him. Not anywhere. We think . . .'

I cut her off. 'Who *with*?' I thought it must be the chef again. *Hadn't they fired him yet?*

'On his own, we think,' she said.

I saw the National Express coach bearing down. '*On his* . . . I'll be right there.'

In the car, all the scenarios replayed themselves over and over again, each more gruesome than the last. And then I told myself to relax. It would be fine. He'd be in the wrong room, or chatting to the chef out the back, or even if he had got out he wouldn't have got far; he couldn't get more than twenty yards without gasping; he'd have found a bench or something; he would be taking some fresh air. *Fresh air? On the Finchley Road? Are you mad?* And I saw him engulfed in a cloud of diesel fumes, choking, dropping to his knees on the pavement, no one around, pitiless traffic careering by.

As I approached the care home in the car I started scanning the road, up and down the pavements. I discounted all the women. A black kid in a T-shirt almost down to his knees – no. A large man with a small fishing hat perched on his head, a shoulder bag across his chest in a sash – no. Two builders in rigger boots, one in a neon-yellow high-visibility vest – no. And then I found myself looking along the gutters.

I pulled into the drive of the care home and leapt from the car. Dashing round the front, I barged through the doors when they buzzed open. As I stopped in the lobby – my eyes trying to settle on someone with some information – I heard a female voice behind me say, 'Mr Watt, it's OK, he's back.' My first thought: *So he did escape; he really did; he wasn't just in someone else's room, or chatting to the kitchen staff; he was out there; on the street; in danger; you fucking idiots.*

I span round. The receptionist was looking at me uncomfortably. 'What? *When?*' I blurted.

'Just now. We heard the bottles,' she said.

'The *what?*'

'We heard the carrier bag. It was clinking as he came in. He's safely up in his room now. With the . . .'

'It was *clinking* as he *came in*,' I said slowly, looking her in the eye. By repeating the sentence and accentuating the key words I thought I could wring some sense out of it.

'He was in a taxi,' she said nervously.

'A *what?*' I was hearing words I wasn't expecting to hear. I was expecting to hear 'ambulance' and 'fall' and 'A&E', and instead I was hearing 'bottles' and 'clinking' and 'taxi'.

'It seems he hailed the first taxi and took it along to Waitrose,' she went on. (The *first* taxi?) 'And it seems he bought some alcohol and then got a return taxi from the rank outside the shop back here.'

I let the information sink in. I had to hand it to him. That was style. Right there. *Right fucking there.* 'Where are the bottles?' It was all I could think of saying. I was picturing him pouring one down his throat right at that moment, up in his room, unattended.

'Here,' she said, reaching down behind the desk. There was the sound of glass on glass. 'We had to confiscate them. Obviously.' She dangled the bag in front of her.

'Where is he now?'

'Like I said. Safely up in his room. You can go up if you like,' she said, putting the bag down again.

Safely? 'How did he get out?' I said. I could feel my brow scrunching up.

'He was in the lobby for half an hour at lunchtime today. He was very sociable. Up by the door. Quite chatty. We think he watched a couple of people coming and going and memorised the code.'

Memorised the code? He couldn't even remember where we *were* last week. '*How* did he memorise it?'

'Perhaps "copied" is a better word, or he might have been hovering and slipped out while the door was briefly open.'

'Why didn't anyone *stop* him?'

'He must have picked his moment when a back was turned. Some of our residents *are* allowed out,' she said, raising her eyebrows, as if to say *it's not a prison*. 'We encourage residents to exercise choice and maintain independence, and they are free to journey out alone if they feel able to do so. Of course, in this instance, it was . . .'

'OK, OK,' I said, butting in. 'I get it. I will speak to someone properly about all this. I'm going up to see him now.'

I took the stairs instead of the lift. Someone was coming down with a hoist and a couple of bed-rails. I flattened myself against the wall to let them pass and flicked them a quick smile. Up on the landing I passed a bucket and some carpet shampoo. I knocked on my dad's door.

He answered almost immediately. 'Come in.'

I pushed the door open. He'd been standing at the window and was turning towards me. The words were coming out of my mouth almost as soon as I had stepped into the room. 'What *have* you been up to? Have you *any* idea of the fuss you've caused?'

A look of boyish innocence and mild incomprehension was on his face. His jacket was on the back of the chair beside the small built-in desk. He was wearing a loose oatmeal sleeveless cardigan over an ironed blue shirt. His moustache had gone. Who had shaved it off for him? The beard at the bottom remained. He looked like an Amish Mennonite sympathiser.

'What are you saying?' he said. 'It's nice to see you.' He edged towards the chair to sit down, coughing.

I sat on the bed. 'How on earth did you get the taxi?'

'What? The . . . ? Oh that.' He eased himself on to the chair. 'Nice driver. Waived the fare. Jazz fan.'

I could hear his chest wheezing quietly. 'How did you *stop* it?'

'He was right there outside,' he said. 'Did you order it for me? Very kind of you. I left the bottles with the concierge. Said they'd stow them. Very accommodating they are here, you know.'

'You can't do it again, Dad. You realise that, don't you? You could have fallen, or got hit by a bus, or anything. They called me. I drove straight here. Everyone's been in a panic.'

'Really?' A look of genuine surprise was on his face.

'Where did you get the money?'

'Not sure. You mother gave me forty quid, I think. Is she all right?' He looked at me expectantly.

'Yes, she'll be OK.' I didn't want to tell him everything yet. 'Not the easiest of operations. But she'll be fine.'

'Oh, good. Tough, she is, that Romany. Like her mother. Though not as miserable. Tell her I asked after her, won't you?' He coughed a little.

I could feel the moment losing its heat, my reprimands losing their urgency. On the one hand, I was agitated, too involved, wearied by the random demands of keeping them safe, keeping them out of trouble, but on the other I realised I was silently cheering him on, willing him not to give up, actually *helping* him into the taxi, *paying* the fare.

'Is it hot in here?' he said. I could hear him wheezing harder now.

I looked at him. He suddenly seemed paler. He eyes were blinking hard. His hand was gripping the edge of the chair. His nails perfectly clean.

'Help me on to the bed . . . there's a good . . . chap.'

I jumped up and slipped a hand under his armpit and lifted him to his feet. I turned him round and got him over to the bed and sat him down. He swivelled and lay back with a grunt. I cupped my hand under his bony ankles and helped them up on to the covers. The backs of his legs felt tight like piano wire. His head was on the pillow now, his eyes closed. He was taking shallow breaths in and out through his nose and mouth. He coughed with his mouth shut. There was no rattle, just a compacted, compressed noise, like air trapped in a creaky harmonium, his whole ribcage lifting and subsiding. It was a dense fibrous sound.

There was a knock at the door. It opened simultaneously, and a carer was into the room all in one movement. She saw me and rolled her eyes. In a second, she seemed to have control. 'Been overdoing it again this afternoon, I hear, Tommy,' she said loudly and directly. 'I've got your *inhalers* here. You left them downstairs again. Shall I give you a puff now? And a blast of oxygen, yes?'

My dad nodded but was waving me away insistently at the same time.

I got up and stepped away from the bed as the nurse bent down to help him up, and then I backed away, loitered for a moment, then retreated from the room, and shut the door. I stood in the quiet corridor and stared at the bucket and the carpet shampoo bottle still at the top of the stairs. Through the fire door came another woman. She had a plastic basket of laundry under one arm.

As she got to me she said, 'You with Mr Watt?'

'I am. I'll be back in with him in a minute. The carer is with him.'

'Give him these for me, there's a love.'

She handed me three pairs of underpants, neatly folded.

I took them and nodded, and she turned to go.

As the fire door closed behind her, I looked down at the underpants in my hand. Each one had a new name tag with 'Tommy Watt' written on it. I remembered that evening hour in hospitals – 'handover' – when one shift of nurses goes home and passes a patient's relevant notes on to the incoming night shift. I thought of the uncomfortable adjustment I felt as the patient, the new faces to get used to, the worry something would get lost or misunderstood, but having to trust the process, to let the moment go. His underpants weighed barely anything in my hand, and in a moment I would give them to a stranger.

My dad's door opened. It was the carer. She came out into the corridor and closed the door behind her. 'He's all right,' she said, under her breath. 'He said he wants a kip now. Long afternoon, what with one thing and another. He asked me to tell you that he'll see you tomorrow.'

I nodded. 'Understandable. Can I give you these?' I held out the underpants.

'Of course.' She took them from me, and turned to go.

'Superman will always need his underpants,' I said.

She stopped, looked back at me over her shoulder and smiled, and then I watched her disappear through the swing doors.

25

When I was sixteen I made my own escape. On a moped. A red Puch Maxi. It was a special birthday present from my mum and dad topped up by weeks of savings from me. During the week I used it to ride to school and back. It had a top speed of twenty-eight miles per hour. I would scoff at the headwind that whipped down off the river.

On week nights, if I'd done all my homework, sometimes I was allowed to use it to go to gigs. I'd leave the tense atmosphere at home and head out across Hammersmith Bridge to the Nashville in West Kensington on the corner of the Cromwell Road and North End Road, and park unknowingly opposite the old Alvic Studios where I was to record my first EP, 'Summer Into Winter', with Robert Wyatt three years later.

Over the next eighteen months I'd stand on my own at the back and watch new bands like Magazine, Black Slate and The Pretenders. I witnessed a thrilling Factory Records triple bill topped by Joy Division, with A Certain Ratio and Orchestral Manoeuvres in the Dark in support, for which – to general amazement – OMD's bassist Andy McCluskey wore era-defying flares and a crocheted patchwork waistcoat. I saw

Jonathan Richman and The Modern Lovers at Hammersmith Odeon – their tiny equipment lost on the enormous apron stage – fully mesmerised by their apparent guileless honesty. At the end of the show Richman got all the house lights turned on and beckoned the entire crowd down to the front for an impromptu question-and-answer session while he swung his legs over the edge of the press pit like a gawky schoolboy. It was another world opening before my eyes.

I got my first proper girlfriend too. Her family lived on the outer edge of Wimbledon in a small end-of-terrace Edwardian house with a pebble-dash extension. Everyone ate breakfast together in the modest dining room – early-evening meals too, sometimes. It was simple hearty home cooking with everyone talking equally and expressing opinions. Her father was a small thin Oxford-educated Yorkshireman with neat grey parted hair and a stiff back who worked for the civil service; he squinted from behind thick corrective glasses and enjoyed putting everyone right at the dinner table in an exacting – often pedantic – but good-humoured way. He played vinyl pressings of Bach on a meticulously assembled high-end hi-fi system, wore open-toed sandals and woollen trousers in hot weather, and in spite of his poor eyesight, took his own black-and-white photographs of church architecture and then painstakingly developed them in the downstairs bathroom, where the windows were taped up with black bin-liners. He voted Conservative. My dad had told me all Tories were toffs and racketeers, but I found that I liked him, and it made me realise people might not be how you first judge them. Her mother was a teacher from rural Essex: broad-shouldered; a mop of short brown hair; also short-sighted, but with a gentle face that took an interest in everything you told her. She cooked up saucepans of food that filled the house with steam, and tended to plants in a lean-to add-on glazed porch that cluttered up the front door. Late at night we'd often find her on her own in the sitting room, the house in darkness, curled up in an armchair with a single spotlight, wearing a candlewick dressing gown, flushed from a hot bath, reading the latest volume of something like Seamus Heaney, her face myopically pressed against the pages. They took a bath together in the evenings – one of their great pleasures. I pictured their bodies crammed into the foaming frothing tub – him, small and wiry; her, all big and fleshy. And I expected, as an adolescent, to find it repellent, but I thought it was touching, and it made me sad that I could never imagine my parents doing the same, although I imagined they must have done once. A long time ago.

I think I had looked to get away from home as early as twelve. I made friends with a boy, Andrew, from school. His father was a script-writer called Dick Clement, who had written – among other things – something successful for television called *The Likely Lads* with a collaborator called Ian La Frenais, although it meant nothing to me at the time. The family lived in a rambling two-storey detached house in Petersham. It had a pan-tiled roof with higgledy-piggledy dormer windows and sat in big grounds with old tumbledown stables, a little fruit garden, chickens and a wide lawn giving way to a copse. I was told Charles Dickens once lived there. The garden was overlooked by a wrought-iron ground-floor verandah entwined with wisteria. Sometimes I'd crush one of its big hanging pale purple blooms in my hand and wonder why we didn't have such graceful flowers in our garden. They had Dalmatians and things I had never seen before: bean bags; duvets; bagels for breakfast; fibre-optic lamps. They took a holiday in California. They went to lunch on the King's Road. They drove a big white French Citroën DS Safari estate. It was a world away from our flat.

I'd play football all day long with Andrew on the huge lawn. He had proper metal goalposts with orange nylon netting; at home I just used a couple of cricket stumps. We'd play for hours, one in goal, one out on the lawn – long matches as imaginary teams. One of us would commentate the whole time as though it were *Match of the Day*: 'We're approaching the eighty-ninth minute. Hollins through to Garland. He's round one man. He's round two! He cuts inside. Here comes Hutchinson! He shoots! WHAT A SAVE!'

Dick and Ian often used to write in the house. Ian turned up in his vintage Bentley – it was said he slept in it – and entered through the tall wooden gates and parked right by the back door, which struck me as showy and a bit daring. They'd lock the doors to the kitchen for a couple of hours in the afternoon and we'd hear their muffled voices laughing and talking. One afternoon Dick called us in from the garden and asked us to sit down and watch something; he wanted to know our reaction to what they had just written and filmed. It was the first ever episode of *Porridge* with Ronnie Barker as the prison inmate, Fletcher. We thought it was funny and he was very happy we got the jokes. Dick had a kind face, and never spoke down to me. He was younger than my parents. Confident. At the end of the weekend he would often drive me home across Richmond Park in the big white Citroën estate with its brown, hole-punched, tan leather trim and hydraulic suspension. I envied all of it. We'd climb up the hill out of Petersham ('That's Tommy Steele's house') and into the park, the sun dissolving behind the trees, cruising past glimpses of red deer, and across its two thousand acres and out the other side to Roehampton Lane.

My dad was withdrawn when I was dropped off, as though he distrusted Dick. Only later did it dawn on me he might have been jealous of him. The self-assured younger man. All that effortless burgeoning success. The world at his feet. Which is where it wasn't for my dad. Ironically, Andrew's parents were going through a bad divorce, but I used to try to close my eyes to it; it wasn't the side I wanted to see. I preferred to submerge myself in the surface luxuries of Andrew's childhood and the boyish friendship we had. One Christmas was spent running around Rolling Stone Ron Wood's house at the top of Richmond Hill – the house that he'd bought from John Mills – where a jukebox stood in the kitchen and I saw my first ever recording studio in the basement. Andrew's family had borrowed the place for the Christmas holiday, but I thought life must be miserable as an adult if even such splendour could leave you as unhappy as his mum seemed to be.

I tried to compare my parents to other adults in our road too. Woodlands Road was a cul-de-sac. All the kids played together in the street on summer evenings – hopscotch, football, sardines, hide-and-seek. The egg delivery van came once a week and we would all jump up on to its cab and hold on while the van trundled along the road, laughing and screaming. We all seemed pretty much the same, but the parents seemed vivid and towering and different. Looking back, it was an extraordinary assembly of high-achieving figures all living next door to each other, but whose accomplishments meant very little when refracted through the optic of my own experience of them.

Two doors down was the arts broadcaster and impresario Humphrey Burton whose first wife, Gretel, scared me with a spaghetti carbonara; I thought spaghetti for kids only came as hoops with tomato sauce. Next door was the opera singer, John Kentish, whose shed caught fire one night, and I watched from my bedroom window as he tried to put it out in his pyjamas using only a watering can. On the other side of us was the eminent British historian and Africanist Basil Davidson; I repeatedly damaged his fruit netting with my football. Beyond him was Michael Hogg from the *Daily Telegraph* (later *Sir* Michael Hogg through an inherited baronetcy); his wife taught me the piano for a couple of years until the sound of her dry nicotine-stained nails clicking on the ivory keys was so unbearable it made me give up. Behind us was a pottery studio run by a small rarely seen nocturnal man in a sailor's cap called Harry Horlock-Stringer, who never seemed to mind if a tennis ball landed in his garden, but whose wife threatened to call the police when my Action Man fell off our back wall into her nasturtiums. Next door to the Hoggs was the TV executive Michael Peacock; he ran both BBC1 and BBC2 for a time in the sixties and then helped start London Weekend Television; I used their trampoline, and his wife Daphne confused me by making me a cup of Earl Grey tea when I was only ten. Next door to the Peacocks was Admiral Sir Caspar John, British First Sea Lord and son of the post-impressionist painter, Augustus John, which seemed to me to make a mockery of ever following in your parents' footsteps. In keeping with the family's pioneering bohemian spirit, the Johns' house was completely devoid of any bourgeois trappings; I can only picture bare floorboards, scattered newspapers, empty wine bottles and nude children. I remember when I was nine, his son Phineas – then seventeen, I think – was sent to borstal for six months for taking part in a peaceful anti-apartheid demonstration outside the South African Embassy. I didn't know what 'borstal', 'anti-apartheid' or 'South Africa' were, but I remember my older half-sister Jennie telling me about what happened to him and saying it was 'disgusting' and being upset. On the corner opposite the verdant shadowy common was a vast yellow-and-white lodge, home to Lord Woolf, Master of the

Rolls, although he was only a simple barrister back then; even so, I lost a shuttlecock over his garden fence once and never dared retrieve it.

Maybe it is just what all kids think, but whenever my paths crossed with any of theirs I only found them intimidating. I couldn't imagine any of them as my parents, except perhaps Mrs Ritchie at the end of the road by the red pillar box, who one day gave me a slice of cake and a glass of lemonade and let me play with her son's marble run even though he was out when I went to call. But in general, I realised I could take no leads or clues from any of them and would have to grow up as quickly as I could and work it out for myself.

26

After my mum left St Mary's Hospital, she joined my dad at the care home, where they spent the next three months. It was like a wind had dropped. They were quieter. Becalmed. The flat sat empty. I didn't have the heart to do much with it except empty the fridge. I even kept the central heating ticking over in case something changed. My dad was spending long hours in his little room. His breathing was becoming very poor. He'd lie on the bed while my mum sat in the window sensing the light gauzily change over the wide terraced garden in a kind of absent contemplation. Her eyesight appeared to have taken a turn for the worse. 'I can see sideways, but your face is vaguer now,' she said one morning. It seemed as if the surgery had left her introspective, devitalised, self-critical. I recognised the feelings – I'd been through a major hospital experience myself ten years earlier – but they only served to worsen her own natural self-absorption. More than anything I sensed an atmosphere of penance around her.

I visited and sat there with them, falling into the same silences. 'You still there, Romany?' my dad would say from time to time from the bed. 'Oh, *yes*, dear. Where else would you *expect* me to be?' my mum would reply, still unable to remove the tone of tetchiness from her voice. Maybe she only put it on for my benefit. Or maybe it was because that is how she now felt. Permanently.

They asked for nothing at Christmas. They did not want to visit anyone – not that my dad would have been able to – and said they'd be just as happy letting the festive days pass uneventfully like any others. They seemed to have accepted the imposed sobriety of life in the care home this time, although they regularly asked for bumper bars of chocolate – the drinker's methadone.

Physically, my mum still looked robust, even after two demanding operations. It appeared she might be quite capable, like Eunice, of fighting on to the end. But what she seemed to be finally coming to terms with was the realisation that she couldn't bring herself to look after my dad any more; not because she couldn't have perhaps rallied one last time and continued with the fetching and the carrying and the constant attention, but because this time she'd had enough. 'No hard feelings, darling,' she used to say in the old days, the morning after another evening of poisonous tit for tat; but now, with the end approaching, it seemed to be *too many* hard feelings.

She'd attempted independent living in an effort to briefly reframe her life, but the guilt at leaving him in care on his own was too much, and he was far too good at making her feel guilty for even attempting it. And of course there was a version of him she still missed. It was a double bind: she couldn't live on her own with him, but nor could she live on her own without him. Joining him in care was all that was left.

When I looked at her sitting silently in the window on those afternoons, as the bronzed autumn light settled over the empty garden behind the care home, I thought all of those things were on her mind, and encircling everything like a hawk high over the fields a sense of unjustness. I wondered if she reflected on the days when it was all still salvageable, when she was younger and more determined, in those days when she was still prepared to haul everything up off the floor because she knew leaving it lying there in its own unhappiness and recrimination would do no good. Did she recall all the new leaves they had turned over in an effort to put the bad days behind them? The notes of apology they left out for each other? The vows of abstinence? Even the half-baked ones of the seventies when they only gave up whisky under the delusion that white wine and strong German lager didn't count?

I shouldn't forget that they had still made good things happen after the bad. Simple things that mattered as they got older: afternoon runs in the car into the summer countryside; a canal boat holiday; a few days on a farm; visits to the local wetlands; days when their own affectionate companionship was fulfilling and untroubled. The problem was that ultimately none of it had ever replaced the *rush* my dad had always seemed to need, and had never seemed able to quell. And so the whole thing had begun again, as regular as the rotating seasons.

I was eighteen when I left for university in 1981. My mum and dad coped in different ways. I'd chosen to read Drama and English Literature at Hull. I was excited by the prospect of the course. Hull had one of the only fully working university studio theatres in the country. My interview had been with the soon-to-be film director Anthony Minghella. The campus librarian was Philip Larkin. Andrew Motion had just left the English Department en route to becoming Poet Laureate. It all seemed like a great secret no one knew about. But my dad – who insisted on driving me – had little interest in literary luminaries or the quirks of my higher education. He was more interested in the four-hour journey up there.

As we turned on to the M1 he started the way he intended to carry on by telling me a story about picking up a couple of old jazz musician friends at Baker Street and the three of them driving north for a gig. All they had to drink in the car was a full bottle of vodka and a full bottle of orange squash; how to mix them became the focal point of the whole journey. By Newport Pagnell, saxophonist Ronnie Ross – who was in the passenger seat – had managed to take a swig out of each, and then, in the rickety, suspension-free Renault Dauphine in which they were travelling, had managed to meticulously pour a capful from one into the other repeatedly for over fifty miles until the two bottles were perfectly mixed together. And he did this without spilling a drop. *These* were the kind of skills my dad thought were worth learning.

The journey wasn't unenjoyable. My dad thrived on re-creating his love of male camaraderie with me. He was often at his funniest and most relaxed, full of stories and bonhomie. Away from home, it was like a weight was lifted from his shoulders. At the motorway services he told me about the time he and a couple of chums had pulled off the road for lunch, and seen the winning line come up on a fruit machine – three cherries all in a row – and just as it rolled into place, one of them had pulled the plug out of the machine at the back to hold the line in position, while another had run to the cashier for a bag of sixpences. With the jackpot payout locked in position, they then fooled the machine into paying out four times.

By the time we hit the Humber Bridge a couple of hours later, we were the best of mates; it was the way he liked it. The bridge was only just over three months old. We'd made a diversion to cross it especially; it seemed to me that it would represent a transformative moment. From one era into the next. At the time it was the largest single-span suspension bridge in the world – a big deal. I regaled my dad with facts I'd prepared: it was well over a mile long; the twin towers were further apart at the top than at the bottom due to the curvature of the earth; the south tower's foundations were over one hundred feet deep because of the shifting sands of the estuary; it could bend more than ten feet in high winds.

As we drove on to it, and the thrill rose up, my dad opened the windows in the Renault 5 GTL. A rush of bracing October wind flushed out the car. Keeping one eye on the road, he reached across me and flipped open the glove-box and fished something out; he'd obviously planned something; maybe it was a little speech he'd prepared. As we hit the middle of the bridge, he depressed the cigarette lighter and put what was in his hand – a small immaculately rolled joint – to his lips. The cigarette lighter popped out, and he pushed a Count Basie Orchestra cassette into the audio player. With one hand, he turned up the volume control, pulled the lighter out of the socket – the orange coil glowing – and touched the end of the twizzled paper. It flared, then blazed. Wind howled in the cabin behind. The languid slow swinging melancholy of Basie's 'Li'l Darlin'' filled the car. He took two small drags before holding his breath, and without a word, passed me the joint, and – as if taking part in a small but perfect ritual – I did the same, as the vast glittering water of the Humber spread out beneath us, and we drove on into Hull with unhurried panache.

Half an hour later we both arrived stoned at my student house. As a first year, I'd been allocated a room by the university in a terraced road next to the campus. My dad parked outside and we rolled into the house like seasoned pros. Six of the eight other students were already there. 'Put the kettle on, fellas,' my dad cried convivially, before sauntering into the sitting room, flopping into an armchair and putting his feet up on someone's cello case. 'And while you're at it, there's a trunk in the back of the car. It'll only need two of you. Thanks, lads.' Mesmerised by his presence, two fresh-faced eighteen-year-old scientists dutifully went out and lugged my belongings up to the first floor without a word. Tea was then poured, and my dad held court for forty-five minutes with gags and stories, before he levered himself out of the chair, made his goodbyes, went for a slash, slapped me on the back and then proceeded to drive all the way home.

In contrast, my mum was momentarily teary, but generally self-contained and quietly supportive. She wished me luck, told me the fact that my girlfriend was going to the University of East Anglia while I was going to Hull would 'work itself out in time' and said she'd write often. And so she did; and with it started a new kind of relationship between us – at a distance, through correspondence, where she painted her life in comic, tender and thoughtful tones. If my dad needed the cut and thrust of a one-to-one alliance to come alive, it was as though the opposite were true of my mum, and it was humour and affection from a distance that seemed to make her more herself. She wrote not long after I'd left:

> The beech in front is bare of leaves, and there are tons on the path. John Kentish tries to move them – one of the labours of Hercules. Had a mini bomb scare in Tottenham Court Road last week. It was a hoax of course. Interviewing Ian Dury at Polydor tomorrow. If you want any records, let me know. Two LPs, perhaps. Also doing Judy Buxton from the RSC, so perhaps we could *blag* them [for tickets] sometime too! I am really struggling to think of anything to tell you.

The most exciting is that we now have all the tits and finches on the bird-feeder on our kitchen windowsill. Eyeball to eyeball confrontation with coal tit during washing-up. We miss you, dear. Christmas will be quiet.

On the one hand I felt her writing flowed naturally with engaging pathos and timing, but also I thought that she enjoyed being unmediated by my dad's presence in her letters, that she could be herself, and there was an element of writing to cheer me up, to make me laugh, to make me like her and miss her. Stuff like:

Was going to finish but might as well drivel on. It's Katie Boyle's birthday today! Gosh, I bet you're thrilled. Kenny Everett was. He mentioned it on the radio. Milkman very late as the Pope was in Roehampton by 7.30 a.m.

Just written 1,750 words on Arthur Lowe for *TV Times* for first week in July, and received my ticket for my holiday in the Pyrenees. Do you want anything? After-shave? Espadrilles? WALLET? GOLD CHAIN?! Glorious day. Garden gorgeous.

Going to a Salvation Army *knees-up* on Saturday at the invitation of its current headman, Brigadier *Nutty*. I joke not. Roly is accompanying me. The invite was for me plus *husband*, but I didn't think it was quite 'TW' [my dad].

Between the jokes, her antennae were still well tuned to others' feelings. She wrote:

We are having great pleasure in sitting in your bedroom window for our breakfast coffee. This is something I have looked forward to for a decade – being able to sit on the sunny side of the house now and again. I have moved the rocker and one other small chair. PLEASE, we are NOT taking over your bedroom. Merely using it whilst you are away. OK?

She could also combine both; she wrote to me 'on impulse' after my dad was told locally that a boy who'd lived in our road had got 'hooked on heroin':

The papers have been full of terrifying stories all week about the rubbish which is being sold so cheaply to kids in London. I always think of you as being mature for your years – so forgive me for writing as an anxious mother! But I do believe it is more important to be aware of the dangers and *care* about what happens to your beloved children, rather than not mention it in embarrassment. Now for the funny bits: *The Mousetrap* party at the Savoy was really rather glamorous and I was on *Nationwide* last night in close-up talking to Bob [Robert] Hardy!! The titles were right across the middle of my face – fortunately. We did a 10p Yankee yesterday and one two weeks ago. In the first Benbow won (collected £8.50). Yesterday Tracey's Special romped in at 12–1 . . . and Bernard Hepton gave me 2,000 postcards last month!

Her collecting of old postcards, like many of her pastimes, endured derision from my dad, as if it were another manifestation of all that was staid and conventional, and should therefore be renounced. But she carried on regardless and I

221

wondered if it began as a way of documenting a life she felt was otherwise invisible. She had favourite, if unsurprising, categories – the theatre, Romany life, Barnes, birds, Fleet Street – and each month the demure *Picture Postcard Monthly* appeared in the flat to vie with my dad's *Jazz Journal* and *Private Eye*. On Sundays, in my late teens, she raided Baldur's, the chaotic antiquarian bookshop on Richmond Hill, which carried a hoard of postcards among its many books. It wasn't far from home and I'd occasionally join her. Baldur's had been run since 1936 by the same man: Eric Barton. He was liverish and curmudgeonly and often greeted us gruffly with the words 'We're *closed*' until he saw who it was. He didn't mind serious collectors. When she wasn't collecting for herself, my mum selected apposite old postcards for family birthdays and occasions: I always got something musical; Tracey, often a female poet or a suffragette. I have many from the Hull days. The card would often be attached to a second-hand present. In Romany tradition – at least that's what I took it to be – she enjoyed recycling family relics and badly gift-wrapping them, imbuing them with a significance that was lost on most of us. A chipped sandwich tray. A pair of 'Gipsy' Smith's braces. Most of us would have been happy with a book token.

During my first year at Hull I began having my earliest success with my music, and then with the music I was writing and recording with Tracey. We'd met on our first day on campus – a meeting of strangers half planned. We were already both signed separately to the same small independent record label in London straight out of school, Tracey with her first band Marine Girls, me solo. It was suggested by someone at the label that we look each other up. A neat coincidence. Two likeminded souls in a remote northern town. Reviews and mentions and then full pages started to appear in publications like *Melody*

Maker and *NME*. Of course both my parents were bowled over in their own separate ways. As late as 1997 my mum faxed me on tour saying that 'to wake up *in* Los Angeles and read a feature on oneself in the *LA Times*' – something that I'd told her had just happened to me – was her 'idea of bliss', so you can imagine how she felt when the coverage first started coming in. It was like an exquisite validation, and symptomatic of what I have often thought about her outlook on life: that any public existence is only of worth if someone is writing about it.

She adored attending our concerts. She requested an AAA (Access All Areas) tour pass and used the stage-door entrance – not the front door – whenever possible. Her desire to then hang around the murmuring inner sanctum of backstage preparations was sometimes as claustrophobic as it was endearing. In her sixties, she arrived like a discreet pearly queen, adorned in badges from previous shows, sporting an Everything But The Girl baseball cap at a spry angle, and I'd turn and find she'd been standing and observing me from the doorway of a dressing room – her face reflected in the Hollywood-bulb mirrors on the opposite side of the room, a picture of composed glee – waiting to catch the eye of her clever famous son. She would ask how the 'notices' had been for the tour ('*Notices* were what you got performing in the theatre after the war, Mum'), and then slip away to her seat for the show, only to return again – perhaps on the arm of the tour manager – to soak up more. Afterwards, she labelled her backstage photographs with arrows and comments in the margins indicating who the 'minor characters' were in the background – somebody's granny, a roadie – in case, I imagine, she thought history might need them.

I used to wish sometimes she had been more *unimpressed* by it all, more outside the circle, less keen to be a character *inside* the circle. I think I would have preferred seeing her a few days after a concert and had her greet me with an artless maternal hug, and a '*Did* you, darling! I almost forgot! How *marvellous*! Let me get that kettle on and you can tell me *all* about it.' Perhaps I was uneasy with the implication that my world was just a variation on her world, that it was all just another kind of showbiz. I was from a new generation – and in particular the year-zero generation of post-Punk. I was naturally keen to distance myself from *any* previous generation, in the delusion that we were somehow different. Now, of course, with hindsight, I see that it was just more showbiz, even if it was our generation's showbiz.

My dad's reaction was more complicated. On the one hand he was just plain proud: our early recordings borrowed jazz stylings; I'd written my first horn arrangements; and we'd featured one or two older established musicians he had introduced me to at the Bull's Head – the alto sax player Peter King, and trumpeter Dick Pearce. Early on he wrote me a rare letter:

Dear Ben . . . I can hardly visit Seal's [the local butchers] without the young staff patting me on the back. You can't imagine the damage done to my suede jacket by hands – which though well-meaning and approving – are fresh from slicing a pound of offal. '*It's Ben Watt's father again.*' . . . It's all great news of you both. I am so very proud for you, and of you. We both look forward avidly to the music press this week. Write again soon, even if it's only a blank cheque . . .

Amid the jokes, I took the compliments. As we progressed, however, I know he wrestled with the pop vocabulary of our recordings, and was more comfortable when the musicianship rather than the concept or intent was to the fore. Backstage I'd sometimes see him struggle to pay tribute to a performance, while remaining true to himself and not hurting our feelings. ('Very direct.' 'You are unique.') Not famed for his diplomacy, at least he was trying. Perhaps in his heart he dreamed I'd be a jazz guitarist – he bought me Joe Pass and Louis Stewart albums when I bought my first guitar. Instead I had moved into the idiom he had rejected, and then made a success of it. It must have left him conflicted, and sometimes – when he drilled right down into it – perhaps just silently and confusedly envious. In later years my mum said that at times of stress in Oxford he would retire to the kitchen and play our music on the stereo – particularly the jazz-inflected albums *Eden* and *The Language of Life* – so I know, in spite of any reservations he may have had, they had great meaning and resonance for him.

Reading back over my mum's letters to me at university, among her quips and ruminations and the excitement over the music, I spot the little nervous pieces of news about unexpected pockets of work for my dad: a few welcome days of decorating for a friend; a chance to conduct a couple of his old arrangements for a local big band; some semi-pro nights at a hotel run by friends outside Cobham. Each mention seems so precious. A thin lifeline. They rise like distress signals, and the letters don't seem quite so funny. I can picture their lives at the time: just enough work at the *TV Times* to keep my mum busy, but long unrelieved days of emptiness for my dad; and all the emptier since I'd left home.

27

October 1983

Monday. 5.50 a.m. *After a wakeful night.*

Another week begins and I wake with those familiar feelings of suppressed dread and anxiety as to what will happen today, tomorrow and the next day.

I heard him come in before 1 a.m., and wonder whether the evening did anything to heal his tortured spirit. Today I go up to my office at the *TV Times* – a pleasure – I am all by myself and busy and interested all morning. By lunchtime, a small niggling thought insists on returning – will the car be in the car-port when I get home? If it isn't, I try to go into neutral – a gear in which I seem to waste a great deal of time at the moment. It is a kind of numbness which means I waste less energy worrying and wanting to throw things, and working up to bouts of tears.

As I lie here in bed I think for the hundredth time how I love and pity this man I have married. I think again and again of what steps I would take to try and fill my mind: I would get my *TV Times* and *Radio Times* and mark daytime programmes I really wanted to watch. I would make sure I could see good series like *Jane Eyre* by changing my timetable. I would look up some *new* ways of cooking vegetables. I would get down some manuscript paper and try to start writing an arrangement for Willie's band. I would get the compost heap ready for us. I would go to an afternoon film. I would try to structure my life differently. Mark books off in the paper and actually buy them or get them from the library. I would ask the Barnes Community Association if I could do anything with my car. But these are PIPE dreams.

My husband does none of these things because he doesn't feel it worth the effort to try – he is too wrapped up in his own more global and personal problems. Basically, life is futile – apart from me and Ben and his music and jazz in general. How am I going to cope with watching the Tory Conference this week? How tragic and pathetic that such a subject should make my heart, physically, beat faster, and a kind of sick despair come over me.

I do not blame him. He is dealing with life in the only way he knows how . . . but with his charm, talent, personality – it's a crying shame.

And I get to look more haggard each day as he gets more bloated.

And finally – each man is an island – what a tragedy. What goes on in his head – how does he feel, really and truly, now that he drinks fairly extensively? I hardly ever get the chance to spend time with him without some effect of alcohol. But I don't believe it is time to call Al-Anon. The fearsome thing is that I do not know when that moment is imminent. Like Jennie, I feel totally helpless and overwhelmed by the enormity of the problem.

It's OK for dear Ben to leave a note saying 'Look after

yourselves', meaning, don't go dramatically off and leave him to fend for himself (even for 24 hours) because it does no good. And he's right. But it's this holding back my real self all the time that is so exhausting. We are always talking on the bloody 'Dear Katie' page about self-respect. Where has his gone? He has so much to be proud of. Why does he make every effort to destroy himself? Is it just a male menopause crisis? This obsession with the world situation is desperately hard to cope with. I feel guilty that I cannot feel as he does – and yet, isn't there something rather perverse about his intolerance. We can no longer watch *Agatha Christie, Reilly*, the news, medical programmes or political diatribe of any kind. How can I broaden my own interests so that my life is not exclusively devoted to him (apart from my work)?

O, the unanswered questions. The defeatist feel to the whole of my life is wearing me out.

It must have been dark outside when my mum sat down in her study and wrote those words. The sun doesn't rise until after seven in October. The flat would have been quiet. Not even the clicking of the cold copper pipes of the central heating as they slowly expanded with the first rush of hot water would have broken the silence; not before six. I picture my dad asleep in the other room, her in a nightie and overcoat at her desk, and the sound of her fountain pen scratching out the pale blue ink on to the large plain pad of ruled paper.

There is no date in the blue ink. Just the day and the time. First thing on a Monday morning. Something pressing on her mind. But it has been added above – *October 1983* – in pencil, and the same pencil has been used on the envelope to write *Personal – Come On, Romany*. There is something about the two pencil inscriptions of the afterthought, as if written a little time later, at the moment the urge to write the rest of it all down had partly subsided, at the point the envelope was sealed and put into a drawer – another sad document for family posterity carefully dated.

But oddly it made its way into my mum's silver-grey Harrods gift box of souvenirs. I found it in there along with other important things like her baby notebooks and the telegrams of congratulations, a tiny red pair of shoes, the letter from Liz Taylor, her Diploma in Dramatic Art, bundled love letters, a postcard of snowdrops bought on the day of her mother's death, and a graphologist's analysis of her handwriting that opens with the helpfully flattering words, *This is the handwriting of a highly intelligent, keenly perceptive woman.*

There is an engaging indefatigable tone to the phrase *Come On, Romany* which seems at odds with the hopelessness of the final line of the letter itself. Together they seem to say so much about her. Soft on the inside. Flinty on the outside. She must have considered the letter important to have kept it among all those other important things, and – as with much of her carefully preserved archive – when I read it I couldn't help but hear a voice that said, *Make me heard.* I should point out that much of her archive is interleaved with additional notes and arrows and codicils that say things like: 'Read these, then throw way'; 'Hadn't the heart to get rid of this'; 'Jennie might like these'; 'Aborted autobiography notes – for family only'. They are signposts that tease and hint and cajole, and ultimately lead to the conclusion that one day she wanted it all known and understood.

I can also be assured the contents of the gift box represent the very heart of how she saw herself, as she was a furious editor as well as an archivist, often weeding out irrelevance and dead wood, throwing away second-rate features she had written, or inconsequential letters, as though she were aware she would be judged soon and was clearing a path to the essential stuff. She made a few wrong calls in my view; ninety per cent of her journalism was purged in the late nineties. She threw away many scrapbooks, keeping only her favourites and interviews with the most famous. I also went in search of one of her much-loved treasures – a first edition of Gabriel García Márquez's *One Hundred Years of Solitude* that I knew had been given to her by Richard Burton in Mexico complete with a dedication to her from him on the title page – but it was nowhere to be found; not among her souvenirs, nor on the bookshelf of any family member. I'd all but given up finding it when a random web search for the words 'Richard Burton' and 'Romany Bain' threw up a link to a second-hand bookshop in Southport, Lancashire. Sure enough, it had the very copy. She must have sold it or given it away to charity in the late nineties along with everything else. I bought it back. For a hundred pounds.

As for the letter, if I felt a prickle of guilt as I opened it, since reading it something *has* been understood, something that I once only sensed has been substantiated: the sheer punishing weight of living with a man with chronic depression. Now, in our age of therapy, and footballers who unburden themselves, it seems so clear that what she endured was beyond what anyone should have had to put up with, and yet no one talked openly about depression back then – especially the depression of a proud Scottish working-class jazz musician. In the year it was written my mum was editing an agony aunt and advice page with Katie Boyle – 'All black dogs, love rats and adult virgins,' she once said to me, 'and tips on how to keep your china sparkling' – but no one was around to give *her* advice when she got home. I'm glad I opened the letter. It made it real. I hugged her when I next saw her; although I didn't mention what I'd read.

I met my aunt – my uncle Glyn's second wife, and yet another 'Jean' in this story – in the spring of 2012. She was eighty-two when I turned up at her tiny terraced cottage in Kentish Town. She had lived less than two miles from me for the past twenty-seven years – Glyn having died suddenly in 1977 and she then remarrying and relocating to London in the eighties – and I couldn't think of a good reason why we hadn't met more regularly, other than our family are experts at keeping their distance. We reminisced about a lot of things, but one thing that stayed with me was when she said she had always thought of my dad as 'quite a sad man underneath'.

'It was in his eyes,' she said. 'I felt he drank to come out of himself, to make himself braver.'

After she'd said it, it suddenly seemed so obvious: underneath the jokes and the charm and the rambunctious exterior was a small melancholy man from Glasgow, who just wanted everyone to love him and his music. I wondered why it hadn't struck me sooner or as clearly. And then I remembered that in 1982 a local London jazz ensemble, the Willie Garnett Big Band, had unexpectedly played a couple of his old arrangements – twenty years after he'd written them – and he'd been invited down and allowed to conduct them himself and bring them to life in front of a small back-room audience in the suburbs. He was home late that night. My mum had gone to bed and left out a note on the kitchen table, asking him how it had gone. He slept in the spare room so as not to disturb her, but not before writing on the bottom of the note: 'I was LION-ISED!' Can we ever be loved enough?

Included with the letter my mum wrote to herself that early October morning, in the same white envelope, was another note on the same paper written in the same pale blue ink, most likely around the same time. She must have written it for my dad to see, although it's not clear whether she left it out for him, or decided against it at the last minute and sealed it up with the other one. Not that it matters. It reads:

> I don't like myself very much, you know. I didn't *want* to be matron – with all that word implies. I would have loved to have someone in charge of me – to make fun of my idiosyncrasies and look after me. But you are teaching me that people are so insignificant, so doomed, so manipulated, so corrupt, that there is no point in anything any more except jazz and Ben. Is our personal life of so little value that it doesn't matter if we both become strangers? I suppose not.
>
> I don't *want* to talk to you about the 'Dear Katie' page.
>
> If you had a *job* – an equally boring 9–5 job – neither of us would talk about our own work to each other.
>
> That is another of my dilemmas. I work here – basically to keep you company – but I know it's all a charade, you being interested in what I do. It's not natural or normal. But what else can I talk about? We never go anywhere – we have no friends – we never go out for a meal or visit anyone. I can't help boring you. We don't go to a play, and now, rarely watch TV.
>
> I am as unhappy and frustrated as you are in many ways. Sorry about it.
>
> R

When I read both of them now they make me sad. And they bring to mind the questions my mum put to Liz Taylor in her two major interviews with her published in 1970 and 1971, questions I now realise she must have asked herself a thousand times. As they sat overlooking the ocean in San Felipe in 1970, she entreats, among a scant selection: *Whose fault is it if a marriage goes stale?*; *Should a woman try to change her husband?*; *How is Richard as a stepfather?*; *Do you have many close friends?* And then, when they met in Rome in 1971, she went on to ask: *Have you thought what you would do if Richard wanted to leave you? Would you try to stop him?*; *Have you ever tried to change him?* In context they pass by in a glamorous whirl of opulence and fame, but extracted on their own they strike me as the saddest of questions.

The summer before the letters – the summer of 1983 – I had come back down to London from Hull with Tracey to finish writing and recording our debut album as Everything But The Girl. We were twenty. The atmosphere between my mum and dad was like an electrical storm. My half-brother Toby said we could house-sit for a few days at his tiny place in Kingston if we needed to. It was right on the Robin Hood Roundabout on the edge of the main A3 in and out of town. Behind us were the vast open spaces of Richmond Park but in front the traffic thundered past day and night. We recorded the final primitive demos for *Eden* there on a tiny four-track cassette deck, waiting until late at night to record the vocals when the roads were quieter. We then stayed uneasily with my mum and dad in early September while we recorded the album in Willesden at Robin Millar's Power Plant studios. We gave my mum some money towards the phone and washed up our breakfast things before we left each day, but we barely saw each other. We'd walk half a mile across the common and catch the train from Barnes to Richmond, then change on to the Broad Street Line and travel up to Brondesbury Park. From there we'd walk the final mile to the studio. It could take an hour and a half each morning. In the evening Robin treated us to a minicab back.

The day after we finished, we caught the train back up to Hull, even though term didn't start for a couple of weeks.

Not long after we were back on Humberside, my mum called me with the news that my dad had drunk his last drink at the Bull's Head. In a confused garbled story it seemed he'd had a public altercation with the new manager and walked out, vowing never to return. 'He said the new manager tried to *humiliate* him in *front of everyone*,' my mum said. 'He'll barely talk about it.' It seemed impossible at the time; the Bull's Head was his home from home. As more came to light, there was a rumour that he was accused of 'being caught with his hand in the till', which, I suppose, while possible, seemed so far-fetched. Others suggested he had become too disruptive and vociferous on a regular basis, and the new manager simply wanted him out, and used the accusation as a ploy to make him leave. I have never got to the bottom of the story; suffice to say it marked a fork in the road, as my dad never *did* return, nor would he drink in *any* of the other pubs in Barnes from that day on. 'Barnes is over for me,' he said casually but firmly a few weeks later. It seemed oddly preposterous.

Instead he took to quietly drinking at home. 'At least I can keep an eye on him,' my mum wrote. 'He gets mildly squiffy here . . . which is so much safer.' With Barnes cast adrift, I was suddenly conscious of a new future looming, and amid all the usual stories of a week away on a farm or a boat, or the annual visit of my dad's mother, or birdlife at the kitchen window, an elegiac tone started to appear in her letters:

The road is emptying. The Kentishes advertised in the *Sunday Times* and the *Observer* last Sunday and the Warhursts are also putting their house on the market . . . Even Anthony and George have sold their house. They are splitting up, I believe. The Paynes' house had a SOLD notice. A young family move in there 'after Easter' . . . We got the tree surgeons to vet the poplar and they say it is *rotten* three-quarters of the way down, so by the end of spring, I think ours and the one [next door] will be felled.

By 1988 our house had been sold too.

28

'Up from London, are you?'

The minicab smelled of Richmond King Size. Lots of them. A glass air-freshener was attached to the air-flow vent on the dashboard sweetening the fag haze with a virulent blast of vanilla. I tried to adjust my position in the back seat so I couldn't be seen directly in the rear-view mirror.

'That's right,' I said.

I could half see his profile. Fishing waistcoat over a black T-shirt. Two indistinct old tattoos in smudged ink on his left forearm. A little bit of eczema on the line of his jawbone. His hair – no hairstyle to speak of, just vaguely cut round the ears – was flattened and smeary on the crown at the back. Straight out of bed and into the cab, I thought. He shuffled on his wooden-bead seat-cover so he could see me in the mirror with one eye again.

'Just for the day?'

How could he tell? 'Yes.'

'What line of work are you in, then?' He cornered the six-year-old Nissan Primera quickly out of the mini-roundabout at the top of the road from Bristol Parkway Station, and I had to stop myself from falling sideways on the back seat. I put my right hand out but the grey velour loose cover – a prerequisite for the leaking curry bags and slopping bottles of a Saturday night's work in town – was badly fitted, and my hand kept moving as the fabric stretched. I had to grab the door handle with my left. As we straightened out, I reached for the seat belt behind me but it jammed in the mechanism and wouldn't come out of the roller.

'That one don't work,' he said, half over his shoulder. 'Don't worry, I aren't going to kill you.' (When my boy, Blake, first heard a Bristol accent, aged five, he leaned over to me in the cab and whispered, 'Is he a *pirate*?')

'No problem,' I said, trying to stay detached.

His mobile rang in the cup holder. He reached out a thick hand and switched it off. 'Only be my mum. I'll call her back when I drop you off.' He pulled a biro from a collection held on by several rubber bands around the sun visor above his head, and scribbled something on the memo pad that was fixed to the windscreen with a suction cup.

We drove a little further in silence.

'You down on business, then?' he said.

'No. Visiting my mum and dad.'

'Can't remember the last time I went out on the A38 up towards Tockington. Live in the village, do they?'

'No. In a care home. Residential. Up out of the village on the other side.'

'I see. Nice and quiet, I bet.'

'Yes, it is. My half-brother lives in the next village along, so he keeps an eye on them.'

'That's nice. You need your family around you.' He gripped the dimples on his racing steering wheel cover, lifted himself up momentarily, reseated himself on his wooden beads, and scratched the tattoos on his forearm. 'My mum's on her own.

Hates it. Gets lonely. Sometimes I'll have her in the cab with me,' he said, his voice brightening. 'Most of the customers don't mind. I have her in the front, up here in the passenger seat, of course. She's not in the back with the customers. Although she *would* be if she had *her* way. She *loves* her talkin', she does. Your mum a talker, is she?'

'No, not really.'

'Ah! The *strong, silent type*, I bet!'

'Yes, you could say that.'

'*Strong* and *moody*.'

'Sounds like you know her.'

'*Do* I?' he said with a note of utter surprise in his voice. He stole a startled, puzzled glance at me over his shoulder.

'Just a joke.'

He moved to catch my eye in the mirror. He was grinning. 'Oh, I get it. That's good, that is.'

He got up some speed on the Gloucester Road, then dropped down the side of Fernhill towards Tockington, the electricity pylons strung out down the valley above our heads, the cables like metal bunting heading west towards the Severn Estuary.

We drove through Tockington and up the hill towards Old Down.

At the care home, after I'd paid the fare, he handed me his business card. 'In case you need to book me in advance, or want a ride back,' he said. 'Mobile's on there. I've got to run a lady to the hairdresser's at 12.15, but I'm free after that.'

'OK. I might get a lift, but thanks anyway.' I shook the card at him as if to underline my gratitude, got out and closed the door.

As he pulled away under the cluster of tall pines that flanked the driveway I looked at the card. It was like one of the ones you can print yourself at a motorway service station. Across the middle, partially covering an image of a Union Jack, in a smart italicised font, were the words *Pinewood Travel*, and below, in smaller print, *Local and Long Distance. Safe, Friendly, Reliable.* At the bottom it said *Karl* with a mobile number and *any time 24 hrs* in brackets. I put it in my back pocket.

My mum and dad looked well. All things considered. It was April 2004. Two months since they left London. Roly had organised all of it. ('There's a place very near me. Seems very good by all accounts. And a lot cheaper than London.') They each had a single room on the first floor. They had their own furniture from the London flat – the bits that we could fit in, anyway. My mum had some of her pictures up on the walls, and their two armchairs were arranged in my dad's room so they could sit together during the day.

'This was the right move,' my dad said. 'Very clever of Roly to suggest it.'

One of the maintenance engineers had even screwed a small CD rack to the wall.

'Are you using it, Dad?' I said, pulling out a Bill Evans album.

'I am. From time to time. If your mother can stand it.' He nodded to the small portable boom-box on the side table.

I remembered when my mum had told me about sitting – at my dad's insistence – in the front row with him at a packed and sweltering Ronnie Scott's for a Buddy Rich gig back in the old days. In the middle of a tumultuous, deafening, thirteen-minute drum solo, Rich had dropped a stick. My mum had leaned over and whispered in my dad's ear, 'Does that mean he has to start *again*?'

We sat and chatted and ate chocolate biscuits. I could hear the crackle on my dad's chest when he strained to reach the newspaper from the table beside him, but their eyes were gentle and their complexions good when compared with their first Christmas at the new flat in London. My mum's red cotton blouse dropped straight down her chest; I tried not to keep looking.

'Can I take your picture before I go?' I asked.

'If you must,' she said, half joking.

As I raised the camera she held a hand up as if to say *just a moment*. She then peeled off her glasses, checked the rise on her swept-back hair and the gold sleepers in her ears, before dropping her shoulders back, pushing one slightly forward and staring straight down the barrel of the lens. While I focused, it felt as though she was taking me on – still the young actress of her mid-twenties, proud, self-aware, the audience watching – and I saw that it was *her* spotlight for a moment, not mine, and she looked strong, and I admired it. And an image came to me – a Sunday morning when I was little, creeping into their darkened bedroom, the air sour, winter light at the edges of the closed curtains, and slipping under the covers on my mum's side, and backing into her warm body, feeling the rough skin on her feet against my legs, the weight of her sleepy arm across me, the sound of her thick breathing behind me, and feeling I was in the embrace of a big noble animal.

With my eye still on the viewfinder, I turned to my dad. Unflustered, he stayed sitting back in his chair but casually rested a loose fist against his cheek, his white quiff thinner but neatly combed, his goatee bushy and recently trimmed. Patches of dry skin on his face were softened by emollient. The back of his hand was brindled with a healing bruise. His nails were spotlessly clean. As usual. And as I looked at him, he gave me the same look he'd given me all those years ago when we threw pebbles against the empty bleach bottle at the Ship Inn: half affectionate; half sizing me up.

I held down the shutter-release button and clicked.

As I put the camera down I thought of the days in the summer holidays when he was decorating and sober. I saw us jumping into the car on an afternoon off and driving up to Palewell Common to play on the pitch and putt course. Parking on the grass. Collecting the clubs and the golf balls and the small coloured plastic tees and the paper score pads from the groundsman's hut. Driving off the tee in the style of different TV personalities. 'Do it in the style of Norman Wisdom, Dad!' We'd stroll up the eighty-yard fairways, the crows calling in the elms, buttercups and daisies springing back through the mown grass. If one of us hooked a ball into Beverley Brook I'd watch my dad miraculously produce a spare from his pocket. 'How did you *get* it?!' We'd cross the footbridge for the back holes and both climb up the verge, and I'd watch a bit of amateur cricket over the fence in the Bank of England sports ground while my dad smoked a fag in the shade, and the people following us round the course got cross because we weren't playing fast enough. After the final hole, he'd tot up the score cards and always say 'Let's call it draw' even if one of us had walked it, and then we'd drop off the clubs and buy choc ices from the café in the nearby thirties park pavilion. 'Call it a reward,' he'd say, 'for all our hard work.'

A little later, Roly arrived to give me a lift to the station. His battered hatchback saloon car was a tip. Although ordained as an Anglican priest back in 1978, he resigned his parish in south London in 1990 and trained at a circus school in Bristol, before embarking on a vocational second life as a touring professional clown telling stories from his slack rope with a Christian punch-line. We've never talked about it much. There's not a lot *to* say. It is so outside my frame of reference that I often don't know where to start. I just tell myself it's a question of belief, and leave it at that. But we get on. We chat mainly about football and the family, and can share a good joke and a pint, and I respect his choices. The back seats were laid flat and all the available floor space was covered in his paraphernalia: red metal frames, ropes, juggling rings, wooden crosses, greasepaint, a foot pump. The dashboard was coated in dust and dog hair. A cold coffee beaker and a half-eaten tub of mints sat by the gearstick. The LCD screen above the radio showed an insistent warning message about the engine. The footwell was home to an empty sandwich carton and a couple of chocolate wrappers.

'They seem to be doing all right,' I said, the hedgerow brush-ing the wing mirror on the narrow lane.

'Yes, they're settling in,' he said. 'Mum seems more relaxed, now there are other people to keep an eye on Tom.'

'I worry about his chest.'

'Of course. It'll be the thing that *does* for him. A bad winter.'

'And Mum?'

'An ox. Like Nunu. She's registered down here now, and they'll keep giving her check-ups, but since the op there's a fair chance she'll be in the clear in terms of the cancer. Something else will have to get her when the time comes.'

We turned on to the A38 heading back to Stoke Gifford and the northern suburbs of Bristol.

'Do they mix with the other residents at all?'

'Did they ever! No, they stay in their room most of the time. Tom *has* to, really. There's an outing to Weston-super-Mare soon. I'll see if I can't get him a wheelchair and get them to get out on the coach for the day.'

'Thanks for doing this,' I said.

'It's fine. You did your bit in London. Jennie's near by now too. Only half an hour for her. We'll get there.'

And I looked at the road up ahead and I realised that was the thing we were all steadying ourselves for: a time and a place somewhere up ahead. When and how it would come we didn't know. Who first? In pain or in peace? Quick? Or drawn out? A future we cannot outrun.

We crested the hill and dropped down off the main road into Little Stoke and turned off by the Rolls-Royce factory – the old home of British Aerospace, where they built Concorde – the windows of the abandoned low-rise buildings on the opposite side of the road shattered with bricks and stones behind boundaries of wire fencing.

He dropped me off at Bristol Parkway Station. As we said our goodbyes and I crossed the road towards the entrance, I passed the minicab pick-up. A few drivers were out of their cabs, chatting and smoking. Near the front I saw Karl's Nissan Primera. Next to him in the passenger seat was an elderly woman. They looked like they were sharing a good joke. His mum. It had to be.

29

As the train back to London picked up speed, passing flooded meadows and fields corrugated with rain, I found myself dwelling on the big move my mum and dad made in 1988 – leaving Barnes for Oxford – and how it had sounded surprising yet so seductive. They told me they'd bought a house on the river. I pictured episodes of *Inspector Morse* and *Brideshead Revisited*: quads and clock towers; cattle grazing on Christ Church Meadow; the punts and the boat-yards; willows lolling over the Cherwell. I suppose it chimed with my enduring idealistic desire to see them miraculously lifted out of their fractious love-hate lives and transformed into well-rounded and contented members of the imaginary happy middle class. Uncomplicated, self-sufficient, loving parents with hobbies and interests. Abiding good health. Cast-iron independence. A state of grace perhaps. I daydreamed about a Strawberry Hill Gothic villa with French windows and a little river frontage, possibly a jetty. They'd certainly made a killing on the Barnes house – sold at the peak of the Thatcherite prop-erty boom. Was it too much to expect? Too fanciful?

As I approached the town from the south and drove across the resplendent gateway of Folly Bridge for the first time – the grandeur of St Aldate's and Wren's octagonal lantern for Tom Tower rising ahead of me – I forked left into the municipal one-way system of Thames Street, away from Christ Church, and turned sharp left again into the shadows, and could sense I was still on the embankment of the river but it wasn't the one I'd idly imagined.

In front of me, an arrangement of new-built narrow modern terraced houses with brown window frames huddled together in a small cul-de-sac. My first uncharitable thought was not *Brideshead* but *Brookside*. Yet as my fatuous dream evaporated I saw that my parents had chosen far more sensibly than I could ever have selfishly envisaged: a low-maintenance four-year-old modern house; warm; convenient; secondary glazing; a decent river view; off-street parking; tiny courtyard garden. In fact, just perfect if you are in your mid-sixties and looking to resettle out of the city. It also emerged that one of my mum's best and oldest girlfriends from her days in the Wrens now lived in the development near by with her husband – an acclaimed professor of radiology. They had personally recommended it. I felt a bit of a fool.

I've often wondered what they must have said to each other to pull themselves out of the bleak Barnes years of the early eighties for long enough to make the decision to uproot themselves. But when I think of it, perhaps it wasn't such an upheaval after all. There was little left to keep them: the children had grown up and left home; Katie Boyle had retired from the *TV Times* meaning the remainder of my mum's writing career was no longer tied to town; my dad had fallen out of love with the pubs. Perhaps it was staring them in the face. Even a snap decision. It was as if all that was left to them was themselves, and they had to choose. Split up acrimoniously. Or start again. With each other.

And so here I was, watching them choosing to start again. Again. Dusting themselves off. Still sustained by each other. Co-dependent. On the verge of a new moment.

My dad was on the wagon. (Again.) My mum had joined him. (Again.) But they had recently bought a dog, an affectionate springy young Irish terrier called Rosie – the same breed my dad had chosen when he lived in Blackheath after he first moved to London after the war – and 'exercise' was suddenly all the rage. It caught me by surprise. Up until then, in spite of his having spent twenty-six years living on the edge of Barnes Common and a mile from the sweeping acres of Richmond Park, walking from the bar to the Gents and back had largely been my dad's idea of a stroll, but now local maps were being scrutinised and new circular walks devised, and soon he was driving every day up to Boars Hill or Shotover to amble through the woods, whistling for the dog, marching with a cane, making small talk with other owners he might bump into, stopping for a fag, leaning on a fence.

Not to be outdone, my mum would pop out with the dog in the mornings. The downstairs kitchen had glazed doors that opened on to a tiny postage-stamp patio garden that she'd neatly stocked with a blackberry bush, a cotoneaster and a couple of vibernums. She'd open the low metal gate directly on to the treeless tarmac towpath, where the swans came right up to the concrete bank, and turn right for a ten-minute mosey past the back of the new developments along Thames Street, and up on to the rusting ugly thirties footbridge that joined St Ebbe's on the north side to Grandpont to the south. It was hardly the Ramblers' Association but it was a start.

After lunch they'd choose outings that satisfied each's interests – not one of their strong points – while steadfastly avoiding a pub. For my dad this meant a run-out in his new Mazda and a chance to enjoy the silent creak-free cabin ('What was *that*? Can you hear that rattle?') and the occasional foot-to-the-floor burst of speed on an empty stretch of country lane, the hedge-rows of the Chilterns racing past the windows. ('Can you feel that *kick-down*?') For my mum it meant a visit to a garden centre – Waterperry Gardens was a favourite – or a postcard fair or a village emporium. A dog show somewhere with an Irish terrier category could be a major highlight.

And they reminded themselves what they liked about each other: the shared sense of humour; the two of them charismatic-ally braced against the world; the daily hugs and the kisses; the gentle teasing; the enduring moments of physical attraction. They'd be back home in time for *Fifteen to One* – perhaps look-ing forward to a little *Bergerac* later on – and on summer evenings, as the sun was dropping behind the new Pembroke College dormitory building on the south side of the river, cast-ing long warm shadows into their cosy draught-free first-floor sitting room, they'd push away the near-overpowering instinct for the first gin and tonic of the evening, and smile at each other over the top of the crossword, and pour another cup of tea, or sip on a sparkling water.

The move to Oxford coincided with a brief flirtation Tracey and I had with the countryside. The same year my parents left Barnes we bought a small thatched cottage in the secluded hamlet of Winwick in Northamptonshire. It was all about the log fire and the muddy walks and the church bells, and getting away from the music business, and for a year – until we soon tired of it and yearned for London again – our lives were trav-elling at similar speeds. My mum and dad would put Rosie in the back of the Mazda and drive cross-country on the A45 for lunch and a walk. Sobriety made my dad subdued but at least we didn't argue. The novelty of it all was sustaining him. And the Christmas of 1988 was one of the happiest I can remember. My half-sister Jennie came too. Five Go Mad In Northamptonshire. Tracey cooked a fibrous nut roast and Brussels sprouts (we were vegetarians then), my dad drank Perrier water while we drank Perrier-Jouët, and by the evening we were all farting merrily round the fire. Even my mum let her guard down. 'Oh all *right* then!' she said, the last to crack during a long game of Trivial Pursuit. – 'If you're all at it, *so am I*' – and she lifted her buttock off the cushion and cut one loose with remarkable abandon. 'I've been holding it in for *hours*!'

In spite of its unforgiving new-build proportions, the new house in Oxford soon took on their imprint. My mum's paintings and posters of Romany and theatre life filled the walls. Dark floral shawls were draped over side tables and chairs. Eunice's remaining antiques – a barometer, a seaman's chest, bentwood chairs – and their own junk-shop bargains softened the corners. Autumnal paint and carpet colours of rust, sage green and apricot appeared. My dad's Ivor Novello statuette took pride of place next to a scale caravan made out of matchsticks. There were embroidered cushions, a terrarium, and in the kitchen my moving-in present to my dad – a vintage seventies Fender Rhodes electric piano to replace the acoustic piano they were forced to leave behind.

If my mum and dad drove to Northamptonshire, we paid return visits to Oxford. All four of us often drove out to Long Crendon at lunchtime where I sank a pint of Flowers while my dad stayed on Coca-Cola, and then we all pottered round the offbeat second-hand emporium next door run by a silly man called Val who wore rabbit-ears for fun, spoke in spoonerisms, and swept breakages up in his 'crush and bum tray'. My mum would find old postcards for her collection among the junk, I'd rummage through old vinyl, Tracey looked for books and ornaments, while my dad stood outside with the dog, smoking.

Perhaps as I caught glimpses of him through the window I should have realised that all of this was not going to be enough for him. It was my mum's new life in retirement we were living, not his. There was still the dog to walk to keep him active and occupied, but perhaps no one should have been surprised when his appetite for another rare plant fair or Pottery in Action soon started to wane and he was calling upstairs to say he was just popping out to 'scout out the neighbourhood'. This of course was not-very-secret code for checking out the local pubs, but he ended up disappointed. The new young Oxford bar managers were unfamiliar and standoffish, and tourists and students in noisy saloons with background chart music were never going to be his style. And so instead, unable to throw off the old urges, he pulled his familiar comforts around him and retreated to the kitchen. He found a local joiner who built him a sturdy storage unit by the back door that held all his jazz records and his hi-fi system, and in the evenings he had soon returned to his familiar routine of cooking and drinking from five o'clock and letting old records make him lachrymose and unsettled. Three hours later my mum would be left with a fully cooked meal in the warming drawer and a husband who had gone to bed while it was still light outside.

It was 1991, little more than two years since moving to Oxford, and they were back with what they had left behind in Barnes.

'Come back, Nunu, all is forgiven! What are you doing to me? Let me do what I want,' my dad wrote in a sour note left out for my mum that barely concealed his underlying unhappiness. I found it among her souvenirs.

'With pleasure,' she'd scribbled tartly on the bottom in return. 'I'd forgotten how *unpleasant* you can be.'

Why did she keep this stuff?

It felt so dark. Almost impregnable. For a while I confronted him, caused a scene in the kitchen, or wrote trite letters of disappointment, too young to realise that you can't beat a drunk with a stick. I thought everything could still be all right, and he would finally wake up and reconstruct his life, and I went on believing it for a long time.

And then in 1992 I got ill.

Very ill.

In fact, I nearly died.

More than once.

When I think of my parents and how they hauled themselves out of their slump and coped – of all the blind commitment and self-commiserating confusion from my mum, all the evasion from my dad and then our poignant reconciliation – it seems wrong to skate over those life-changing few months so quickly, but the whole story is documented in detail elsewhere, in the book I wrote about it, *Patient: The True Story of a Rare Illness*.

But when I think *past* those weeks in hospital, and think of the aftermath – when I was out of the woods, and through the awful internalised months of convalescence, and how my mum and dad visited me, still shell-shocked at the whole thing, still startled by my weight loss and shamed by my resilience – I see a beautiful photograph that Tracey (a self-confessed technophobe) took on Hampstead Heath in 1993, a year after I left hospital, and it is one of my favourite photographs: the place we all finally got to for a while.

My mum and my dad — sixty-nine and almost sixty-eight — and Jennie, then thirty-nine, had all come up to London for a Sunday roast to celebrate my dad's birthday. It was a cold bright late October day, the green leaves of summer drooping in the trees, and after lunch we wrapped up warm and walked the long Boundary Path that cuts across the Heath from the Pryors over to Highgate Ponds, beneath the broad-leafed shelter of the avenue of lime trees, past the replanted saplings from the hurricane of 1987. We turned south-east along the viaduct road, past the football pitch and the metal open-air changing room by the old brickworks, and found a park bench on the path, looking south-west down over the shallow valley and the course of Hampstead Brook below. The sun was low: amber and coppery in the western sky. Tracey took the camera and the rest of us assembled like a football team for a photograph. My mum and Jennie stood behind the bench, my dad and I sitting on the bench itself in front.

When Tracey clicked the shutter she captured my mum in a belted teal-blue trench coat, her charcoal hair tumbling out in natural waves from her crimson beret, her face set strong and serious and wilful, like some kind of resistance fighter. Jennie, in a borrowed coat and corduroy hat, has her head cocked slightly on to her shoulder, diffusing confrontation, her hands lightly and protectively on my dad's shoulders in front, her dark-lidded eyes both ardent and tender-hearted. My dad is wearing a navy storm-jacket with a white fleece lining that I bought him once for his birthday on a whim, not knowing if he would like it; it became a major winter favourite. The pale lining reflects the sun up into his meek, stone-cold-sober face. In his right gloved hand is his walking stick planted between his legs, as if gently marking the spot, as if he is saying, 'We are all here. In this moment.' He is wearing round, wire-rimmed

Lennon glasses and his hair is crinkled from the damp autumnal air. He has one of the gentlest smiles I think I can ever remember seeing on his face. An adult and a boy in one. I am sitting beside him in jeans and a woollen hunting cap and a black-leather oil-rigger's jacket, all gaunt and bearded and glint-eyed. And the low cupreous light from the October sun illuminates the faces, and the figures glow like a kind of formal religious painting. Connected. Steadfast. And when I last looked at it, I realised that all of the photos of my dad that I cherish are the ones in which he is sober.

30

A few weeks before the photograph was taken, my dad was driving the long way home to Oxford after a walk with his dog, Rosie, up on Boars Hill. The late-summer sun was shining and he had the Duke Ellington Orchestra on the stereo. In the outside lane of the motorway he gear-shifted contentedly up into fifth and eased the car up to seventy-five miles an hour. He loved driving; he always had done. He spent hours poring over technical specifications in *Car* magazine. It was such attention to detail that had recently convinced him to replace his groovy French Renault 5 with a coolly efficient Mazda 323F, and in so doing to make a radical and decisive break from years of loving voguish European cars to loving his new sportily aerodynamic yet reliable Japanese car. In fact, he was loving driving it right at that moment. And then, with no warning, his right arm fell off the steering wheel and lay like a dead weight in his lap.

In the mirror he could see two container lorries on his inside, and found he had only one arm to operate a manual car travelling at almost eighty miles per hour in the outside lane of a three-lane motorway. Instinctively he steadied the wheel with his knees and, using his left hand and the clutch, managed to swerve over two lanes of busy traffic and on to the hard shoulder, where he braked and stopped in a hail of flying grit. He sat in a daze for a few moments. Coaches and lorries thundered by. The car shuddered in the side-draught. He remembered staring at the litter and the dandelions along the crash-barrier. After a while – he couldn't recall how long – some feeling came back into his right arm. He restarted the car and drove gingerly home, where he made an appointment to see his doctor.

Unfiltered Turkish tobacco had been one of his pleasures for fifty years. In the week running up to the scare in the car he had been persuaded to give up cigarettes and try nicotine patches, after his doctor had finally succeeded in scaring him with phrases like 'onset of smoke-related asthma' and 'loss of cognitive functioning'; but it was never going to be easy. I remembered other occasions when he'd tried giving up: one time, in the seventies, he grew a beard to 'feel different', hoping it might help the transition, but it just left him quiet and morose, as though he was being forced to wear a costume and the real him was hiding inside it; a small creature in a hedge. He shaved it off within days. On another, he took up chewing gum, but it made my mum laugh as soon as she saw his jaw start moving.

At the appointment he told his doctor that on the day his arm dropped from the steering wheel he had felt his craving returning, so had tried 'doubling the dose' by wearing an extra patch. The doctor checked him over. It was clear he'd had a shock. In the end he doctor stopped short of using the word 'stroke' and instead told my parents (in language that wouldn't frighten the living daylights out of them) that he had simply 'given his nervous system a bit of a jolt', and that the unexpected extra release of nicotine had momentarily affected his driving. Even after they told me, I still thought *stroke*, or at least a mini one.

The whole episode explained why he looked so sober and clear-eyed in the photograph taken that October day on Hampstead Heath. He'd been on the wagon and off the fags for several weeks in the run-up. The 'loss of cognitive functioning', however, first flagged by his doctor, had started to shadow him.

Over the next couple of years, he started to find his morning crossword puzzles harder and he put off morning walks; getting showered, dressed and climbing one flight of stairs seemed difficult enough. Eventually in the late autumn of 1996 he went in for a scan and he was told the main carotid artery in his neck leading to his brain was 'all furred up like a kettle'.

'What next then? *Viakal?*' he'd asked the specialist drily.

'Well, we need to take it out of your neck, pop it on the table, descale it with a little wire brush and pop it back,' came the reply. (Every major procedure is treated like a tummy-ache by the British medical profession.)

'And if you don't?' my dad asked.

'A scaly piece could detach itself, get lodged in the artery, and potentially block blood-flow to the old brain. And we don't want that, do we?'

'I wouldn't have thought so.'

He was booked into the John Radcliffe Hospital in Oxford. We all knew that the procedure itself – an endarterectomy – was risky. The chance of a 'scaly piece' breaking off *during* the operation and triggering a major stroke had been mentioned, but we tried not to talk about it in the days running up to it.

I drove up with Tracey on the day. We were trying to play it all down a bit to keep my mum upbeat; it helped that we'd both been in hospitals before.

When we got word things had gone well and he was on his way back from the operating room, I went out into the hall to meet him. I'd forgotten how wide hospital beds are. Porters and nurses were pushing him along the corridor. On the outsize bed he looked old but seemed no bigger than a boy – a silicone model by Ron Mueck. His head was rolled to one side on the pillow, his eyes lolling under the effects of the anaesthetic. A square of gauze was secured around the side of his neck. His throat and eye-socket were purple and yellow with bruising, the colours of freshly cut irises. His hair was rumpled and sweaty. He looked like a featherweight ferried from the ring by his trainers after a colossal beating. I slipped alongside the moving bed and bent down so he could see me, and touched his arm. He opened his eyes. They were soft and glazed. He smiled weakly. Apparently he had said to the anaesthetist at the pre-med, 'If you turn me into a cabbage, have the decency to turn off the heat and pull out the plug, there's a good chap.'

He made a great recovery. The new year of 1997 was met with 'elation' according to my mum – not a word you would commonly associate with either of them. She wrote in a fax of 4 January: 'Dad in buoyant mood. Had his stitches out. Got a bear sticker for being brave, then flirted with receptionists.' That sounded like the old dad – masculine charm mixed with a boyish need for being looked after.

The fax machine was a new present that I'd given to my mum a couple of weeks before for Christmas 1996. She was seventy-two. I bought it in the hope it would help us keep in touch while I was away on tour, as she used to worry every time I boarded a plane, and a trip to Australia and Japan was looming. I wasn't wrong. For the next two years until it broke

– possibly from the sheer volume of traffic – she sent me more than a hundred and fifty faxes. It was more than four times the number of letters she had sent me in my entire life.

At the beginning, in early 1997, they came through at the rate of two or three a week. If we were away, she would often track down where we were staying. I checked into a hotel with Tracey in Sydney to be told a fax was waiting for us in the hotel's business centre. We had been expecting an urgent message detailing the complex promotional schedule over the next four days concerning our new album, and asked for it to be sent up to our room. A bellman arrived. 'Your schedule, sir.' The cover page was written in thick black felt-tip pen: *Fax for Ben Watt. Everything But The Girl. Welcome to Sydney! To await arrival! This page plus 2 from Mrs R. Watt, Oxford (England)*. It began: 'Sorry to have missed your call but Dad nodded off early while watching the Italian Football . . .'

Reading back through them, I am struck by the transparency of her feelings. They read almost like a live unmediated blog feed of her life at the time. There are jokes ('Main excitement here is our plumbing. We are being "rodded" right under the house. Number One stoppage but responding to treatment. Send me a fax sometime even if it is just to say HELLO') and strings of quick-fire news bulletins: the latest birdlife outside their window ('grebe in residency'); films she intends to go to *without* my dad, and reviews of ones she's seen ('Saw *Wings of a Dove* last night and felt, tho' beautifully shot, it would probably have been better left as a Henry James novel'); reactions to actors' performances on TV ('Jacobi was *riveting*'); descriptions of her new hairstyle ('On a good day Dad says I look like [the saxophonist] Peter King'); reports of visits from other members of the family; commentaries on little trips out of town on her own. All of them are delivered with a likeable, indefatigable immediacy. 'Tom and I love each other to death,' she wrote in one high-spirited and unusually perky fax of that year. 'Our relationship is built on a huge reservoir of love and affection, and at least once a day we tell each other so.' I really hoped so.

Yet in the background she also methodically outlines the slow decline of my dad in the wake of his endarterectomy; the momentary euphoria she reported when he first got home from the operation is soon replaced by plaintive requests to 'call him sometime' and the careful itemising of his forgetfulness, lapses into depression, and worsening breathing problems. In all of it, she rarely holds back from saying what she's feeling. She could dash off a page of despondency on her way out to the shops ('Dad is no longer the dozy man who says he is quite content. I have never seen him this depressed before – unsatisfied with his life, and with us') only for the opposite to arrive a few days later ('Dad starts every day by announcing how well he feels') and as a result I lashed out on a couple of occasions – under pressure and often away from home – admonishing her for expecting me to follow and respond to every little rise and fall. She wrote wounded and prostrate apologies by return. It was often impossible to keep up with, but perhaps, with hindsight, all the noise was her way of saying that she wasn't coping at all, and she was fearful of the future, and what would happen to them.

She left home for a weekend in Cumbria in 1997 to attend a special Romany Society meeting in honour of her father. She said Tom had seemed happy to let her go, and was even fine on the phone when she called twice from motorway service stations on the way back, but on her return at eight o'clock on the Sunday evening – after a six-hour car journey trapped in the back of someone else's car – he 'snapped' (as the doctor later said) and subjected her to a corrosive self-pitying attack about leaving him alone, the pointlessness of her journey, the vacuous eulogising of her father's memory, and the futility of being a socialist in a world gone mad. He then slammed the door and disappeared to his bed. He stayed there all the next day too. It was only after an emergency home visit from his doctor and a subsequent consultation with a psychiatrist to which he willingly agreed that he managed to right himself, and he fully apologised, and they stumbled on.

The doctors laid the blame on his delayed reaction to his worsening health, and we were encouraged to sympathise – and of course we did – but I remembered the way he had gone at my mum that night she got back from Rome in 1971, and it sounded as if it was exactly the same. The same depressed man. Still stuck. Still threatened. Twenty-six years later. Unable to get past himself. Now also troubled by ill health. It seemed as if they would just muddle on from crisis to crisis in ever decreasing circles.

In one of her last faxes on Valentine's Day 1999 before the machine broke and was never repaired, she wrote:

I have just given Tom my Valentine present – Sixteen solid milk chocolate figures and a solid milk chocolate winning goal. It's called 'Football Fever' and costs 99p from M&S. He has offered me lunch at Waterperry. It was today forty-one years ago that I received an anonymous Valentine and took the envelope to Brian and Elspet's to check the writing! Heigh ho. All love xxxx. *NO* reply needed!

31

stepped down from the carriage on to the platform at Paddington and realised the last bit was now out of my hands. I pictured them in the new care home near Bristol. Someone else was looking in on them, putting new name tags on their laundry, wiping the custard off the table. The uneaten tray would be cleared away unconditionally. A new doctor would reassess their tablets. A new hairdresser would do their hair. And Roly, with all his courteous, muted fondness, would be there to usher them through the next doorway. Old age is a series of halting-places. From this flat to that room. From that room to this smaller room. From that chair to that bed. Furniture is slowly consolidated and sold off, possessions shrink, until the world – more than ever before – retreats, and we live inside our own head, where we increasingly become an unreliable witness to everything we've ever done. A life finally imagined.

I thought all of that on the platform walking to the barrier and I just wanted to get back on the train and travel back up the line and put my arms round both of them, and stay until it got dark, beyond the visiting hours, beyond the moment when all the trivial catching up is done, into the moments when you can just sit there quietly not speaking, just content to be in someone else's presence who knows you, and you know them. But that stuff is so hard to get to. Life in all its awkwardness drops like a fallen tree across the track.

And even if I had pushed it, and *made* it happen – insisted on travelling, insisted on staying, insisted on being affectionate – there would still have been a moment when I would have had to get up and walk out and shut the door on them, and slip back into my own life. In the end, as in hospitals, the final visitors have to go home, and there will still be hours left in the day – and in the night – and the ones we leave behind have to get on with it. Each on their own.

It was six months before I went back. I went with Blake; he was three and a half. It was a warm late-summer's day. We caught the same train, passed through the same stations, looked out over the same fields, the embankments invaded with dense thickets of lilac buddleia, the canal boats and launches and the swollen river at Tilehurst, the sewage works, the railway workers in their orange jackets trudging, sheep and cattle unmoved near the line.

I took photos of us to show we were enjoying ourselves. Blake had had his hair cropped close for the summer – a little suedehead – and, after putting his fingers in his ears and sticking his tongue out for the camera, he sat back reflectively and silently watched the fields pass by, his favourite bear under his nose. I sat and watched with him for a bit: the open bags of aggregate, rusting unused rails in the long grass, the copses on the hilltops, the paddocks with the pony jumps and pole fences, wildflowers in the cuttings, barbed wire around the superstore, the steaming cooling towers, a Union Jack in a cottage garden, skips and pallets in the business park, cartwheeling wind turbines. Everywhere the light was hitting the green undulating land bright and clear beyond the sealed windows of our carriage. And all the while, I couldn't shake off a feeling of dread and sadness that this journey would be the one I would be making and remaking from now until I didn't have to make it any more.

At the care home, my mum and dad were surprised to see us. Roly had warned them twice and someone had looked in to remind them earlier in the morning, but when I pushed the door open to my dad's room he was dozing on his bed and my mum was at the window, her arms splayed across the sill, her face pressed to the glass as though she might be estimating how high it was to jump.

'Mum . . .'

I saw her start, then turn stiffly. 'Who is it?'

'It's me. Ben. I've brought Blake to see you too.'

My dad lifted his head off the pillow. 'Who's there?' he said.

'Oh, goodness, you startled me,' my mum said. 'I thought you were coming tomorrow.'

I could feel Blake push in close to my leg and take the fold of my jeans in his hand. 'Didn't Roly tell you? Well, never mind. We're here now. Brought you some chocolate truffles.'

Within five minutes I had helped my dad up and over to his chair, and we were all seated in a group. Blake spoke in a clear small piping voice.

'Is that your real hair?'

'What's left of it,' my dad said.

'Are you old?'

'Yes. Too old.'

On the table was a framed photograph. A crisp blue-swept day. My dad in a wheelchair in an Everything But The Girl baseball cap; it looked as though it had been put on his head by someone else, but he was beaming straightforwardly into the lens. My mum was on the handles behind, no hat, shoulders back, tight-lipped and withdrawn. Weston-super-Mare's iron promenade railings and wide sandy beach rolled out behind. Roly had warned me they might be going. It seemed implausible, as though they had been Photoshopped on to the background and had never really been.

'How was it?' I asked them, gesturing to the photograph.

'Ludicrous,' my dad said.

Fifteen minutes later he had chosen to climb back on to his bed while the rest of us went down to the garden. Clouds had drifted in from the west and the sun was gone. An autumnal coldness was in the air.

'Chase me,' Blake cried, spying a small ornamental rose garden surrounded by a tall yew hedge.

'I think Granny is too tired to chase you.'

'Chase me!' He darted towards the roses.

As if responding to a challenge, my mum unlinked her arm from mine and padded towards the hedge.

'You OK, Mum?' I said. 'You don't need to.'

She walked on heedless. 'I'll catch you! I'll catch you, I *will*!' she said loudly. It sounded almost stentorian.

'Granny's chasing me!'

And I had an image of myself in the garden in Barnes – a little boy. The rockery rose up at the back. I could run up the steps past the low firs to the poplars along the back wall and hide behind the trunk of the one by the compost heap, and I saw Nunu in a straw bucket hat creakily clambering up towards me to find me, and me counting out loud to ten and thinking she was too slow, and it would be more fun if it was my dad and he was roaring like a lion.

My mum picked her way along the back of the hedge then appeared in the archway on the opposite side of the rose garden unexpectedly. 'I can *see* you!' she cried abrasively. She had lifted her arms up and had crooked all her fingers into claws and contorted her face into an awful grimace.

Blake squealed. He hadn't seen her. He span round. 'No! Not *that*. Not *that*! Not a *monster*, Granny.'

The game was spoiled.

Never quite the appropriate gesture or response: how many times had I said that to myself about her over the years? Too much this. Too much that. Too much effort. Too little effort.

'Is the old man still up there?' Blake said, his face still damp with tears, as we were walking back.

'Yes, the old man is still up there,' I said. 'He's my daddy, you know.'

'Oh,' said Blake, not raising his head.

The three of us slipped back into the lobby, into the miasma of ammonia and cooking oil and air fresheners. I helped my mum up the stairs, her body all squidgy and heavy under my hands.

'Don't let me keep you,' she said as we made it back to the room. This was her way of saying she'd had enough already, however brief a visit might have been. It was as if returning to her own thoughts were more preferable and less exerting than having to share them with other people.

'We're in no hurry, Mum.'

'Oh. I thought you'd gone,' my dad said from the bed, as we pushed the door open. 'Did you miss the train?'

'We were just down in the garden for a few minutes, Dad.'

'*Were* you now. How very civil.' He was still lying looking up at the ceiling, the back of his hand against his forehead, as though we'd caught him in the middle of a deep reflection on something.

'They're just leaving, Tom,' said my mum loudly.

I looked at my watch. We had been there for thirty-nine minutes.

'Thirty-nine,' said Roly later, as he gave Blake and me a lift to the station. 'That's good going. They kicked Jennie out after twenty last week.'

In 2005 they moved into rooms together. The care home had a ground-floor suite for couples that gave them a small bedroom each and a shared sitting room overlooking the garden. Another halting-place, I thought. And my dad's chest got a little worse. And my mum's eyesight got a little worse. Roly would take my dad to the local memory clinic for pep talks on 'functioning better'. (As opposed to getting better, perhaps.) I learned new words like 'personhood' and phrases like 'empowerment through advocacy'. I started to think about having to officially take over all the important stuff – the paperwork, the bank accounts. It starts with the furniture, and ends with the bank accounts, I thought. The courses of antibiotics for chest infections came and went like vitamin supplements.

And I wanted to applaud and respect the wholehearted efforts of the care home – the emphasis on human dignity, the wry humour mixed with compassion – but every time I arrived I struggled with everything I saw although I tried not to show it. I'd slip along the corridors, mouthing the first names and last names on the residents' nameplates on the doors, and glance uneasily into any rooms with the doors held open. A figure stationary in a chair. A shape in a bed with the curtains half drawn. A room with nobody there. And I hovered at the door to my mum and dad's room not wanting to knock and push it open for fear of seeing stripped beds and their belongings gone and someone replacing the carpet.

One morning I woke from a dream in which all the residents were slumped in the chairs in the lounge, wearing white T-shirts with the words *I may have dementia, but I still have a life* and my dad was playing the piano for them but his fingers were splintering on the keys while my mum was loudly reciting from the poems of John Betjeman: 'Come, friendly bombs, and fall on Slough! / It isn't fit for humans now, / There isn't grass to graze a cow. / Swarm over, Death!' I lay in bed and wondered if I should be there with them, and got up and started looking up train times until I recognised it as the absentee's guilt. In such moods I felt I could agree to anything that would ease their pain, as really I would be easing my own.

Yet somehow as I pushed the door to their room open each time it was like the volume in my head dropped, as if a car with bass bins pumping had finally moved off down the road, and a new quiet descended, everything muffled by the soft furnishings and the double-glazing, and in my head I heard the slow ticking of the pendulum of an imaginary clock, and there they were, my mother in the chair and my father on the bed, in a silent limbo. And I would open my mouth to speak, and our worlds would merge again.

'Don't rush,' I'd say to myself. 'Don't rush. Go at their speed. Take your time.'

32

n the half-light I knelt by the bed, the air vaporous with the smell of pine-needles, cinnamon and menthol in the high-ceilinged, cool, north-facing room. Nail scissors and an emptied Karvol capsule lay on the bedside table covered in stickers. Three sheets of folded tissue paper were stained with amber droplets next to a plastic beaker of water with a spout. Under the feet at the head of the bed two fat books lifted the frame off the floor a few inches: *Non-League Club Directory 2004*; Donna Tartt's *The Little Friend*. Perfect choices in their matching heights. Behind me the summer-evening glow still edged the outer seams of the long curtains. The sound of a jetliner passed high across the house and garden.

Rolled away from me and close to sleep was Blake – four years old – his duvet pulled up under his chin. I could sense him quietly running the silk strip of his bear along his top lip.

'Story?' I whispered quietly, my head now resting on the pillow behind him, my knees still on the floor.

'Mmm. But not the flying bed,' he murmured.

'No. Not the flying bed.' (Not the bed that lifted off the floor and sailed out between his curtains into the night sky. Not even if it did return safely. I pictured him lying there worrying about it after I'd left: *Could my bed really fly? Would it? Uncontrollably? I might never come back.)*

My face was inches from the back of his head. 'When he was four . . .' I said softly, beginning an imaginary story of the same imaginary boy, who lived an imaginary life in an imaginary house, as I had done almost every night that summer, half kneeling, half lying behind him in the soft shadowy light; I'd made up stories of tall trees and fields, boys and caterpillars, catapults, bikes, duping grown-ups, cheekiness and misrule, crossing busy roads and getting lost in crowded shops; a moment of danger, but a safe resolution; and an ending steeped in affection and protective tenderness. Always that.

When it was over, I lay there a little longer and heard his breathing lengthen and deepen, and smelled his freshly washed hair, and closed my own eyes, and wanted to follow him down the tunnel of sleep, away from my nagging melancholy and irritability. It was as if I could be him, not me. Wondrous. Charmed.

Did I have a memory of my dad putting me to bed? Not that I could remember. Only a memory of him standing silhouetted in the doorway ready to go out in a well-cut suit. It made me wonder whether I was lying there listening to my son sleep because my own dad hadn't; not that it was probably expected of him back then; perhaps he did that thing that men do in movies when they look in on their sleeping kids in a moment of crisis, and it is supposed to signify immense love and trapped emotions. Yet still I asked myself why I needed these moments with Blake so badly, why I felt so entirely enveloped in them, as though I could swim through him and have everything about him – his clear skin, his small smooth feet, his unclouded blue eyes, his sense of fear and wonder – all around me, like the waters of a pool. Sometimes it felt as though I needed them more than he needed me – which of course I looked on as a flaw, a parental flaw in me – for as soon as the thought crystallised I sensed I was hovering above the bed, observing my own mawkish scene of great self-involvement below, and a voice was saying in my ear, 'There is no place for self-regard in this. You signed the parents' contract. No conditions.' What did my dad feel when he stood silhouetted in the doorway? Perhaps he saw in me – tucked up warm and safe in flannelette sheets under a flat felt roof, a gentle night-light burning – an idealised image of *him*self as a little boy, watched from the landing by his own father. Or maybe it was more complicated than that.

I breathed in the comforting menthol air and felt the warmth of Blake's body on my face until I was hit by that deep jolt of imminent sleep. My neck muscles loosened and I sensed my head go heavy on the pillow.

Twenty minutes must have passed. I woke to feel Tracey's hand on my shoulder in the darkness. I stood up, heavy-lidded, slothful, and followed her out on to the landing into the bright light.

'You all right?' she said.

'I don't know.'

Looking back, I did know. I was running on fumes – the motor turning, the needle on zero. An accident waiting to happen. Each day I just felt wretched and withdrawn. Absent. A dark daydreamer. Often joyless and intolerant, I was forgetting appointments and errands, putting things off until the last moment, loitering distractedly in front of the family, there but not there. Falling asleep on the bed next to Blake seemed to be a kind of fragile narcotic escape.

Why so sad? Because back then I had been unable or unwilling to accept, and then act on, obvious patterns of depression in my own life, even though I'd been happy to point them out in others. Tracey could see them; she'd lived through most of them. For years she'd watched them bubble up like clouds over clear skies. I could bore you with all the perceived injustices and insecurities that have left me tearful and guilty, or paralysed and bleak, for days or months on end, but I have gradually learned it is better to see them as part of an injury I carry. Like a bad back. Debilitating but now generally treatable. How I have longed at times for more wry wisdom, an elegant stoicism, an indomitable black humour – such attributes fly in the face of dark days – but let's just accept that we are all credulous and soft, encircled by the casual affectlessness and unkindnesses of real life, and it just gets to some of us more than others.

Having said that, it is hard to avoid the violent sadness that has gathered over the heads of various members of my family. There is a black-and-white photograph from the twenties of Sandy – one of the brothers of my grandma Jean, my dad's mother; if I'd known him I suppose he'd be my great-uncle. He is sitting outside on a flight of steps. Everything is covered in thick snow; it covers most of his boots. He wears a dark-wool winter Mackinaw jacket with the collar turned up, and gloves and a flat cap. On his head is balanced a large snowball, and flecks are tumbling on to the peak of his cap. His is smiling shiny-cheeked into the lens of the camera. It is a picture of winter fun. On the back it says: *Jean's brother, Sandy: drowned himself in river (love affair?)*.

My mum's brother, Glyn, killed himself too. In 1977. My aunt Jean found him. They'd been married since the fifties when they first met working in different departments at the

Coal Board. Glyn had striven against unhappiness for years. They moved to the countryside near Cambridge shortly before his death in an attempt, Jean said, to alleviate the perceived stresses of London life. She told me how she came home from work one evening. The first thing that struck her was the silence around the house. She went in and found their dogs locked in a room in which they wouldn't normally be kept; if Glyn was napping, she'd thought, he would have taken the dogs with him, and they'd have been curled up on the bed beside him. She went upstairs and found him in their bedroom. He'd used a shotgun.

I was brought up to believe it might have been an accident, that he might have been cleaning the gun, but as Jean said, 'Who locks the dogs in a strange room before they clean a gun in the bedroom? And anyway, it was always coming. If it hadn't been the gun it would have been something else.'

Perhaps closest to home is the story of my half-sister Jennie who lived with neurosis and depression for pretty much all of her adult life. She was twenty-two when our mum let her come back home to live briefly in the flat downstairs after Nunu's death. I was thirteen. I'd pop down in the evenings after I'd done my homework to see her and her new cat. She didn't seem to have very many possessions. Although she was my half-sister she seemed unlike anyone I knew – quiet and far away yet gentle. I never understood why my mum was reluctant to have her stay. I didn't really know any of the drug and psychiatric stories then. I knew she had had a breakdown at nineteen – not that I knew what a breakdown meant, except that it had left her sad and without a job or A levels. It was only later I learned that, by the time she moved in downstairs, while my half-brothers were getting university degrees and finding their first jobs, she'd already lived with an ex-junkie, been arrested for possession, had an abortion, survived an overdose and an attempted strangulation, and experienced two long spells at Long Grove Psychiatric Hospital living among schizophrenics and addicts, where she'd undergone electro-convulsive therapy and something called desensitising where they confront you with your phobias in an attempt to cure you of them.

She stayed in the flat only a few weeks. It was the long hot summer of 1976. She played me Lou Reed's 'Satellite Of Love' and J. J. Cale's 'Magnolia' with the windows open, and when we talked she made me feel grown-up.

Aged thirty – long after she'd moved out and tried holding down her first half-decent office jobs – she was still capable of being fearful of her own family and could still hear voices talking to her through the radio, voices that could drive her from a house in the middle of the night, and make her run down an unlit country lane with bare legs to be found curled up in a cold remote barn by Ken, her distraught father. She lived on and off with a handful of unreliable, sometimes violent men, or had dead-end affairs with ones who were married and bored, but when she finally got herself sorted out and got married herself to a lovely bloke in a windswept country church on the Somerset Levels at the grand age of fifty, she asked me to be the 'father of the bride'. Her own father was no longer around – Ken died just after Christmas 1984 – and Tom was by then housebound in the care home near Bristol. I was forty-one. My daughters were bridesmaids. I was very proud.

Of course these stories make my own seem tame by comparison, but when things were then to take a turn for the worse for me with my own depression, Jennie was one of the few people I felt able to talk to.

*   *   *

I travelled heavily that summer of 2005. I flew out to Palm Springs and DJ'd at the Coachella Festival. The manicured grass of the polo fields and the vast picket-fenced business class of the VIP section made me nostalgic for the mud and unruly hedonism of festivals back home. I went on up to New York and Boston, joining the club circuit, and then headed south-west again taking in Houston, Los Angeles and San Francisco. Part of me was travelling to escape myself. I was down and I couldn't shake it off. We will always take our hang-ups with us wherever we go, but at least we can keep them moving. The itinerary helped stupefy and nurse me: comfy beds; room service; taxis; airline check-in staff; travel accessory shops; massage chairs; moving walkways and vast windows of light; airports as cathedrals to the pining journeying heart. And at the other end – for those of us lucky enough to make a living out of our self-expression – a kindly stranger who wants to promote our work is there to drive us into town, pay for our hotel room, buy us dinner, set us up in front of a supportive crowd, give us drinks, offer us drugs. What's not to like? Not much of course. A life seemingly gilded. Except that I hadn't addressed why I'd left in the first place, what it was I was running from, rather than towards.

It went on back home. At the Homelands Festival I arrived after nightfall. I drove through swirling mist and silent woods west of Winchester, my headlamps shooting ahead into the darkness, the tents and rides appearing suddenly like an extra-terrestrial circus had landed in a hollow in the land. In Paris I was led into a club in the hull of a huge moored ship on the Seine. Then Edinburgh, Malmo, Ibiza. The Electric Picnic in Ireland. Berlin and Brighton. And then back for more: a return to New York in December with San Francisco, Seattle and Hollywood thrown in for good measure. And of course, in the midst of it, were the gigs themselves. Two or three hours of indulgence and escape; glass-rattling bass and air-punching exuberance, burnished with moments of pathos and blurred melancholy; and all the time the drum, the drum; a ritual where the room is bigger than any one individual within it; a fire that gets stoked then self-sustains; societal and infectious. Clubland is a world largely without language, in which fragments of song replace narrative, text messages and gesture replace conversation, feelings replace ideas. For someone who all his life had written songs that had often been performed in hushed auditoriums to crowds clinging to every syllable, it represented something that suddenly seemed to express the way I was *actually* feeling inside at the time: inarticulate; messed up; introspective; my mood rising and falling in waves; grateful for a room of people who seemed to need the same thing.

I stepped off a plane from Los Angeles at Heathrow after a week of dawn finishes and a final night-flight of broken sleep and intermittent sinusitis on the first day of November 2005. It was as if I was testing myself. How much sleep did I not need? How many decibels could I stand? How far could I run? It was the day after my dad's eightieth birthday and I knew I needed to see him. At thirty-seven thousand feet just before I'd tried to close my eyes, I had leafed through a catalogue from The Sharper Image and dwelt on all the useless executive man-toys I could have bought him for a birthday present – an indoor golf-swing improver, fog-free travel mirrors, a bagel splitter, a shiatsu belt massager. What *do* you buy old people? Slippers? Chocolates? A rug? They seem so comforting and sensible, yet also somehow insulting.

The kids were thrilled to see me back, rushing at me, pawing at my suitcase for presents, jumping up at me with paddling hands like terrapins at the side of a tank. Wasn't I meant to return home refreshed and invigorated, ready for the resumption of normal life with equanimity and renewed zest? In reality I felt the same as before I left, if not a little worse. Shrink-wrapped in my own world. Jangly. Apprehensive. Not helped in the least by being down on sleep.

Forty-eight hours later, jet-lagged and guilty, I got into the car to drive out to see my dad and my mum in the new care home near Bristol. By the time I reached the M4, my eyes felt sand-papered and my hands were trembling on the steering wheel. The tissue inside the back of my head seemed to be flexing involuntarily, pushing into the hard bone. The traffic slowed then stopped near the junction to the motorway from the Hayes bypass. I was staring at the concentric rings on a flyposter wired to a lamp-post by the crash barrier: *Back To 88 Old Skool House Rave All Dayer You Know It's Gonna Be Fireworks*. A van honked behind me. A gap of three cars had opened up in front of me, I hadn't noticed. I signalled an apology into my rear-view mirror.

I drove round the roundabout under the motorway and missed the exit. I drove round again, hugging the inside rail, and missed it again. This time deliberately. And then I did it again. This time indecisively. And then I just wanted to lie down and sleep. A metal signpost in the tall grass of the roundabout flashed by amid the trees and the underpass: *Welcome to the Field of Hope*. And then I was shouting at myself inside the car, 'Why, why, why?' and had started to drive back the way I came. Another lamp-post: *Cash Paid 4 Cars*. And then another – dead flowers wilting in cellophane. The barriers were strewn with litter – split sandbags, styrofoam cups, Lucozade bottles, empty plastic bags wafting like little ghosts. I kept driving, retracing my steps. When I got home, having managed only fifteen of the one hundred and twenty-two miles to Bristol, I went upstairs and climbed on to my bed fully clothed and pulled my knees up and lay there for a long time. So this is what a wall feels like, I thought.

I told Tracey I still had to go to Bristol, so two days later I pulled myself together and took the train instead.

'It's not been good,' said Roly, collecting me from the station. 'Mum's near silent. They've had to change the carpet. Tom can't get to the bathroom quickly enough. He can't see it coming. It was all over his slippers yesterday. The smell has been awful.'

I looked out at the fields. First I saw an image of my parents forgetting the small, often comic, insignificant things, such as where they put the car keys or the name of that face on the television. Then must come bigger, more significant things: what day it is; how to work the cooker. Until finally must come the dangerous and demeaning things they didn't think it was possible to forget, such as what thirst feels like, what being cold feels like, what needing a crap feels like. Can you just forget to drink? Forget to keep warm?

At the care home I sat with my mum in the window of their room.

'You needn't stay long, dear,' she said. 'It's all beyond comprehension.'

'Where's Dad?'

'In there, I expect,' she said, gesturing with her hand, her fingernails as grey as a winter sea.

I got up and walked towards the doorway to a little darkened room. In the shadows I could see the bed. A shape was rolled away from me. I took two or three steps. The shape stirred. As my eyes adjusted I could see him lying on his back.

'I heard you arrive,' his voice said. 'Sit me up.'

I got him upright and swivelled him round. Wilting skin. Mismatched pyjamas. We sat on the edge of the bed side by side in the shadows, neither speaking for a moment. His breathing was laboured.

'Happy birthday. Belatedly,' I said, looking at the floor. 'I didn't know what to bring you. So I brought . . . myself . . . eventually.' And as the words came out of my mouth so did an unexpected heavy breath, following the words out like a tremulous gust ushered by a closing door. And then there were lots of tears in my eyes, spilling over on to my cheeks and my shoulders were rising and falling, and I didn't think I could stop easily. And I felt his arm come round my shoulders, and his other hand squeeze my forearm, and his head came close into me, as if he was about to tell me a secret, and he rested his cheek on my shoulder and his voice was saying quietly, 'I know.' And then again gently, 'I know.'

Christmas came and went, and then I had my breakdown.

33

On 18 May 2006 I was sitting in a large dark ground-floor room in Harley Street crying at the unknown bald man in front of me. I'd tried to tell him all I knew: how I'd driven Tracey to think about leaving me; how I'd trampled all over the few days she'd set aside for recording her first solo record in twenty-five years; how I was unable to pick up a pencil or plug in a guitar; how I considered myself a false, inhibited parent; how I lacked any authenticity in my work; how violence and pain on the TV made me cry, especially the newsreel footage of that man trapped under a collapsed roof in Poland, his torso rising and falling like a hand-puppet; how I was shouting at the children all the time; how I couldn't even face seeing them, the way I felt yesterday, and slipped out of the house when I heard them come home from school, and drove the car aimlessly in slow-moving heavy traffic, before pulling over on the side of a busy road and watching a set of traffic lights change over and over and over again, and closing my eyes and falling asleep for forty-five minutes to shut it all out while the mollifying rain drummed on the roof; how I felt I was never catching up; how I could not cope with the detritus of home life, the endless tidying, the clutter, the dishwasher, the loose socks, the sweeping, the fingermarks, the chipped paint; how I hated my bald patch, and the little bits of knobbly skin appearing on the backs of my hands; how I couldn't taste or smell anything; how I'd been to see a counsellor recommended by a friend a few times and not liked her very much but learned new things that troubled me even more like *somatising* and *resistance* and *adult child* and *narcissistic parents*; how my father was in hospital on a nebuliser and couldn't really breathe any more, and how I'd just been to visit him on the train; how I thought both my parents suffered from depression; how I had been unable to effect any change in their lives when I thought I'd be able to; how my uncle had killed himself although I barely knew him; how I'd been through bad periods before – going right back to the eighties – but got over them, although I'd twice been prescribed Venlafaxine and it'd calmed me down but left me feeling vacant and packed in cotton wool; how I knew it was all just a chemical imbalance in the brain, but it didn't feel like that; how my half-sister had been in Long Grove Psychiatric Hospital; how I'd survived a life-threatening illness that I wasn't expected to survive; how I still had flashbacks; how some days my black mood invaded the house like a fog; how I was having bad dreams that were making me sit up in the night and shout; how I was brimful of tears and as soft as a peeled egg; how I often felt I was lying at the bottom of the deepest barrel looking up to a tiny patch of grey sky; how Tracey was overwhelmed and frightened, and the other night didn't know who or where we were any more.

He made notes with a blue fountain pen while I talked. I had only stopped because the tears had made talking impossible. There were tissues sprouting from a square box on the table next to me. I was sitting in a wing chair. It was protective.

He put the lid back on his pen and clicked it shut, and leaned back in his chair.

'Well, you'll be pleased to hear the prognosis is very good,' he said with a smile. 'You have a recurrent depressive disorder. How serious? I'd say moderate to severe. You are extremely vulnerable. The shorter the gaps between episodes, the heavier the depression. Soon they will happen spontaneously without a trigger if untreated. You have a strong family history. To be honest, you probably should have been on anti-depressants twenty years ago.'

I walked from his room that day into the undimmed London afternoon, clutching a prescription for tablets that were to leave me car-sick and somnolent for days, with the promise that when I'd taken them for a few weeks and settled down I could talk to someone properly, someone sympathetic he could recommend who would understand and help me get on top of it all.

That night I wondered if the clouds hadn't lifted a little, and I gave the kids the biggest hugs that left me wet-eyed over their tiny shoulders. Blake drew a picture of a lion, a tiger, a palm tree and a lizard with a massive tongue that curled round and round the page before ending in a speech bubble that said *The End*.

'Were you five once?' he said, apropos of nothing.

'Yes,' I said.

'Were you happy when you were five?'

I felt myself start to cry. 'Yes, I think so.'

'Was Mummy five?'

'Yes, she was.'

'Did you know her then?'

'No, we hadn't met.'

'How old was I?'

'You weren't born yet.'

It was clearly another fact he thought he needed to take away and ponder. He blinked a couple of times.

'Oh,' he said thoughtfully, and I pictured him walking back from the rose garden after being chased by my mum with the same look on his face. And I could hear the girls laughing and playing in their room and I thought how they all thankfully still seemed so happy in spite of the chaos I had brought.

Then Tracey got home from the studio and we sat and talked.

Two days later I was woken early by the sound of the phone. As I reached for the receiver I glanced at the clock. It was 6.33 a.m. No good news ever arrives at 6.30 in the morning.

'Ben, it's Roly.' He sounded different. Quavering. 'The hospital just called. They said that Tom died in the night.' He couldn't quite pronounce the word 'died' properly. It came out with a squeak.

'OK,' I said. I felt in neutral. 'What else did they say?'

'It was a staff nurse. She just said, "Is that the Bain residence?" Not much else.'

'OK.'

'They've asked me to go down. Do you want to see him?'

'I don't think so.'

That's all I can remember of the conversation. Perhaps not much more was said. Just the bare facts for now. I said I'd call Jennie. Roly would tell our mum and his brothers. I hung up. Tracey had guessed, but I said it anyway, 'My dad died last night,' as if to make it real. She reached out to hold me and I leaned in for a moment awkwardly, but then rolled on to my back and closed my eyes. If I was aware of anything, I seemed to feel relief. Even though I'd been told to wait two weeks before I could expect any change, I wondered if the pills from the psychiatrist could be doing anything yet to dampen my reaction.

I thought of my dad a few days earlier when I had last seen him: the gnomic face; the stick legs; the nebuliser; the coffee stain. It seemed like an outlying memory. Distant and still. And then a train of thought led me to the photograph of us all on the park bench on Hampstead Heath in the low orange October sunlight and I saw the someone I was going to miss, and I felt the first few confused tears trickle on to my cheeks.

We lay there for about an hour watching the light at the window, exchanging a few words, and I couldn't help thinking how the creaking scaffolding on the front of the house had kept me awake in the night; and how I'd lain there for a couple of hours between two and four, and at one point heard a strange noise downstairs like the sound of the letterbox slamming shut on its spring – even though there'd been no wind – and wondered if it had happened around the time he had died, and it was a message; but then I felt stupid because I'd never believed in ghosts.

Blake and Alfie appeared – Jean was at a friend's overnight – and got into bed next to us, and I told them what had happened.

'Are you sad?' Blake asked.

'Yes,' I said.

'It was sad when Miss Steele at school died too.'

'Yes. That was sad as well.'

'Is Granny dead too?'

'No, Granny is still alive.'

'Oh.'

There was a moment's silence. I could smell Alfie's hair, still so fresh and clean even after a night's sleep.

'Are you sure he is dead?' Blake said. 'He might wake up.'

'They're sure.'

I went downstairs and made coffee and took it back to bed. Tracey cried a little bit. I went upstairs to call Jennie from my studio. She was in the village shop she now ran with her husband Eddie, near the north Somerset coast. Eddie was out on a delivery.

'Hello, Jen,' I said. 'Bad news, I'm afrai . . .'

The words were barely out of my mouth and I could hear her convulsing in tears and choking on her words at the other end of the phone. It seems it was on everyone's mind. I gave her the simple facts I knew. She said she'd only been in to see him the day before and how distressing it had been: the oxygen; a little banana and some grapes to eat; the few words he had said were lost inside his mask. And then I heard her compose herself and say, 'That'll be one pound twenty, please,' and I heard the till open and shut.

I rang Roly back and said I would catch a train down in a couple of hours. He'd already been to the hospital and back and picked up a few belongings. He said they'd told him he'd died peacefully in his sleep. A little unexpectedly. His breathing had been shallow yesterday but they hadn't been expecting him to die.

I was at the care home by lunchtime. My mum was alone in her room. I sat close to her. Roly stood in the doorway already talking loudly about funeral arrangements. I wanted him to shut up. My dad had only been dead a few hours. It was impossible to tell what she was feeling. She seemed largely unmoved, no different to any other day.

'It's hard to know what I'm supposed to miss,' she said a little sternly. 'He has been away for so long.'

Afterwards as we were walking to the car, I heard her voice calling us. She had come out of her room and was at the far end of the car park. 'Roly, are you coming tomorrow?' she shouted, projecting her voice.

'Yes,' he called back.

She cupped her hands up to her mouth in the shape of a megaphone and called out matter-of-factly, 'BRING ME SOME PAPER TISSUES.'

34

I n the small car Tracey was sitting in the back. I was driving, and my mum was in the front passenger seat. It had been a largely silent fifteen-minute ride from the care home. The lanes and dual-carriageways of South Gloucestershire slid by unremarkably. I kept to the speed limits; it felt oddly respectful to drive within the law; and a speeding ticket wouldn't have looked good, not on this day of all days.

I've watched as hearses and funeral cortèges with their back-seat sombre faces drive solemnly along city streets, turning heads and slowing traffic; it seems to be the only time such deathly speed is tolerated in the frantic tarmac-grab of city driving. It is as if, as passers-by, we recognise it as an attempt to bend time to our will, to slow it down, to stave off the final death-y part of death – the burial part, the cremation part, the sound-of-soil-on-wood part – to delay it a little longer, to tidy and formalise it into an orderly moment that happens at our own speed, in our own time, not randomly and unfairly. Yet here we were bowling unexceptionally along the A38 at forty-three miles per hour, no coffin up in front with *Dad* in flowers along the side, just a lorry with *Peter Green Chilled* printed on it slowing us down, making me think for rather too long about the potential for compilations of soothing early Fleetwood Mac tracks.

'Where are we going again?' my mum said, breaking the silence.

'To Tom's funeral, Mum.'

'Yes, of course,' she said thoughtfully, her finger pressed to her lips, her eyes loosely on the road.

It was the third time she'd asked the same question in the fifteen-minute journey. Of course the care home had warned me she was confused, that we should bear with her, that the week had taken its toll, and one lapse I would have understood, but three now startled me. It seemed unfair. And so quick. As if she'd been clinging to a ledge for so long and had now just let go. And I wondered if it felt like being stoned or drunk. Dreamlike and disconnected. I reached out with my left hand and squeezed her arm.

'We'll be there in a moment, Mum. All the family are coming.'

'Where to?'

'To the funeral.'

'How kind. How did they find out about it?'

I kept it brief.

Vaguely Dutch, and isolated in the surrounding fields, the huge steeply sloping tiled roofs of the modern crematorium buildings rose out of the sleepy landscape. Viewed from the approach, it was as if four giant Lego tents had been huddled together in a paddock beside the road. The place looked barely used. Roly had said it had only just opened. Spindly young trees needing twenty years of growth to achieve the right amount of dappled gravitas lined the approach road and car park. It could have been a new superstore. I hovered, deciding where to put the car. *With those other cars over there, or was that for staff only? In this easy space right here, or is that too far away and looks like we want to make a quick getaway?* I settled on something near the main pathway to the chapel to make it easier for my mum. I say 'chapel' although not in a religious sense. Roly, who had hand-picked the location from his weekly experiences in the local funeral game for its light and airy aspect, had made it clear – having spoken to the office – that the ceremony did not have to have a religious angle. We all knew it needed to be godless; my dad wouldn't have had it any other way. I liked the way the website put it: *The chapel can be altered to create a suitable environment for a service of any religion or belief.* I presume athe-ism is still a belief. 'We might make room for a prayer,' Roly had added. 'For Mum's sake.' Or perhaps because he couldn't im-agine it all going by without one.

It was colder than I was expecting when I opened the door of the car. Winds were gusting across the empty beds and manicured hummocks of grass. The chill only accentuated the instinctive humble walk and cowed head of funeral attendance in the figures I could see approaching the building, as they hurried, not too disrespectfully, hands in pockets, shoulders forward. Rain was starting to spit. My mum was wearing her 'best coat' again – the same all-enveloping cream duvet that she wore to first visit flats in London five years earlier. Before it had seemed like a statement of flamboyance; today, it seemed like a comfort blanket. As though she were a shock victim being led from an explosion.

It was a relief, once inside, that the chapel – in spite of the disappointing weather – was indeed as light and airy as Roly had promised. The imposing steeply tiled roofs on the outside were transformed into sharp white vaults on the inside, with a near vanishing point where the seam of glazing met the bright sky high up; quite heavenly for some, I'm sure, but enough to lift the sceptical heart too. The rest was blond and amber wood, flagstones, breeze-blocks and rough-cut stone pillars: part Scandinavian-modern; part Celtic barn. 'If you don't believe in God, what do you believe in?' I once asked my dad. 'Nature,' he said. Exactly what he meant I'd never been sure. The here and now, the immutability of the seasons, perhaps. We come. We go. We flourish. We die. I looked around the room and wondered if it was OK on that basis for him. If he'd been attending someone else's funeral in the same room, I could picture him running his hand over the stone pillars and leaning into me and whispering, 'Nice job. Shame about the cross on the wall.'

I imagined him in his coffin. Jane, Roly's ex-wife, had wanted to put him in something smart for the occasion; she'd chosen his double-breasted blue blazer and tartan trousers and had helped get the body dressed. It wouldn't have been my choice – not that I could have gone through with it – but if I had, I think I would have picked one of his snappy bird's-eye-check Savile Row suits from the late fifties, with a knitted tie, and perhaps a ciggy between his fingers. The smoking may have killed him, but one last defiant stand might have seemed appropriate.

I looked out into the largely empty chapel. The website said there was room for ninety. We must have mustered about eighteen. Almost all family. A couple of faces from the care home. I'd taken out a 'death notice' in the *Guardian* at 48p a word:

WATT, Tommy. Bandleader, arranger and jazz pianist. Died peacefully on 20 May 2006 aged 80. A much-loved husband to Romany, father to Ben, and stepfather to Simon,

Roly, Toby and Jennie. Funeral – Friday 26 May, 1p.m., Westerleigh Crematorium, Bristol. Flowers – R. Davis and Son.

It hadn't attracted much of a walk-up.

I read some extracts from my book *Patient* during the service – the bit about when I was a kid and we went to football together, and then another bit about us all as a family having Saturday lunch after the customary visit to the pub, and I made reference to the obituaries that had been commissioned by the broadsheets in the week. I even read from the one Steve Voce had written that had already appeared in the *Independent* that morning:

No one had heard of Tommy Watt and then suddenly here he was leading a big band made up from the cream of the very best jazz players in the country. An exaggeration? Not when you say Tubby Hayes, Ronnie Ross, Tommy McQuater, Bert Courtley, Jackie Armstrong, Phil Seamen and the other names. And they didn't just play for Tommy on his records; they appeared under his leadership in broadcasts, clubs and concerts. Amazingly gigs with the Tommy Watt Band seemed to take precedence over all their other work and if they ever did have to send in deps then the deps were top-liners too. At a time when rock 'n' roll permeated everything Tommy Watt somehow managed to get his band before the audiences . . . Over the years Watt was revered by musicians in many fields, but pretty well obscure to the general public.

I'd rung the papers a few days earlier saying I was preparing the death notice and would any of them be interested in an obituary. I wasn't sure if he meant anything to anyone any more. They said they'd speak to their jazz writers and get back to me. Within an hour, I'd had calls from Dave Gelly at the *Daily Telegraph*, Peter Vacher from the *Guardian*, and Steve Voce. I was quietly thrilled at the speed of their response. It had seemed somehow necessary to me to get him acknowledged. After all, all that obscurity had done for him in so many ways. Or perhaps I was just channelling my mum: we don't exist unless someone's writing about it. Brian Rix had rung me that morning to say what a great and accurate portrait the *Independent* had painted, so I guessed it had been worth it. Either that, or part of Brian is the same as my mum.

We played some of my dad's music. I'd unearthed a crackly ten-inch acetate cut at a live radio session of a tune he had written for my mum in the early sixties called 'Wholesome Girl' – a description that perhaps described the woman he wanted, rather than the woman she may have wanted to be – but, title aside, it is a beautiful piece of writing, especially when stripped of its rather treacly lyrics (written by someone else) and returned to its original soaring and romantic instrumental melody. The version I found was recorded solely with an orchestra; the pops and crackles on the recording lent it a time-trapped authenticity as it pealed out in the chapel, and as it was playing I wondered if all couples who live together for a long time can pinpoint a moment when things were at their most perfect, and in which they felt they were most themselves, because that was what the music seemed to be saying about my mum and dad.

We played some Billy Connolly and there was a prayer for those who wanted it, and then it was over. I'd thought about playing 'Bring Me Sunshine' from the *Morecambe and Wise Show* to round it off, but in the end I chose the ballsiest of the four Forty-Two Jazz Band recordings, and the curtains finally closed around his coffin during a rather fine tempestuous Bert Courtley solo.

Outside, people were gathering in the covered walkway. The wind was sharp and biting. I was surprised to see so many flowers had been delivered, all laid out along the trellis fencing; perhaps the death notice had worked after all. I bent down to read a few and didn't recognise any names until I realised almost all of them were from the previous funerals that morning. As I was straightening up, one caught my eye; it was the only one for my dad not from the family. It was from Bobby Wellins, the Scottish tenor saxophone player. I unclipped the card from the cellophane bouquet and slipped it in my pocket.

There were a few tears and clinches and kind words but it was too cold to stand around. Within five minutes we had all dispersed to our cars.

An hour later we were gathered together in Roly's sitting room in his unostentatious fifties brick vicarage paid for by the Church Commissioners, with plates of food on our laps. Someone suggested putting on some of Tom's music, but no one had any. We fell into familiar roles: Roly softly shepherding; Jane briskly serving food; Toby breaking the ice with one-liners and hearty laughter; teenage children prowling self-consciously; me sitting quietly on the sidelines. And everyone was gently laughing at Jennie – still the butt of so many jokes, padding round in her stockinged feet. Jennie sitting in the wrong place. Jennie speaking with her mouth full. Jennie forgetting what she was saying. It must have been like that since she was a child. And now she was fifty-two. And I could see Eddie, her husband, biting his lip. And suddenly I was angry for her, and when she came over to thank me for the 'lovely words' at the service and tell me that she wanted to write to me to express properly what she felt about it all, I gave her the biggest hug, and our eyes were glistening with tears.

Across the room, my mum was sitting silently in an armchair staring into space. She still had her coat on. She had refused food and was on her third large whisky.

'I'll get her back in a minute,' Roly said, as I passed him in the hall. 'She's not used to being allowed *three* any more.'

'Is she OK?' I said.

'Who knows. She's definitely confused. She has no idea where she's been today. Whether it will settle down, only time will tell. You'd hope so.'

'What about Tom's ashes?'

'Yes. That needs sorting. He talked about having them scattered somewhere.'

'Here?'

'No, maybe in Barnes, in the river. Or he talked about somewhere in Oxford. One of his walks with the dog.'

I went back into the room to see my mum attempting to lever herself out of the chair. Someone steadied her. Once she was on her feet, Roly scooted over and got his arm under her armpit and I could see him saying something in her ear, and she was nodding. 'Whatever's best, dear,' I could hear her say. 'Whatever's best.'

When she was settled to go, and we were focused on her leaving, she looked up at the assembled room and said, 'Thank you for a lovely day, whoever you are.'

Everyone laughed. Half in jest. Half not.

went back to see my psychiatrist. I told him my dad had died since I last saw him. It seemed comically unfortunate.

'And how does it make you feel?' he asked.

'I think he'd had enough.'

'So?'

'So I suppose I am pleased. For him.'

'And you?'

'I think it's too early to say.'

He asked me about the medication. I told him that it was leaving me stable and sleepy during the day but wakeful at night, that I was forever yawning, that my ears were ringing in the silence of the bedroom at night, that my shoulders and legs felt cramped and I was sleeping face down and outstretched like a skydiver, and that I dreamt the upper floor of an imaginary house I was living in was haunted and it had made me wake shouting and crying.

'Anything else?'

'Isn't that enough?'

'All pretty normal, and it will settle down,' he said, jotting some notes. 'Give it a few more weeks. You'll get there.'

Back out on the street with more prescriptions in my hand I

told myself this was the new normal, and soon there would be a better normal, and hopefully, in time, things would go back to normal normal.

A couple of weeks later I got into the car to make a journey I'd been quietly dreading. The route was a familiar one: out on the A40 past Northolt Aerodrome and the Polish war memorial and on to the M40 past Beaconsfield and High Wycombe. It was the same journey I'd made to Oxford in the nineties, wondering what mood my mum and dad would be in, yet always optimistic. I reached the Headington roundabout and took the usual ring road out to the south past Cowley, counting the roundabouts in the same way I had counted them when I first ever visited them, scanning the sky for clouds, hoping for a fine morning, but when I got to the Abingdon Road turn-off and the road up to Folly Bridge I carried straight on heading for Boars Hill, where my dad used to walk his dog.

I'd agreed to meet Roly in a pub car park near by; he was driving from Bristol. It took me a while to find it. I drove up and down the same country road a couple of times. I got there first. When he finally pulled in it was like we were involved in some kind of undercover operation.

'All OK?' I said.

He was out of the car by then. He tapped the boot lid, signalling to its contents. 'Yup.'

'Come on then. You follow me.'

He went for a piss in the pub and then we got back into our cars and pulled back out on to the country lane. Within five minutes I had found the twisting climbing narrow road that I'd remembered from the only time I'd been up it. At the top by a slatted gate and woods and a bridleway I pulled over, and

Roly pulled in behind me. I got out and walked round to the back of his car, as if we were second-rate criminals handing over a smuggled firearm. I wondered if anyone was watching us, but there was no one around. Rooks cried harshly in the woods. I expected him to open the boot and there would be a shotgun wrapped in a towel.

He already had the back of the car open and was reaching inside when I got to him, and then he turned to me and in his hands was a large green plastic container with a screw lid. My first thought was its shape was like the sweet jars in the corner shop where I used to spend my pocket money as a boy. They'd come down from the shelves and be tipped, in a cloud of fine white sugar, into the stainless-steel bowl on the scales. Kola Cubes. Drumsticks. Barratt's Shrimps. Only the jar in his hands wasn't transparent. It was a solid colour. More like the plastic from which a garden bucket might be made.

'Is that it?' I said.

'As far as I know,' he said smiling. He went to hand it over.

I took it from him. It was much heavier than I expected. The static on the plastic had attracted a fine grey dust.

'How do they know . . .' I said, faltering.

'. . . That it's all him?' Roly said.

I nodded.

'They claim they rake it out after each cremation, so you can be pretty sure it's at least *mostly* him.'

I smiled. 'Come on then, let's get on with it.'

We walked a little way back down the hill to the entrance to the woods. There was an Oxfordshire County Council Map showing some trails. A woman in a bright blue ski hat was coming out through the gate with a dog on a lead. It was the middle of June but the sky was overcast and a fresh wind was on the top of the hill.

I'd walked through the gate once before, more than ten years earlier, with my dad and his dog Rosie. It was one of his favourite spots: a sleepy hamlet; bluebells in April; a short stroll, not too exerting; a contemplative view over Matthew Arnold's Field and the distant sandy spires of Oxford. We'd driven up in his Mazda, green wellies in the boot. Rosie was a lovely dog with a kind inquisitive face. Once out of the car she'd turned for a look of approval from my dad before bounding away and springing after squirrels. He doted on her. It struck me that a dog is the jazzman's ideal sideman: the unquestioning, willing companion; no need for language, just gesture and tone; prepared to journey where you journey. It was a tragedy when Rosie died so unexpectedly, aged only eight, tumbling down a flight of stairs on a routine evening at home, witnessed only by Roly's son Sam who was six at the time and visiting with his family. She'd had an undiagnosed thyroid condition and suffered a heart attack. Sam walked into the sitting room where all the adults were talking and said, 'Rosie just fell down the stairs.' Within a couple of hours, and a fruitless run to the vet, there wasn't a sign in the house that my mum and dad had ever owned a dog. My dad had insisted that everything was either taken away by Roly or dumped. Only a few photographs were kept. One of my dad's favourites was one of me, lying on my back looking up at the sky, with Rosie still on her lead looking out to sea, on a wide empty shingle beach at Cley on the Norfolk coast during a brief holiday in 1989, when I drove up to see them for twenty-four hours. On reflection, Rosie seemed to symbolise the good years: bought just before they moved to Oxford; a shot in the arm; tugging them eagerly through their short autumnal renaissance. They never replaced her, although they talked about it once, but within a year my dad's health had worsened and then there was no question of it.

We'd walked a little way into the woods and stopped by a stone seat in a hollow surrounded by the exposed roots of the trees above.

'Do you want to do this on your own?' Roly said.

'Perhaps I should,' I said, although I didn't know what I wanted.

'I'm fine with that. Really.'

We made our goodbyes and he walked off back along the path. I watched until he was out of sight, thinking how he'd driven all that way to hand me the jar – should I call it an urn? – and was now going to drive all the way back.

It felt lonely in the woods. The sky was grey. I kept looking up in the hope that a patch of blue might make me feel better about it all. The wind was between the trees. I looked all around but could see no one approaching. Standing by the bench I began unscrewing the lid. It turned crunchily, and then there I was looking at the contents, full almost to the brim, like the rakings from a winter fire, of mixed consistency, part powdery, part unburnt. Why I had chosen to stop by the bench I wasn't sure. In my mind's eye I had imagined a sunlit hilltop that I could have slowly encircled – young lush sappy grass, buttercups, Christ Church visible, livestock grazing – but here I was in unspecific overcast woods by a random stone seat of no particular meaning other than it triggered an instinct. Seat: rest. Stone: enduring.

I walked behind it and tipped some of the ashes on the ground, like flour from a jar, and then made a circle around it. It left a grey trail. Clearly visible. It made me think of *The Railway Children* and the boy with the bag over his shoulder who leaves the paper trail through the fields for the runners and then injures his leg in the tunnel. I began to walk away from the bench and along a path to a fence and the edge of the wood, attracted by the light from the field beyond. I kept pouring. When people said 'scattering ashes' I'd envisaged a handful, not this, not a huge jar full of them. Tiny pieces of bone tumbled out too, and the wind blew ash on to my trousers as I walked, and I involuntarily brushed it away before realising what I was brushing. I half leapt back, a little spooked, and some of the ashes slopped out, but I kept going until I got to the fence.

I looked back. It was as though I'd laid a trail of gunpowder. I questioned if I was even in the right spot. Perhaps he'd hated this part of the woods. It was too late now. The urn was half empty. Along the edge of the fence ran a bridleway, muddier with the imprint of horses' hooves. I walked a short way along the fence line, emptying the remaining ashes before reaching another bench, this time just an ordinary wooden municipal bench, the kind seen in parks in every town. I stopped and sat on it. Right in the middle. It felt right. Simple. The field was empty but for a lone grazing horse.

To my left, at the end of the field where the bridleway stopped, I could see the slatted gate close to where I'd parked. Another car had pulled up facing the field. Inside I could see a middle-aged couple looking out. The man – who was sitting in the driving seat – was pouring something hot from a thermos into his cup. The woman in the passenger seat was eating a sandwich. Under the damp matt grey light everything seemed silent and remote. All I could think of was the mess I had left through the woods, and I worried that people would come across it later and wonder what it was. I wondered if my dad had experienced this view – like this – the hushed wind in the woods behind, this stillness, this silence, this matt sky, these uneventful minutes. And then as I stood up to go, the empty urn under my arm, I saw the horse move into the centre of the field and raise its head, framed by the sunless clouds behind, and it looked majestic and proud.

36

'He still visits me, you know,' my mum said, her pallid eyes turned to the window.

It was September 2006, almost four months since my dad had died.

I sat close to her on the footstool beside her chair. 'Does he?' I said.

'Oh, yes. Quite often lately.' She ran the tips of her fingers gently back and forth on the velour of the armrest.

'How does he arrive?'

Her fingers stopped. I saw the answer appear in her face before a faint wrinkle of doubt flashed across her brow, and she seemed to question what she was about to say. Then she dismissed it and said quite plainly, 'Through the curtains. Just there.' She gestured to the long curtains by the locked and alarmed double-glazed PVC door and window at the end of the room.

It was a narrow single room on the ground floor, perhaps fifteen feet long and about nine feet wide, the door and window in the end wall overlooking the car park, and the kitchen staff on their smoke breaks and the fields beyond. She'd been moved in not long after the funeral. A single bed and the last few pieces of her furniture stood along the walls: a tall narrow bookcase of scrapbooks and photo albums near the window; a small red metal office chest of drawers; two armchairs (the green leather one of my dad's she never used); the large square footstool in a dark William Morris floral print on which I was sitting; the TV that she never turned on; and a slim sixties side table topped with ceramic tiles depicting musical instruments, which I knew from Barnes and brought to mind my dad's blue *Senior Service Satisfy* ashtray, flecks of ash, his retractable Sheaffer ballpoint pen and a copy of *The Times* folded into quarters to show the crossword puzzle. A teak dresser that I didn't recognise full of photos and a few ornaments took up most of the space inside the door; maybe it belonged to the previous occupant and they couldn't get it out. Roly had hung some pictures of caravans and one of my dad's Centre 42 jazz posters on the pale apricot walls papered in woodchip. An adjustable-height invalid table on wheels with a lip around the edge to stop things sliding off was parked near her chair in the middle of the room.

'Through the curtains?' I said.

'Yes. It sounds strange when you say it, but he just slips in.'

'What's he wearing?'

'One of his suits, I think. Very smart. Always.'

'Does he speak?'

'Oh yes. He could always do *that*. A gift.'

'And what do you say to him?'

'I usually just lie there in the bed listening.'

'And what does he say?'

'Oh, this and that. He's getting married again, you know. To another woman. I hope he's told her about the drinking.' She was now speaking the way she had always spoken, head turned away, as if addressing the middle distance. Her tone was slightly detached, as though she had tumbled the ideas for hours around her own head, rinsing them of any detectable feeling until they could be voiced like simple yet vaguely baffling facts to get used to.

'What do you mean?'

'Well, she ought to know beforehand, don't you think? I mean, it's not right, is it? It's just so unfair to spoil someone else's life like that.'

I heard muffled voices out in the car park. A greenfinch was at the bird-feeder outside the window, then it was gone.

She turned her face to me. 'I would have liked some looking after myself, you know. Someone who took me for who I was.'

There was a knock at the door, which was half held open with a rope attached to the radiator. I looked up. It was one of the carers.

'Just brought you your laundry, Romany,' she said loudly, already half into the room, the corners of the words curled and whorled by the West Country accent. 'Shall I pop them in your drawer for you?'

'Yes,' said my mum, half over her shoulder, stretching the word a little patronisingly to make it sound like *as usual*.

The woman zipped into the room and slipped a couple of things in the chest of drawers. 'Nice of Ben to pop in and see you, isn't it?' she said, still loudly.

'Don't. Shout,' said my mum, clipping each word short, putting a full stop between them.

The woman shot her a smile, then winked at me. 'Lunch'll be along in a moment,' she said, already almost out of the door.

'How *thrilling*,' my mum said, pulling a face just for me.

I waited for the footsteps to disappear, then said, 'You were saying about Dad . . .'

'Who?'

'Tom.'

She rummaged around in her head. 'Was I?'

'About his visits.'

She sat still for a moment. 'A handsome man.'

I watched her face. I could picture a carousel of images in her head, coming and going, in and out of focus, faces on a fairground waltzer, random in time and space, and every now and then she was able to slow the movement down and bring something into focus and freeze the frame before it floated away again like a paper fire lantern.

'Can you remember when you first met?' I said.

'Who?'

'Tom.'

'Not really.'

'It was at Brian and Elspet's party. New Year's Day 1957. Only a few nights after Tom had started at Quaglino's. Ring a bell?'

Her eyes widened. 'I think you're right.'

It had been a sketchy fact I'd known growing up, one my dad had bragged about. 'Why did you kiss her?' I would ask him. 'I couldn't *stop* her,' was his stock reply.

'Can you bring it to mind, Mum?'

She closed her eyes and wrinkled her brow as though I'd asked her the name of a South American capital city. 'He was at the end of the room,' she said after a moment. 'And I thought, Who is that man making everyone laugh with the lonely face?'

'And you kissed him that night?'

'I must have.'

'Although Ken was there?'

'Yes.'

'Why did you kiss him?'

She shrugged. 'People do.'

*   *   *

She and Ken had married a little over eight years earlier in 1948. He was on the staff at the left-wing weekly magazine *Tribune* as their theatre critic, and had spotted her acting in London not long after she left the Royal Academy of Dramatic Art.

'He took such a shine to me,' she said to me one evening as we walked by the river in Oxford. 'He began following me everywhere. He even travelled down to Devon to see me in a tiny church hall. I was in rep. It must have taken hours. He had to walk across the front of the stage to get to his seat after the curtain went up. Clump, clump, clump. I was so embarrassed.'

The ceremony took place at 11 a.m. at the Hinde Street Methodist Church in central London on 2 October with the reception at the Mandeville Hotel. Her brother Glyn gave her away, her father having died five years earlier. She wore a white satin Victoria gown with a bustle and short train, the Swedish lace veil was bound round the brow with a gold circlet studded with pearls, and she carried a posy of crimson roses; the brides-maids wore Wedgwood-blue gowns and coronets of fresh white flowers, and carried bouquets of white carnations and gladioli.

Eunice, her mother, kept a meticulous list of attendees and no-shows, and their respective wedding presents. The list is a brilliantly comprehensive vision of forties domesticity:

dinner wagon and kitchen scales
coffee percolator
toast rack and napkin rings
canteen of cutlery
cheque for £5
bread fork
biscuit box
book of poems

tea knives
cheque for £2
recipe book and doily
Victorian bon-bon dish
Daleware mixer
fireside companion set
Shetland rug
Staybrite tray
wool tea cosy
fish knives and forks
biscuit barrel
cheque for £3.30
waste-paper basket
whisky decanter
Pyrex set
two soup ladles
pair of double sheets

The list went on. And yet if my mum was to be left in no doubt that she was preparing for domestic life, it was clear she was also unwilling to sacrifice everything.

In April 1951 she was asked to write a talk for one of the clutch of new afternoon programmes on the BBC aimed at women in the immediate post-war years. Wartime broadcasting for women may have been typified by programmes such as *The Kitchen in Wartime* and *The Factory Front*, but 1946 had seen a new emphasis on the home with the advent of *Housewives' Choice* and *Woman's Hour*. Writing for the newly launched *Mainly for Women*, she defended the right to seek work and look after the home at the same time. In an essay entitled 'Housewife at Stratford' she wrote about the months immediately following her wedding:

When I got married, just over two years ago, most of my friends thought I should give up the stage. My relatives and in-laws took it for granted; my actress friends sighed, rather smugly I thought . . . But my husband and I had other plans. He is a theatre critic, so he understood my love of the stage. We decided when we were engaged that it would be foolish to waste my two-year training at the Royal Academy of Dramatic Art, and my two years' experience in repertory, and that if any jobs turned up I was certainly to take them.

At first, overwhelmed by setting up home with Ken in a small mews cottage in west London, she found it hard to do both, only acting in 'one or two Sunday night shows' and 'a few odd weeks of repertory in the suburbs', but in the spring of 1949, after six months of nest-building, she began looking in earnest. She 'pestered all the agents and wrote an average of ten letters a week'. Every management company she could think of was contacted, but it was tough going; work was scarce. After three months of dispiriting rejections, and more in hope than expectation, she aimed high and travelled to the Globe Theatre in London on a summer morning in August to audition for the director Anthony Quayle, who was preparing for the following summer's season of Shakespeare plays at the Memorial Theatre in Stratford-upon-Avon. She nervously delivered speeches by Hermia and Cleopatra, was thanked, eagerly agreed to accept walk-ons or understudies or small parts if required, but left disheartened. The following week, much to her astonishment, a nine-month contract to act with the Shakespeare Memorial Theatre Company alongside John Gielgud and Peggy Ashcroft arrived in the post. When she'd first started looking for work she'd imagined small repertory tours in the provinces lasting two or three weeks; leaving home for nine months had never crossed her mind. Newly married, she was torn, but she also knew it was a huge chance. It took several days to make up her mind, but with encouragement from everyone, she accepted. She went on to write excitedly:

> The next few months went all too quickly. I looked at everything with a new eye. The store cupboard was stacked with tins of soup and spaghetti, the local dairy coaxed into thinking my husband needed lots of eggs and sympathy, the best blue taffeta counterpane folded in tissue paper and a cotton one put in its place. Every garment was dry-cleaned, every sock darned and every button sewn on as if he were to suffer a great siege.

Rehearsals started in the cold early months of 1950. She confessed 'the leave-taking that bleak February afternoon was awful' and she was bitterly homesick for the first three weeks, but she soon grew to love the work and the routines; and the view out over the foggy river and the fields from the big white Georgian house where she lived among other actors, two miles from the theatre, fired her with a galvanising romantic enthusiasm. In June, midway through the season, Ken had 'tired of his tinned diet and solitary life' and travelled up to join her. He stayed for three months, even though she was still often rehearsing all day and acting all night. When work called him back to London in September, she stayed on to finish the season alone. And then, on 28 October, shattered but elated, she finally headed back to London herself. She wrote:

> Oh, the excitement of seeing my little black-and-white mews cottage again, with its red window boxes and little tub trees! The delight of not having to go out in the evening, of just

sitting by the fire, of looking in all my cupboards and finding things I'd forgotten! And above all, the companionship of my sorely tried husband, who had never once complained, but who never wants to eat stewing steak or kippers again!

I don't doubt that she was happy to get home to the quiet comforts of her husband and the fireside after such a tumultuous and exhausting year, but it's also clear the whole adventure had been deeply fulfilling on a profound and potentially life-changing level. 'The most marvellous experience I ever hope to have' is how she reflects on it in her written memories; it was also how she spoke of it in later years to me, when we'd talk about it sometimes if my dad was not around, and she could relax and not feel judged. It's not hard to see how she thrived on the unrivalled attention it brought and the heart-stopping thrill of it all; it was what she had perhaps always dreamed of ever since that first day recording a broadcast with her father. Certainly the life of a housewife in a little mews cottage in west London could not have been more different. And then, ten months later, their first child, Simon – my eldest half-brother – was born, and everything changed.

'Were you and Ken both keen for kids?' I asked, as we carried on walking by the river that same evening in Oxford.

'Of course,' she said. 'Although at the time I think Ken was more concerned about getting called up for the Korean War.'

'What do you mean?'

'He was carrying a *gas mask* wherever he went. He was quite convinced war was around the corner. So he said we *ought* to have one. Just in case.' She gave a gloomy laugh. 'Not sure if you can call that romantic or not.'

Two swans cruised up to the bank, their necks poised, droplets of water resting on their furled wings.

'Why do you laugh?'

She stopped to look at the river. 'Did I ever tell you about our honeymoon?'

'No.'

'We went to Florence, Ken and I. Took a plane. We had to fly via Switzerland; it was very different back then. We stayed in a small hotel near the river. Very pretty, it was. Windows that opened right out on to the city, and that *view*. All very E. M. Forster.' She let out a little laugh through her nose. 'But to be brutal about it, that was about as romantic as it got.'

'What do you mean?'

'Sex, darling,' she said crisply. 'Or lack of.'

The swans had lost interest and had pedalled back into the middle of the stream. The shadows from the buildings loomed on to the surface of the water.

'But that's what honeymoons are for!'

'You would have thought so, wouldn't you. But no. I think we must have seen the inside and outside of every single church and duomo in the whole place. My feet ached. And the little guide book and everything. Renaissance this, Renaissance that. Beautiful, of course, but, well . . .' She trailed off.

A man passed us wheeling his bike, cycle clips pegging his trousers to his ankles.

'Ken was in heaven, of course,' she said. We walked a little further and up on to the footbridge. 'And I made such a fool of myself at Stratford.'

'How?'

'I didn't get half the jokes. I'd been married for twelve months but had no idea why the audience all laughed at Paul

Hardwick's line "Hard all night". I actually asked what it meant in front of a number of people.'

'You didn't!'

'I did.'

We stood laughing. It wasn't often that she was like this – forthcoming and confiding, and I felt close to her, like she was letting her guard down for a moment. Mingling. Gossipy.

'What about before Ken? There must have been others,' I asked, as we headed back.

'Oh, yes. A whole string of them during the war. Pilot offi-cers on leave or suffering fatigue – that sort of thing. I was a Wren of course. I nearly followed one back to New Zealand! Mother had to talk me down. She was always telling me I had a tendency to go *off at the deep end* about everything. And before that, when I was eighteen, I went to an old girls' school reunion at the Craiglands Hotel and fell for a thirty-four-year-old married man called Reggie. He was very good about it. But it was all very chaste. All of it. All of them. Kisses and cuddles. That was as far as it went in 1942. Not like it is today.'

I've tried to picture her arriving at Brian and Elspet's New Year's Day party in 1957, aged thirty-two, and what she was thinking as she pushed through the hallway of people with a drink in one hand. I talked to Elspet, who became my godmother, over lunch not long after my dad died, and she painted it in simple strokes. Close friends with my mum since meeting at RADA in 1945, she said, 'Romany hadn't been happy. Life wasn't very exciting. She loved the children to bits – the triplets were *adorable* – and Richard [the name she gave to Ken – as many did – after his pen name Richard Findlater] was such a *nice* man, very bright, but she wanted – how should

I say it – more *pizzazz*. It had all got rather sterile. Perhaps she wasn't even aware of it.'

'But then Tommy wasn't very happy either,' Brian had interjected. (Elspet had always been my mum's advocate, and Brian my dad's. It was odd to think they'd each known one of my parents separately since the mid-forties, and then circumstance had brought the four of them together in the mid-fifties.)

'How so?' I asked, half knowing the story already, but wanting to hear Brian say it.

'He was married as well. June, her name was; we never saw her. He'd married her right after the war. They had a flat in Blackheath. She had a condition. Awful business.'

I pressed him. 'What sort of thing?'

'Nephritis, by all accounts. To do with the kidneys. Couldn't have children, or so we were led to believe. Often bedridden.'

I pictured my parents both there at the party, each already in their early thirties, almost six years before I was born. On the one hand there was so much going for each of them: my mum with the family, a celebrated husband and a new career as a journalist; my dad as a bandleader at Quaglino's on the cusp of glittering success. But on the other, they must have felt as if there was so little: each adrift in awkward, idling, passionless relationships, fettered and unfulfilled.

Were they really on a collision course?

37

As the weeks and months went by at the care home, my mum's hallucinations got worse. She was convinced there was a rifleman on the roof outside her room, and would sit back from the window or lie on her bed to keep out of the way. One morning a carer found her with her shoes off in front of her small pink basin trying to splash little cupped handfuls of water on to her bare feet. When asked what she was doing, she said, 'Can't you see them? My feet are covered in wasps.' And before long, Tom had changed from the smart lover appearing through the curtains to a skeleton, sometimes under the bed or sometimes in the chair as she woke.

She lost sense of day and night. Often she dozed and got herself into bed during the afternoons only to fall heavily asleep, and then found herself wide awake in the middle of the night. The night staff would find her wandering the corridors, using the handrails as a guide, as a mountaineer uses ropes, but then often she'd try to break into a determined run, which was all the stranger as during the day she could only shuffle unsteadily from chair to bed. One night it was said she burst into another resident's room – up on the first floor – and was all set to wrestle her from the mattress, convinced Tom was under the sheets beside her. How she got upstairs no one was sure. They didn't like to give her sedatives unless it was completely necessary, but sometimes it was the only way to keep her under control, and she'd zone out in her room for twenty-four hours, and then be calmer.

Yet in the midst of it all she had brief periods of great tranquillity and lucidity where random parts of her memory were sharp and her sense of humour undimmed, and I hoped as I pushed the door open on a visit that I'd catch her on a good day.

Leafing through some old photographs one morning I asked her for her strongest memory of my dad. The skin on her face was furrowed as though a fork had been pressed into clay or plasticine, her eyes grey-blue and gauzy. She opened her mouth to speak and moved her hands together under the blanket over her knees. Her face lit up. 'He was very *loving*,' she said, half girlish and fond, half cheeky. 'So *alive*. And *very imaginitive*.'

She twinkled, as if she'd said something naughty.

Something must have detonated inside her during those opening few months of 1957. 'It's a deep pool,' my dad had said on the eve of their first tryst in March at his flat in Blackheath over tea and gin. She had instigated it, phoning to suggest an 'interview' for the *Evening Standard* with 'one of London's top young bandleaders', but the subtext was abundantly clear.

I have no memories of being told much about the affair while I was growing up. In fact, when I discovered, only recently, that it had started as early as 1957, my first thought was one of shock that it had gone on so long; they weren't married until late October 1962, six weeks before I was born; that's an affair lasting five and a half years. How was it sustained? Who knew? Why so long?

When my dad died, Roly handed me some souvenirs that had been kept in his loft since my parents' move from the

London flat to the Bristol care home. He hadn't chosen to look at them himself. There was a banana crate of Tilly's Romany china wrapped in newspaper, archived folders and cuttings, and the old grey cardboard fifties Harrods gift box with its Festival of Britain design, in which I knew my mum kept her special keepsakes and mementoes. I filled the boot and drove them back to London on a rainswept afternoon.

In the gift box I found a sealed envelope marked *Memories – Very Private – For Tom Only*. The handwriting was my mum's. I looked at it unopened for a few days, my mind full of unanswered questions. Was it right to read it while my mum was still alive? Did her cognitive collapse make it OK? Was I allowed to open it, as my dad was now dead and I was his son? Should some time elapse first? If so, how long? On a long walk one afternoon I decided if I were to have any final appreciation and understanding of my mum before she died too, I needed to know the full story. What was the point in saving it? To only regret opening it when it was too late?

I remember how the old sealed envelope sat lightly in my hands, the paper softened by years of storage among other papers. The dried-out gummed edge was puckered. Sitting at my desk at the top of the house where we lived at the time, in the lavender twilight, I slid a small brown kitchen knife under the envelope's edge and carefully cut a clean straight line. Why I was being so careful, I wasn't sure. It felt as if I were picking a lock. I was aware I might be leaving fingerprints. Tiny flecks of white paper clung to the knife with static and a few tumbled on to my desk like feathery frost or the first flutters of snow. The folded paper sat neatly and tightly in the envelope; three or four sheets, I guessed. As I pulled them out I wondered how long they had rested in there private and undisturbed. It felt like an exhumation.

Putting the envelope down I pushed back my chair and unfolded the sheets of paper. The creases were as resistant as stiff old unoiled hinges. I could hear children playing on the neighbour's trampoline in the next-door garden below and a helicopter passing in the distance. The paper cracked like a knuckle.

The words were typed on a proper old-fashioned typewriter, the font retaining all its quirks of misaligned spacing and over-blotting from the imperfect action of real machinery striking on real ribbon, hammered with the real feeling of real hands. The opening words jumped off the page in all their startling candidness like a tight heart unbuttoned. They read:

I kissed you for the first time on January 1st 1957 because you looked lonely. I kissed you again on January 28th because I couldn't help myself.

The paper drooped in my hands. I looked away. I felt as if I had prised open a locket.

The three pages of captured memories are vivid and impressionistic, by turns wistful and defiant, written it would seem in the middle of 1959, some two years after the affair had begun. 'I have no diary for 1956 or 1957,' she begins, and there is a sense, by the end, that by writing the memories down she is trying to trap and preserve something she fears she might lose, or worse, forget. Of the early days she eye-catchingly reminisces:

March 3. Prelims. Scones for tea on the trolley, with honey . . . Unromantic humorous musical medley on out-of-tune piano. Offer of gin. Offer of another gin. Shoes off. The rest is history.

And then:

Opening Phases. Spring '57. Sitting on the piano stool . . . the sun shining into your flat in the late afternoon. The sun at the Yacht [in Greenwich]. Sitting pressed close together against the wall at the Yacht and you saying you thought you loved me for the first time . . . Driving from the tea shack on the heath to the Plume. Following you down the hill . . . My black cotton dress. Your grey suit. My gold bangle . . . Driving round St James's Square. Journeys to Blackheath at night when the world was ours. Tea in Hampstead. Tea in the Chinese Restaurant in Brompton Road. The visits to your tailor. Buying my coat in Harvey N. And collecting June's from Fenwick.

They met illicitly for four months – riverside pubs and stolen afternoons, a little hotel (the Paragon) and sometimes bolt-holes engineered with the help of friends – but beyond the surface clandestine excitement, it's clear from the beginning that it was a door opening on to a new and profound secret world for her: a world that was carnal, adrenalised and consuming; unlike anything – at the age of thirty-three, with four children and nearly nine years into a marriage – she had ever known before. A few letters preserved from the period are unblushingly frank and unposed, as if this time she really had – as her mother used to say – 'gone off at the deep end'. It wasn't long before she was describing it in a letter to my dad as 'the most overwhelming, beautiful, tender, savage thing that ever happened to me'.

Looking back now, and bearing in mind the changes and loosening in the divorce laws that have taken place since 1969, it is hard to imagine what entangled years lay in store for couples who met as ardently and dramatically as my parents did in 1957. The rights of the married individual have long since displaced antiquated notions of moral fibre and dangers to the fabric of society, but back then the divorce laws of the day permitted annulment only on the grounds of adultery or cruelty or desertion lasting at least three years. Even when the Royal Commission on Marriage and Divorce 1956 was set up to review increasing pressures in the post-war years to see marriage merely as a companionate alliance between two people in an increasingly individualised world, as opposed to a legal binding duty that involved the state as well, no changes were made. A relationship that 'broke down' was not enough. In fact, clinging steadfastly and conservatively to the past, the report stated:

> We are convinced that the real remedy for the present situa-
> tion lies in other directions [i.e. not easier divorce]: in
> fostering in the individual the will to do his duty in the
> community; in strengthening his resolution to make
> marriage a union for life; in inculcating a proper sense of
> responsibility towards his children.

It was against this background on 2 July 1957 – four months after the affair had begun – that my dad's first wife, June, found out.

My dad broke the news to my mum in the tiny Grenadier pub on Wilton Row near Hyde Park Corner. He vowed it would make no difference, and they talked themselves into renting a flat for six weeks in Sussex Gardens in Bayswater to continue their secret assignations. Quite how soon afterwards Ken found out is unclear, but the affair was fully exposed by the end of August, and my mum and dad seemed unable to sustain the duplicity. In early September, they were preparing to reconcile with their respective partners. On the final night before the lease ran out on the Bayswater flat, my mum stayed up late alone while my dad was out performing at Quaglino's, and wrote an open letter to herself:

Written to the strains of Jack Payne on Eve's lousy wireless. On this night of Sep 4 at 11.30 sitting in this strange girl's flat in which I have been since Monday, I feel, for the sake of the future and the past, I must write a couple of things down. Tomorrow I give in the keys. The oddest thing almost, is that I should be so besotted in the business that *we* have a flat – us – he and I actually have a flat of our own and have had for six weeks. 'I am so steeped in' now, that I can entirely neglect my children – my lovely lovely triplets and my awkward heart-rending nervy Simon – can entirely and utterly banish them from my thoughts. That Ken – my dear husband of almost nine years is a stranger to me as a piece of furniture – a thing – not a person any more. And I realise I am doing all this – for what? For my lover – for this boyish, randy, sensitive, needful man . . . What is it I see in him? I know what he sees in me, but there is a terrific core of gentleness, thoughtfulness, passion, vanity and need there, that I find irresistible – plus humour (often violently simple), gaiety and, I suppose, though I hate to admit now that it has any bearing on the subject, glamour. I love him because he has a creative life of his own – he is above me and brilliant in his own field, and he loves me, I think, because sexually he finds me stimulating and I am a 'whole' person, he says – developed, he thinks! But emotionally I am pretty unstable. He talked to me about music again tonight – the things he's playing in the first programme – 'Sally', 'You're Driving Me Crazy' and 'They Can't Take That Away From Me' – which when he said it last time, on this very bed – with tears choking – it seemed the saddest thing I'd ever heard. They're playing 'Jennie In Love'. Poor little girl – will she go through all this after the years of apparent stability, security and happiness? I feel I must be such a worthless person to be so wrapped up in this – so unaware of anything else – so vital, so important, yet, unless I can be adult enough to remain his mistress and also a good wife and mother . . . But I can't believe I am strong enough or without conscience – and yet I love him *absolutely* still, and tonight I am happy – but tomorrow I must take up the threads and responsibilities again – and the house fills me with foreboding – please may everything work out – and yet why should He bother when I am so wicked.

If it is a portrait of my mum in crisis – crazily in love for perhaps the first time in her life – it is also a portrait of the time: a post-war moral maze where her love for her children, duty to her husband, respect for the institution of marriage, and fear of Christian judgement run parallel with unstoppable feelings of awakened passion and free will. Reading it now, I find it difficult not to hear its continuous background soundtrack of late-night London jazz and sentimental show songs, spilling through the radio, running through her head, articulating every surge of feeling, all interlacing with the many versions of the same songs she must have heard performed for her in restaurants and clubs and studios by her own lover. If it weren't my own parents' story, I'd say it reads like the overwrought synopsis of a bestselling fifties potboiler.

*   *   *

I sometimes drove my mum to Paddington Station when she came up to London to visit me after they'd moved to Oxford in the late eighties. We'd turn off the Marylebone Road before the flyover and cross the Edgware Road, and she'd go quiet on Sussex Gardens.

'Is it *all* hotels now?' she once asked.

'Looks like it,' I said, as we passed the strung-out illuminated porticos of the two- and three-star conversions set back from the road.

'Funny to think I rented a place up there with your father.'

'Yes, Dad mentioned it once,' I said, keeping the tone in my voice unembellished, wondering what she might say next.

'I *bet* he did. He probably said something *rude*.'

I laughed. 'He probably did.'

We turned up Norfolk Place towards the station.

She was still looking out of the window at the passing buildings. 'It was all just so desperate,' she said quietly. 'You never mean to hurt people, do you?'

At first, after they left the secret Bayswater flat in early September 1957, there was an immediate breaking-off. My mum returned to Ken and the children, and my dad to June. Yet within a fortnight it was clearly an insufferable state of affairs. In an attempt to exert some control my mum wrote to my dad; her letter was headed, a little comically, *RB's 2nd Sensible Manifesto (Rules for Anguished Lovers, Part II)*. Nevertheless, she writes earnestly and clearly:

> Statement: This last two weeks has been intolerable, unproductive, desolate, blank and quite untenable. No work, no love, no nothing. Tears, rows and dead hopelessness.
> Cause: A complete cessation of a six-month love affair

(which on Saturday included 'for ever') is too drastic and
cruel for ordinary mortals of which we are two.

Reasons For Abrupt Cancellation: Of the highest conscien-
tious principles – love, duty, honour and [the] pain we
were causing our legal partners and the intolerable strain
of running a double life.

BUT in actual fact, our utter misery is making us much
crueller and bitterer than we need be and we are taking it
out on 'them', the very people we have done this thing for.

Suggestions: (1) We continue this enforced separation until
such time as we are all more settled in mind – till then,
the body must want. (2) You *must* get on with your work
and rebuild your musical life and concentration. You're
on the threshold of success. (3) I *must* make my family
happy and be kind to Richard [Ken] and take an interest
in ordinary things again.

It must have been such a tense and volatile stalemate. June
had responded with implacable anger and entrenchment. Ken,
on the other hand, soon understood that nothing of value
would come from such enforced deprivation, and – much as it
must have pained him – reluctantly advocated 'something less
drastic', in the hope it would all come to nothing if left to run
its course. If required, he was also ready to meet Tom and write
to June to edge things forward. In a letter from the time, my
mum calls him 'the strongest and best of the four of us', the one
prepared to 'wait and see' and 'face what comes'. Was it just his
measured pragmatism that impressed her? Or the fact that he
was quietly clearing the way for my parents to meet again?

It was six months into the first year of their affair and the
slow walk towards an uncertain resolution had begun.

38

'We went driving, Tom and I.'

Pale autumnal light was at the window. A hoover could be heard in the corridor. I leaned in and smelled the fading red cut freesias in the vase on the chest of drawers. Soap. Strawberries.

'Did you, Mum? When?'

'Yesterday.'

I turned and pushed the uneaten bowl of apple crumble to the side of the invalid table, and slid the coffee towards her. I'd learned to stop correcting her; if it was true in her mind, it might as well be true. 'Really? Where?' I sat beside her on the footstool.

'Oh, here and there, you know. The countryside. It was dark. Very romantic. We were late back. No one saw us come in.'

The lake and willow trees in the green ghost light at Sonning. The dovecote, swans, my too high heels, the red buttons on the sofa, the journey back under the stars of peculiar brightness.

(From my mum's letter of private memories with Tom)

'He was unsure about coming here,' she said, slowly slipping her lightly trembling finger into the handle of the cup and raising it to her mouth. She took a sip of the tepid coffee. 'I thought he wouldn't arrive. But I saw the lights from his car.' She put the cup down and gestured to the car park of the care home beyond the window. 'Out there.'

Henley. Waiting, watching the bridge for your car. Rowing up the river. Dinner when my nerves overwhelmed me. Lying smoking cigarettes in bed at one in the morning and me crying. Darts at the Turville pub, and me in a blouse like June's, and even at that stage the knowledge that I must make you drive up the avenue of meeting trees and just belong under it for always although you were already in an agony of doubt and conscience.

(From my mum's letter of private memories with Tom)

'And where is he now?'

She hesitated for a moment. 'Around.'

She looked out again towards the car park and as she did so, it suddenly hit me why in part they'd chosen to move to Oxford in the late eighties: it wasn't just for the little modern house on the river, or the recommendation of an old friend; it was because it was the hub for so many places where much of their early elopement had taken place – the towns and villages along the Thames Valley, in the Chilterns, beside the Ridgeway; before all the years of compromises and mistakes; in those days when it was all about them; in the green ghost light; up the avenue of meeting trees; when it was all intoxicating and alive; under the stars of peculiar brightness. Oxford was to be remade as something of their own again.

* * *

1957 bled into 1958. My mum was still with Ken and the children at the family home in York Avenue in East Sheen. My dad was still at his flat at The Lawns in Blackheath with June, albeit sleeping in separate rooms. With his quintet continuing in nightly residency at Quaglino's, he began his new much-anticipated Wednesday lunchtime show (*Time for Watt*) with his jazz orchestra at the BBC on 8 January, which was to run for two months. Ken tried to turn a blind eye to the affair, hoping it would fizzle out, but he knew my mum and dad kept meeting.

How did she find the time with four children? It's something I've often asked myself, but with nannies and baby-sitters and her own mother now living near by in East Sheen, she did. Her written memories for my dad are studded with intense images and place names that stand witness to their resolve: 'Thame and everything it stands for'; 'the dream child ring I gave myself for us'; 'the violets you brought to the Grenadier, the anemones last week'; 'burying the wine bottle at Burnham Beeches'; 'the birthday card and record in the Adelaide Rooms, and Fitz playing "Our Love Is Here To Stay"'; 'you asking me to marry you at Henley and on Hammersmith Bridge'. Yet for all their gameness, her letters of the time also reveal she worried that it might all burn out with the fervid intensity and effort; that my dad's interest would fade if enforced duty and domesticity kept them apart in between. 'I can't bear the thought of you falling back into the old pattern,' she wrote. 'I feel you *will* move back into the bedroom one day, out of pity . . . and you will, out of circumstance and pressure, let things go on as they were.'

If she was anxious in 1958, by the following year it had been replaced by a creeping despair. There were momentary highs ('March '59: The night I sat waiting for you with the Modern

Jazz Quartet as background . . . and we decided we must tell them that we wanted to leave them') but they were outweighed by the thick stagnancy of intervening weeks with little progress.

If Ken lived on in the slim hope of a reconciliation, he also knew, as the days crawled by, that it was increasingly unlikely. He wrote in a note left out for her:

> You say you must be able to see a gleam of light, but it's there, isn't it? What you want will probably happen within two years. Perhaps before. Who knows? I can't give you a date. At heart I hope – however stupid and selfish and naive that may be – that somehow or other it will never happen. But of course I couldn't tie you to me, indefinitely, feeling as you do.
>
> I daren't look ahead. I know you feel desperate, and that you often wish – as you say – that you were dead. But at least you have two things to look forward to: love, and the children. I lose both. I just don't see a gleam for me.
>
> It's all so much more complex than a few typed sentences can suggest. But this is meant, in a hamhanded way, to give you comfort. And I do hate to think of you being unhappy.

Tom's wife, June, meanwhile, had simply dug in for the long haul; if the law said three years for a divorce, then as far as she was concerned, three years it would be. If not more. Unwell, she was spending more time with her parents away from the flat in Blackheath, but wouldn't countenance any discussion. My mum couldn't help but be scornful. 'Neurotic' and 'small-minded' are words she uses to describe her in an early letter to Tom, yet no sooner has she written them on the page, than she feels a pang of sympathy: 'God knows she feels the same as us, poor soul', she inserts above the line.

*   *   *

Looking again through the three pages of her private written memories of 1959, it is not hard to understand the tone of dreamlike reminiscence and elegiac melancholy with which many of them are set down, when one considers that the rest of her life must have still felt so stuck; no further forward, two years on, from the tense deadlock of that first autumn after June found out. She ends with words for my dad: 'I promise I will read this through and *draw on it* as you suggested, whenever I am niggly enough to be miserable again.'

It must have seemed at times as if memories might be all she could be left with.

I moved the apple crumble off the table and put a small portable CD player in its place.

'I've brought you some music, Mum.'

She said nothing, just eyed my movements. She'd lapsed into one of her dazes and we hadn't spoken for five minutes or so. Pressing the play button brought the familiar chimes of 'You Make Me Feel So Young' from Frank Sinatra's *Songs For Swinging Lovers*. Released in 1957, it had been the soundtrack to the early years of my mum and dad's affair. 'Every song was written for us,' she'd once told me. I hoped she'd remember it.

She squinted as the music played, trying to recognise it, and then suddenly she tuned in, and her head started bobbing as though a familiar pop song was playing on the radio, but she couldn't quite place it. As the music registered with her more clearly, her eyes brightened and she started to mouth some of the lyrics. And then, quite unexpectedly, she started to sing the ends of lines, in a beautiful soft fluting voice, touching lightly and delicately on the words, her head gently wagging to the rhythm: '"Picking up lots of forget-me-nots . . . A wonderful fling to be flung . . ."'

As the music faded, her head sagged a little and she looked down at her hands.

'Another one, Mum?'

'No. No more.' She looked at me. 'Is it too sad?'

'For me?' I said.

'Yes.'

'A little.'

'Me too.'

In the summer of 1960, three years after the affair had started, June's resolve began to weaken. 'Please let the holiday be happy,' she asked of my dad in a letter, as they spent a sickly week in St-Tropez, in what she must have realised would be their final summer away together, 'and then we'll see.' In December of the same year my dad jumped at the chance to decamp to Manchester as the new conductor of the Northern Dance Orchestra – the prestige of the appointment only matched by his keenness to leave the grim atmosphere of Blackheath – but if it eased the residual pressures at home it did little to dampen the affair.

My mum prepared pre-paid lick-and-seal postcards for him, to be used as love dispatches from the north. She even added her name and address on the front in her own handwriting, so as not to alert Ken. If my mum's preserved letters are lucid and thoughtful, the few cards and letters of my dad's in her collection are blunt and endearingly corny and heartfelt. 'I LOVE YOU WITH ALL MY BEING!' is all one of them says, all in capital letters. 'My desire to be your husband is IMMENSE' and 'We must just *hold on*, my darling' are typical of the economical style of the rest.

But perhaps the most spectacular gesture of commitment saw my mum leave home in London not long after darkness fell in January 1961 seemingly for an evening out with friends. Instead she took the ring road north out of London, and drove on her own – using only long, foggy, single-lane carriageways – all the way to Manchester, where she spent one passionate hour with my dad, before driving all the way back before dawn in time to get the children off to school. In the days before much of the English motorway system was built, it must have amounted to a four-hundred-mile thirteen-hour round trip.

The story was told lightheartedly by my dad during my growing up as further evidence – 'if any more were needed', he would joke – of my mum's supposedly unquenchable lustful desire for him, and he would paint a lewd and humorous portrait of them getting it on in a tiny Didsbury kitchen, before she'd turned round and driven straight home again in the pouring rain, but it is clear from the letters that something else was on the agenda that night: she went to tell him she was pregnant. But not with me.

Back in London, she wrote to him:

Darling, I sometimes have fearful pangs that I should never have involved you in this at all. That I should have kept the secret to myself until this week – as I have from Ken – that I oughtn't to have burdened you with it – that it spoils our particular happiness. But I am such a part of you now – I couldn't *not* tell you – and yet I feel I have let you down in a strange way. I cannot be entirely unfeeling about it and treat it as a slip – and yet I must not treat it desperately seriously. It's Harley Street and the law that makes it seem an enormity.

I never knew about it all the time I was growing up, or even as a grown adult until researching this book. They never mentioned it once; not that you'd have expected them to, even though they were often open and jokey about things; I suppose it's not something you could be open and jokey about. I am certainly not morally offended, but it seems oddly touching that – as their only child – I was actually preceded, albeit only briefly. I now picture my mum in that car on those roads in a different light to the one my dad had always irreverently cast.

As it was, with divorce still distant, a termination seemed the only realistic option. Yet if the divorce laws of the time threw unreasonable obstacles in the way of ordinary people, then the abortion laws did the same. It wasn't until the Abortion Act of 1967 that terminations were regulated as a free provision for all through the National Health Service. Until then, a professional abortion was a luxury only few could afford, but even then a private practitioner had to be found to perform it, and risk to the physical or mental health of the mother through continued pregnancy or childbirth had to be proved. Inevitably, in an unregulated era, paying doctors for 'proof' was not uncommon. In early February 1961, Ken composed a letter to a specialist London surgeon:

> I am writing to ask you to terminate my wife's pregnancy. She suffers from poor health, is most highly strung and over-imaginative. It took her some considerable time to recover from the birth of the triplets in 1954. And during the last three months she has been deeply depressed and emotionally disturbed at the prospect of enlarging the family still further.

Such economy with the truth was fairly standard in such circumstances, but there is a further postscript typed solely on

329

to the duplicate carbon copy attached underneath that has somehow been preserved in my mum's souvenirs; it does not appear on the original top copy of the letter. It reads:

> As I am not the f. of this c. I feel it would be better that she should not have it. And sub to your advice I hereby give my permission for . . .

It trails off. It is hard to believe from the articulacy of Ken's other letters that he was genuinely lost for words. On the contrary, I think every word was very carefully chosen. The coded abbreviation ('father of this child', presumably), the implied but unspecified permission he grants, the use of the secret duplicate – they all seem dismally designed to help sidestep any possible legal recrimination, while pushing the whole thing through with a quietly efficient and determined endurance.

In the upshot, three psychiatrists were required to sign affidavits testifying to alleged 'suicidal tendencies' in my mum to permit the procedure to go ahead. Her subsequent preparatory consultations were needlessly undignified, the formalities punctured more than once by the surgeon's desire to make it perfectly clear he had a very low opinion of her occupation; journalists, in general, were not high on his list. Only after the final meeting, just before the operation, does she plaintively record, 'He was much more human yesterday.'

It must have all felt like so much wretched subterfuge.

By that summer – the summer of 1961 – my dad was back from Manchester after a tempestuous early exit from the NDO. Unable to face returning to Blackheath, and with divorce proceedings finally moving forwards, he began to take advantage of Ken's absences from the family home on York Avenue in East Sheen, not just visiting regularly, but staying overnight too. It was a step too far for Eunice.

Perhaps surprisingly, given her strict Methodist views, Eunice had been supportive of her daughter's affair when it first came to light. She had never warmed to Ken – not that she naturally warmed to anyone – judging him indifferent and cerebral and only weakly concerned with family life. At first, Tom had represented a fresh start – a man who, by all accounts, loved her daughter with the very passion she considered Ken lacked – and as a consequence, she colluded in a number of my mum's stolen visits to see more of him.

Tom's increased presence at York Avenue, however, became a flashpoint. Not unreasonably, it pricked Eunice's conscience to think that – with the divorces still officially unfinalised – he should be, as she wrote, 'sitting on Ken's chair, lying on Ken's bed, and using Ken's belongings'. As far as she was concerned, it was at best overhasty, and at worst, dishonourable, not to mention risking scandal with the neighbours. My mum felt betrayed. Just when she needed her mother's support at a critical time, it was withdrawn. It was not an uncommon feeling – I think she had felt criticised and undervalued by her throughout her life. 'You haven't shown me a loving, warm feeling in years,' she wrote astringently to her that summer, pitching into her 'bitter, stark morals and cold and sterile ideals'. Eunice unsurprisingly replied in kind. 'If, as you say,' she wrote back snappishly, 'these unkind thoughts have been in your mind *these last few years*, how could you have been so two-faced as to have used me in a thousand ways to further your affair with Tom?' The long-running triangular battle between Eunice and my parents that was to carry on all the way until her death in the mid-seventies had had its first testing encounter.

Throughout it all – judging from his few eloquent and unpresuming letters to my mum, written on brief trips with friends, or from the new flat he took on for himself in Paddington as the divorce was finally crystallising – Ken maintained great humility and grace. Not long before everything reached its slow conclusion, he travelled with his friend and fellow journalist at the *Observer*, Anthony Howard, to Switzerland in a self-confessed comic attempt at learning to ski – although more, I'm sure, to take his mind off things – and from the distance of a hotel room was able to identify the qualities that perhaps did for him in the end. He writes to my mum a little too ruefully of his 'elusive identity', his 'doggy devotion' and his 'slobbish, phlegmatic and all-too-familiar exterior'. As characteristics, they were, of course, the obverse of Tom's. They were so obviously *not* what my mum had set her heart on. With his guard down, he also confessed openly to his sadness and desperation in his final letters, yet was proud and honourable enough to remain magnanimous right to the end. In July 1962 he wrote:

My dear Romany

As our marriage is at last being ended this week, by the law – years after it ended, for you, from other causes – I feel I should mark the event in some way. So before I go on a holiday and you go on yours, I am daring, with my usual originality, to write you a letter – or, rather, to finish and post it; because I spend too much of my off-duty time writing letters to you in my head.

This one, no doubt, will turn out to be pointless – as they are – and because the underlying motive behind them all is to say: 'I am lonely. I am bitter. I am hurt. I never thought anything could hurt as much as this, in so many ways, for so long.' And what good does that self-pitying do? I know. But I might as well write it now because to pretend – on this occasion – that I am sitting happily and philosophically in a kind of stoical bachelor coma would be silly. Having uttered it, I will not *think* it at you across the ether so much!

The worst thing is that – having accepted the inevitable – I can't look back on the past yet, any more than I can think of you all together in the present. We had what was, for me, a happy marriage; and I look forward to the time when I *can* look back, as it were, without dissolving into tears, without regrets at the waste, at my own inadequacy. But I wanted to take this chance of saying thank you from the bottom of my heart for all the past happiness, years ago; and to say how grateful I am for that marriage, obviously the most important thing in my life (and how I will not have a word said against it or you), to apologise for the pain and boredom I have caused you; and to wish you – with the deepest sincerity – happiness and contentment and peace of mind in the new life you have already started.

I found the letter in amongst a few others kept by my mum from the years they were married. They were in the box of souvenirs, near the stuff of Tom's, folded together inside a sixtieth-birthday card he had sent to her in 1984, a few months before he died at the age of sixty-three. The card depicts English garden birds – appropriate for my mum, of course – and on it, in her handwriting in biro, it says: 'Ken's Lovely Letters'.

'It was all a terrible shame in one way,' Elspet said, at our last meeting. 'People loved Romany and Richard [Ken] together. But your mum and dad were *magnetised*. It was unstoppable.

It could be terribly embarrassing sometimes, but that was them.'

'True. And they loved to dominate a room,' Brian recalled. 'In a crowd – on more than one occasion – Tommy would spy Romany over all the heads, and put his hand to the side of his mouth and call out loudly "I LOVVVE YOUUUU" – just like that, down the room, exaggerating and lengthening the words so the whole place noticed. It made us cringe. *Awful.* Sometimes we'd throw a party, and friends would ask who else was coming, and if we said Tommy and Romany, there would be – you know – *looks*.' He winced to illustrate it. 'But what could you do?'

'Romany *loved* it of course,' said Elspet. 'She'd preen and laugh. All that attention. Who *wouldn't*? She wasn't used to it.'

'What happened to June – Tom's first wife?' I asked.

'I think she died,' Brian said glumly, looking at the table.

'When?'

'Not long after. It was never mentioned.'

And that is how I remember it too. June. A name. Nothing more. Written out of the story. It took Brian to tell me she'd had nephritis, and it took my own research to look it up and realise how debilitating it must have been. All that was said when I was growing up was that she was 'an invalid'. That she had 'tricked' my dad into marriage. That her parents were 'demons'.

I tracked down their marriage certificate. She was born 'Jeune' not June. Her middle name was Rhoda. She and Tom (I expect she called him 'Tommy') were married on 13 May 1947 at St Thomas's in Old Charlton. She was twenty-three. My dad was twenty-one. She was a sales assistant. Her father, Arthur, was a civil servant. My dad was just out of the RAF. All I could think was that they were very young.

And I pictured my mum in the car on that journey to Paddington after she'd come up to see me in the eighties and heard her words again: 'You never mean to hurt people, do you?'

On 24 July 1962 June was finally granted a decree nisi on the grounds of adultery. Ken was granted the same. In anticipation of the final paperwork, my dad and my mum – already four months pregnant with me – had been settled into the new flat at Woodlands Road in Barnes for over six months with the triplets and Simon. Eunice was living on the ground floor. Ken had moved from Paddington to a more permanent flat on Ladbroke Grove.

'Did you know what was going on at all with Tom and Mum?' I asked Roly, the afternoon I collected the souvenirs and crockery from his loft.

'No, but then you don't understand when you are a child. You sense something is odd but you can't work it out,' he said. We were outside in the garden behind the vicarage. A brisk late spring breeze whipped across the weathered picnic table and harried the long grasses at the end of the rambling lawn. 'I remember one day being told out of the blue that we were moving from York Avenue to Woodlands Road, with Mum and Tom, but not Dad. We must have been eight. We went away on a holiday with Dad, I think – Jennie kept calling him "Tommy" in the car and then correcting herself – and when we got back we were taken to Woodlands. I can remember running round the new house exploring with Toby and stumbling across a pram in the hall and asking Mum what it was, and that's when she said we were going to have another little brother or sister.'

In among my mum's papers, I found a short telegram to my dad from his solicitor, Blanche, confirming the ratification of the divorces that July of 1962. It reads: 'All's Well That Ends Well'.

39

'Is my mother still alive?'

We were sitting as we always sat, in the solitude of my mum's little room, the TV off, the brightly lit soft hubbub of the communal lounge with its ring of upright armchairs out of earshot. The direct question seemed to deserve a direct answer. Unsure how she would respond, I answered simply, 'No, Mum.'

'No, I thought not,' she said lightly, with a small nod of the head, as though she were pleased to have worked out something that was true and concrete in everyone else's real world, and not just in her imaginary one.

'How long ago did she die?'

'Over thirty years ago.'

She stared ahead. A cloud passed across the sun and the light shifted in the room. 'How odd,' she said, momentarily perplexed. 'Was she not *here*?'

'No.'

'What is this place?' she said, her face earnest.

'The care home. Near Bristol. Where you live now. You've been here over five years.'

She said nothing at this, and after a moment's silence, tucked the nail of her index finger in between the gap in her two front teeth, and flicked it out making a clicking noise. Her eyes darkened. 'Who are *you*?' she said, turning to look at me fixedly.

It startled me, but I tried to see the moment from her side: dealing with the slow decrements in capacity; the illusions and the uncertainties; the fleeting facts; the mutating faces; shadows on the wall; snipers on the roof. 'Ben,' I said gently. 'Your son. Your youngest.'

'But you are *thin*,' she said, with a tetchy exasperation. 'If you were *fat*, like you were as a little boy, I might remember you more easily.'

I laughed. 'Thanks, Mum.'

'And your hair. Very short. And you're *bald*. At the back. When you turn round. I'm not used to it.'

'Oh, thanks,' I said sarcastically, still laughing. 'Thanks for reminding me. Not sure why it all fell out. Dad – Tom, I mean – had *lovely* hair.'

At the mention of Tom, she turned towards the window and fell silent. I sat still. Someone marched past the half-open door. Outside, a car edged slowly off the green verge.

'He's not been lately,' she said quietly. 'He's away.'

'Who?'

'Tom.'

'Where is he? Do you know?'

'In prison.'

At 8.45, on a cold quiet Saturday morning on 27 October 1962, at Surrey County Council Register Office, opposite Norbiton Station, in front of no one except two witnesses, my mum and dad finally got married. After all the years of waiting, all the desperation, as an occasion it could not have been more low-key. No invitations were sent out. There was no reception. There are no photographs. I knew my mum was almost eight months pregnant with me. Was she camera-shy? It seemed unlikely. Did they just not plan it in time? They'd certainly had long enough. All those letters, all the anticipation – didn't they finally want to tell the world about the love that couldn't be extinguished? It would seem not. So what happened?

I knew one version of the story: it started just over a month earlier in the small hours of a Tuesday morning on 18 September 1962. My dad had left the old Ronnie Scott's jazz club on Gerrard Street in Soho with trombonist Ken Wray, after a night out watching the Tubby Hayes Quintet. It was a five-minute walk to the car. They turned right into Newport Place and right again into Lisle Street. Safely inside the parked car, Wray had the beginnings of a joint in his hand when a face appeared at the window. My dad grabbed the cigarette paper and the crumbled hash, but it was too late; the police officer was already tapping on the windscreen. Confiscating the cigarette paper and its contents, the officer then found twenty-eight grams of 'Indian hemp' in my dad's possession and arrested both men. 'Look, I am a fairly important man,' my dad was reported to have protested. He suggested the officer was taking it all a bit 'seriously'. It made no difference. The officer *was* taking it seriously.

'The first we knew about it was when Romany rang the next day,' Elspet said, when we last met.

'She was in a terrible state,' added Brian. 'She said Tommy had been arrested and had already been down to Bow Street Magistrates' Court, and he'd been convicted already, and they'd given him six months. He'd lodged an appeal but he needed the bail money.'

Brian leapt into action. He rang his friend and colleague, the theatre director-producer Wally Douglas, and the two of them headed immediately for Bow Street.

'We just had to get him out of there,' Brian went on. 'Wally had been a prisoner of war. He was very, you know, stiff-upper-lip, and he'd seen everything, but he couldn't take the seediness of it all. There was talk they'd thought Tommy was a dealer. It was like having fifteen teeth out without anaesthetic for poor old Wally; but we signed the forms and paid the money, and got Tommy out.'

The next day *The Times* ran a news report. Under the head-line *Composer and Musician Had Indian Hemp*, it read:

Thomas Mitchell Watt, aged 36, a composer of Woodlands Road, Barnes SW said by Detective-Constable W. Huckleby to be earning between £2,000 and £3,000 a year, was sentenced at Bow St Magistrates' Court yesterday to six months' imprisonment for being in unauthorised possession of Indian hemp in Lisle St, Soho, W.

With him on the same charge was Kenneth Wray, aged 35, a musician of Fairhazel Gdns, Kilburn NW, who was sentenced to four months' imprisonment. Both pleaded guilty.

The *Daily Mail* ran a similar, but longer report the same day, mentioning the appeal, and soon everyone knew. Letters arrived at Woodlands Road from concerned friends offering to help. Aunts wrote hoping it was all a 'silly mistake' and it would all 'turn out for the best'. Tom's father wrote – a great rarity – referring to it as a 'sordid matter' that he was relieved hadn't made the Scottish newspapers or been the subject of gossip on the factory floor.

The court appeal, when it came, not long after the sentence, featured two brilliant cameos from Brian and Wally who stood up and, in matchless theatrical aristocratic voices, vouched for my dad's first-rate character and RAF record, while drawing touching attention to the imminent birth of his first son, his essential work for the BBC, and his recent effective adoption of four stepchildren. It was, by all accounts, a tour de force. My dad – much to everyone's ample relief – got off with a fine of £150 and the sentence was quashed. Ken Wray got off too. 'Brian' was also later inserted into my middle names (for a long while it was only going to be 'Thomas') as acknowledgement of his selfless and sterling efforts to clear my dad's good name at the eleventh hour.

So surely there was great cause to celebrate. Why didn't they? What prompted my mum and dad's long-awaited marriage to take place on that cold inauspicious early Saturday morning before breakfast, opposite Norbiton Station, squeezed in before all the day's other well-planned ceremonies with their limousines and flowers and hats and happy tearful relations?

The answer came when I was researching this book. I found out the *date* of the appeal. I'd assumed – and my parents had implied – that it was within a couple of weeks of the original sentencing back in the September, but it was in fact on *31 October 1962* – not only the very day of my dad's thirty-seventh birthday, but also four days *after* the wedding. They married because they didn't know if my dad might be going to prison a few days later. They married so that there wasn't a chance they might have to do it *in* prison before I was born. They married in the hope that it would read well at the appeal and with any luck I'd be born without my father in jail. No one was at the ceremony at Surrey County Council Register Office that morning because no one was supposed to witness that hope; it must have felt so threadbare; as if, after all those years of waiting, nothing could be properly celebrated.

In the end, I was late. Reluctant to come out. Story has it that no amount of sulphurous baths or heart-thumping walks up and down the stairs at home could tempt me. The sub-zero temperatures of the bitter winter of 1962–63 were probably to blame; but finally, with London gripped by a murderous fog on a Monday night in early December, my mum took herself to the old Middlesex Hospital in town, where she was sure I must emerge at any minute, while my dad played the piano at Grosvenor House, clock-watching nervously.

The next morning, Tuesday 4 December, a thick layer of acrid, green-and-yellow smog was covering the whole of London. It was to stay for three days. As Wednesday stumbled into Thursday, two hundred and thirty-five people were admitted into the city's hospitals. The government was recommending 'do-it-yourself' masks made from thick cotton gauze or woollen scarves. Coal fires and bonfires were banned. Windows were kept closed. Black ice covered the roads. By the Thursday morning ninety people had died, and the fog was spreading across the country.

Inside the relative safety of the Middlesex Hospital on the Thursday afternoon I was finally induced. My dad was rehearsing an episode of Brian's new TV series, *Dial Rix*, for which he had written the music. My mum managed to get a message to him and he crawled across town by car in near-zero visibility just in time to be at her bedside as I finally emerged at 7.35 p.m. on 6 December 1962.

My mum remembers the look on my dad's pale face as he

first saw me – one of adoration, disbelief and relief. I've wondered if it wasn't dissimilar to the look on his face as I greeted him that last time I ever saw him in hospital a few days before he died. As he reached out to pluck me from the cot, it's said he stumbled over the oxygen tank, half dropped me, then caught me again inches off the floor.

40

I n December 2009, three and half years after my dad died, my mum was diagnosed with DLB, or Dementia with Lewy bodies. It sounded confusing. I looked it up on the Alzheimer's Society website. *Dementia with Lewy bodies (DLB)*, it said, *is a form of dementia that shares characteristics with both Alzheimer's and Parkinson's disease.* I learned that the Lewy bodies – named after a doctor, Frederich Lewy, who first identified them in 1912 – are tiny protein deposits that when found in the brain's nerve cells disrupt the brain's normal functioning. I scanned down the specific symptoms, saying yes in my mind to all of them when picturing my mum: *problems with attention and spatial orientation; a tendency to shuffle when walking; detailed and convincing visual hallucinations, often of people or animals; can fall asleep very easily by day, and have restless, disturbed nights with confusion and nightmares.* Roly, who pops his head round the door several times a week, said it rang very true for him too; all of which was heartening, given that it is said to account for around only ten per cent of all cases of dementia in older people and tends to be under-diagnosed. At least her carers know what to look for now, and there is medication to take, although none of us are under any illusions

– DLB is a progressive disease. And over time the symptoms will only become worse. I am pleased, though, that her long-term tendency towards depression has been tackled too with extra medication, and it seems, at least in part, to have relieved her of the more ghoulish aspects of her hallucinations.

I never know when I get on the train to Bristol quite how I will find her – alert, or sometimes mute and self-absorbed. Her abilities can fluctuate by the hour. Some days she is almost completely unresponsive; it is rather like talking to an elegant owl. And she is still so beautiful, in that hawkish way she has always had. Other days she is positively skittish.

'I was a good actress, you know,' she said, by way of nothing at all recently, on one of her chatty days.

'You were. What can you picture?' I replied. I try not to ask her if she can *remember* anything any more, or what the weather was like this morning, or what she had for breakfast. I know she won't have a clue. But climbing into her head at a particular moment can unlock memories we might share.

She wrinkled up her face, as she often does now, trying to focus on and articulate her fleeting thoughts. 'Smoke,' she said. 'Smoke in the corridor. And Sir John coming for me. For our scene. To dance. To dance with me.'

'Sir John Gielgud? At Stratford?'

She snapped open her eyes. 'What?' Her voice was pettish, prickly. It was as if she were cross that I'd broken a spell.

'To dance with Sir John Gielgud?' I asked.

'What?'

'Gielgud. To dance with Sir John Gielgud.'

'I've no idea what you mean. *Who?*'

'Never mind, Mum. It was just a passing thought.'

I told her about this book, and relayed scenes and moments I was writing about, and she closed her eyes, as a child might listen intently to a vivid story, occasionally throwing out a comment ('Ken – a dear man') then gesturing for me to go on, still with her eyes shut. ('I can see the house in Halifax now . . . yes, the cemetery. And the tower. Very good!')

'You *have* been doing your research,' she said, opening her eyes as I finished. 'Oh, I shall look forward to reading it immensely when it comes out.'

I smiled at her, knowing she never would, but cherishing her good manners.

'I do like it when you come,' she went on. 'You *remind* me of so much. Most of the time I live in a dreamland, you know. I was quite interesting once. I am proud of my Gypsy connections, you know. But now I need to stand up. And when I stand up, I shall fart. Very tiresome, but I wanted to warn you.'

I helped her up from the chair.

'There it goes,' she said, expelling a sharp retort. 'Quite nauseating, but it can't be helped.'

I was still laughing about it on the train several hours later.

As for my own depression, I have slowly got on top of it these days. The worst is behind me, I hope. I did get to see someone as the Harley Street psychiatrist had promised – someone to whom I warmed, and shared a lot of stuff with. And some of it I seemed to have known for ever but just had in the wrong order, but I learned some things I had perhaps never thought of before – that my dad might well have been jealous of my success, for one thing. But most of all, I began to see the mum and dad that I grew up with not only as people who I loved and who undoubtedly loved me but also as just two people I happened to know, for whom life was still as complicated in middle age as it was for me as a child.

346

What do I see when I look back at them now? In my dad, I see how the war offered the social mobility he craved as a precocious ambitious Glasgow boy. 'Tommy' was such a classless name. Approachable. Unpretentious. It was as though, on top of his natural skill as a musician, he acquired a key to a door, a route to imagined sophistication and acceptance on merit. He never went to the Scottish Academy of Music as he claimed to the BBC when accepting his appointment with the NDO, even though it went into the press release and was reprinted in all the newspapers. He faked his CV. He was venturesome. The boy who blagged the piano stool with Carl Barriteau. Leaping from opportunity to opportunity. Blending in. Having us on. The great charmer.

When the fusty old general confronts the young upstart Army medic and opportunistic rebel leader, Percy Toplis, in Alan Bleasdale's 1986 First World War TV drama *The Monocled Mutineer* at the peak of the training-camp riot, and demands, 'And who are *you*?' Toplis replies, in so many words, 'Anyone I want to be. And who are you . . . any more?'

There was something of Toplis in my dad. Confident, nimble, amoral, repudiative. And friends of mine, whose lives he passed though – in backstage dressing rooms or on family occasions – have said what a laugh he could be. Drink in one hand. Fag in the other. Stylish. Assertive. Charismatic.

And yet, I asked Brian to describe him in a single word. 'Bloody-minded,' he said. 'Chippy. Brilliant but bolshy. He always had the talent but he didn't have the personality, in that his single-mindedness led him down a blind alley.'

'And he didn't spend the time with Romany that she might have liked,' added Elspet.

And I had to agree. For all his charm and swagger, I also saw his self-absorption and the disillusioned musician he became:

sulky when things went wrong; intimidated by the outside world after failure; with only my mum to 'understand' and 'forgive' him.

When I played 'Wholesome Girl' at his funeral, in honour of his love for her, I was struck by how wrong the adjective 'wholesome' was. What did he mean? Virtuous? Decent? Fully rounded? It is strangely suppressive. It was as though the image he wanted of her was not exactly the person she was. Once all the exultant sex was out of the way, and his career was in jeopardy, it's as though he needed looking after too much, but then would accept little in the way of affection, while counting on her to be there through the mess that followed.

Yet the curious thing is, she fell for it. Certainly at the beginning. In Elspet's words, 'She loved the bad boy image.' For all her thoughtful agonising and Wesleyan self-reproach she's always been a quiet thrill-seeker and a sucker for glamour. Her pin-board was a gallery of hunks and brooding leading men. Even now she'll swoon over a high-contrast black-and-white photo of a young Anthony Hopkins. All that bruised Welsh passion. 'But she tried to rein him in,' Elspet continued. 'And that was fatal.'

If my mum ended up applying a brake on my dad, perhaps she was destined to be the more prudent and cautious partner. It was certainly never going to be easy to throw off the sober conscience of her upbringing, especially with her condemnatory mother forever watching from the wings. Her children also made her involuntarily watchful and maternally protective, and for all her flirting with danger and passion, she was mindful of the damage being done by a tortuous spun-out divorce, and bothered by guilt in its aftermath. I think a part of her – even with Tom – also still just yearned for a stable life with known boundaries, where she was appreciated and respected. Not much to ask. Although he couldn't have made it harder for her sometimes. It struck me that she used the same contented phrase to describe her time at Stratford in 1950 as she did for her period working at the *TV Times* in her later years as a journalist in the eighties: 'I was just happy to be a cog in a wheel,' she wrote, in different notebooks at different times.

In 1986 Elspet suggested she and my mum, and Tom and Brian, meet socially but was knocked back. 'It's family only now,' my mum replied cryptically. Elspet remained mystified for years. 'We had been so close,' she said to me recently.

'I think she thought it was safer,' I ventured. 'Tom was such a loose cannon by then. Only the family would forgive it. Anything else risked too much embarrassment. The sad thing is – all too often – it soon became just *Tom* only; and then she became a proud captain prepared to go down with her ship.'

My mum was writing short travel and nature features as a freelancer for the *Observer* at the time. Instead of meeting up, she invited Elspet to travel up to Scotland with her on a commission – a birdwatching trip to Skye. 'It was a wonderful few days. We were very happy there,' said Elspet. They took a car over on the old ferry. It was October. In gale-force winds and driving rain they rented a chalet overlooking the sea-loch, and sat with binoculars watching gannets nesting in their thousands on the opposite cliffs, as cormorants and shags plunged vertically into the sea below. In the calm purple-and-amber-lit evenings sea otters played in the shallows near the rocks. Trudging across a peat bog one afternoon they crested a rise in the hill only to meet a wide field of grey-lag geese. Swans arrived from Iceland overhead, among buzzards, sparrow-hawks, merlin and a great golden eagle. They ate and drank contentedly and talked long into the evenings. The early eighties were among the hardest of times with Tom. I like to think of my mum on this trip around that time too.

It strikes me that my mum and dad imparted little advice, and offered few pep talks or manuals for life. They just let me be and get on with it, working it out for myself, guessing my way through the mistakes. If they had one thing in common, it's that they vowed never to repeat the child-rearing they'd each experienced, with all the attendant rectitude and stricture. 'Live and let live' was another of my dad's great battle cries. Of course he regularly defaulted on that one. 'He can be a right bastard to those who love him,' my mum once said in a letter to me. But at least I never had to controvert their authority. And they never raised a hand to me. And a lot of the time they were very funny.

I pieced together their golden years, and some of them shone very bright, but mostly I saw ordinary people trying hard, which is all we can hope to do. As for the downhill part, it can't have been easy. It's the descent that is the tiring bit. 'How old am I? Eighty-eight?' my mum said the other day. 'Too long. Too long.'

When she was in one of her skittish moods recently, I took her hands and helped her up from her seat and we shuffled out into the small sunlit lounge beside the lawn, where we settled in a couple of chairs overlooking the soil-filled skips and loaders and metal fencing of the new extension going up at the care home.

'Tom's downstairs now, you know,' she said.

'Is he?' I said, knowing there was no downstairs as my mum's room was on the ground floor, but wondering if she half pictured our old flat at Barnes with Eunice below, or perhaps even Oxford, where you'd hear the front door open and close from the first-floor sitting room.

'Yes, he's on the board here now. Very important.'

'Do you get to see him?'

'No. Too busy. But he's around.'

I waited to see if she would add some more, but she seemed content to leave it there, as if knowing he was 'present' in some way was a kind of solace. It seemed oddly spiritual and comforting, if a little comical – Tom, the man who conducted Tubby Hayes and Phil Seamen in full flight, on an imaginary board at a rural care home outside Bristol – but maybe it sat well with her to think he was about the place, looking out for her, overseeing her daily life in some way, her interests at heart. And that was good, wasn't it?

'Do you remember the day when I was little,' I said, 'and we walked hand in hand through the fields at Walberton, past all the wheat, pointing out all the wildflowers, and down the hill, across the bridge and up to the church, and you recited that poem by Yeats, out loud?'

She wrinkled up her face, and closed her eyes. Then she opened them. 'No. I don't,' she said.

'Never mind.'

I tucked in the label that was sticking out from the collar of her cardigan, and took her hand, and we sat a little longer.

AUTHOR'S NOTE

While writing this book I had to settle on whether to use the word 'Romani' or 'Romany' when describing my mum's background. Although 'Romani' is now becoming the more accepted modern spelling – and the term adopted by large bodies including the United Nations – the spelling my mum used, and the one I grew up with, was the older variant, 'Romany', and for this reason it is the one I have chosen to adopt.

ACKNOWLEDGEMENTS

I would like to thank my godfather Brian Rix and late godmother Elspet Rix for their memories and kindness, my half-brother Roly for sharing the load, my late beautiful half-sister Jennie who had so looked forward to this book and whom I miss every day, my aunt Jean for her tea and insight, Karen Levy and Jeremy Pfeffer for their helping hands, the late Eric Monteith Hamilton for his unexpected emails, Sir Arnold Wesker for sending me his Centre 42 souvenirs, my agents Kirsty McLachlan and David Godwin, my editor Alexandra Pringle for having me back, Mary Tomlinson and Sarah Barlow for their eagle eyes, Bobby Wellins for remembering, Graham Kaye for helping me uncover some crucial court details, Marianne for holding the fort, Beach Hut A for a place to think and write, the British Newspaper Archive at Colindale, Bodil Malmston for her encouragement right from the beginning, all the staff at Windmill House, and lastly, lovely Tracey and our three kids, everyone out there who has chosen to read this book, and of course, my mum and my dad.

A NOTE ON THE AUTHOR

Born in 1962, Ben Watt is a musician, songwriter, DJ and author. His first book, *Patient: The True Story of a Rare Illness* was a *New York Times* Notable Book of the Year, voted a *Sunday Times* Book of the Year by William Boyd and shortlisted for the *Esquire* Non-fiction Book of the Year. He is perhaps most well known for his twenty-year career in alt-pop duo Everything But The Girl (1982–2002). He is also an international club and radio DJ, and since 2003 has run his own independent record labels Buzzin' Fly and Strange Feeling. Having recently returned to songwriting and live performance, his first solo album for thirty years in expected in 2014. He lives in north London with his wife Tracey Thorn and their three children.

Follow him on Twitter @ben_watt
www.benwatt.com